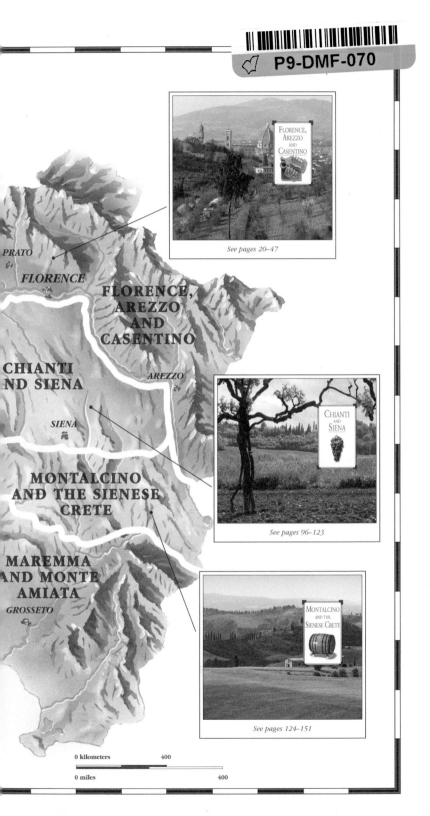

P9-DMF-070

PRATO

FLORENCE

FLORENCE, AREZZO AND CASENTINO

AREZZO

CHIANTI AND SIENA

SIENA

MONTALCINO AND THE SIENESE CRETE

MAREMMA AND MONTE AMIATA

GROSSETO

FLORENCE, AREZZO AND CASENTINO

See pages 20–47

CHIANTI AND SIENA

See pages 96–123

MONTALCINO AND THE SIENESE CRETE

See pages 124–151

| 0 kilometers | 400 |
| 0 miles | 400 |

EYEWITNESS TRAVEL GUIDES

A TASTE OF
TUSCANY

A TASTE OF
TUSCANY

Edited by: GUIDO STECCHI

LONDON, NEW YORK,
MELBOURNE, MUNICH AND DELHI
www.dk.com

Produced by Fabio Ratti
Editoria Libraria e Multimediale, Milan, Italy

TEXT Guido Stecchi, Maria Cristina Beretta, Marco Scapagnini
EDITORS Diana Georgiacodis, Laura Recordati,
Federica Romagnoli

DESIGNERS Massimo Costa, Carlotta Maderna

MAPS AND ILLUSTRATIONS Massimo Costa, Carlotta Maderna,
Alberto Ipsilanti, Daniela Veluti, Oriana Bianchetti,
Roberto Capra

Dorling Kindersley Ltd.
EDITORS Felicity Jackson, Fiona Wild   PROOFREADER Stewart Wild
ENGLISH TRANSLATION Richard Sadleir
DTP DESIGNER Jason Little   PRODUCTION Marie Ingledew
SENIOR PUBLISHING MANAGER Louise Bostock Lang

Reproduced by Colourscan, Singapore
Printed and bound by South China Printing Co. Ltd., China

First published in Italy in 2000 by Arnoldo Mondadori Editore
S.p.A., Milan and Fabio Ratti Editoria s.r.l., Milan as Guida
Gourmet Toscana

First American Edition, 2001
04 05 10 9 8 7 6 5 4 3 2

Published in the United States by
DK Publishing, Inc.,
375 Hudson Street, New York, NY 10014
Reprinted with revisions 2004

ISSN 1542-1554
ISBN 0-7894-9735-2

The photographs and information in this book are intended to
help the reader select produce, particularly mushrooms, in a
market, and are not intended as a guide to picking wild produce.
If you are in any doubt about the edibility of any species,
do not cook or eat it.

**The information in every
DK Eyewitness Guide is checked regularly**.
Every effort has been made to ensure that this book is as
up-to-date as possible at the time of going to press. Some
details, however, such as telephone numbers, opening hours,
prices, and travel information are liable to change. The
publishers cannot accept responsibility for any consequences
arising from the use of this book, nor for any material on third
party websites, and cannot guarantee that any website address in
this book will be a suitable source of travel information.
We value the views and suggestions of our readers very highly.
Please write to: Publisher, DK Travel Guides, Dorling Kindersley,
80 Strand, London WC2R 0RL, Great Britain.

CONTENTS

How to Use this Guide

This guide uncovers the best of Tuscany's food and wine for visitors to the region. Tuscany has been divided into six areas or zones (see the map inside the front cover). There is a brief description of places of gastronomic interest: shops, wineries, vineyards, and estates, and restaurants with local character. To make it easy for travelers to find them, there is a map and a *Places of Interest* section for each of the areas. There is practical information about the most important *Traditional Produce*, such as wine, cheese, and *salumi* (cured meats), all clearly illustrated. *Wild Produce* with its descriptions of truffles and mushrooms, herbs and wild fruits will encourage excursions into meadows and woods to search for them (or at least to keep an eye open for them in the markets). The delights of the local cuisine are highlighted in a selection of traditional dishes from each area, and the region's restaurants are assessed for quality, atmosphere, traditional dishes, good service, and value for money.

A Taste of Tuscany Area by Area

LUNIGIANA, GARFAGNANA AND VERSILIA

The guide has divided Tuscany into six areas, each of which covers a geographical area based on the local produce and the gastronomic traditions.

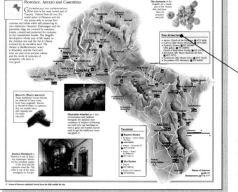

The title page *for each area illustrates one of the most important local products.*

Star Attractions *indicates important artistic and cultural sights no visitor should miss.*

The map illustrates the area dealt with in the chapter and illustrates the region's most important produce and places.

*In the traditional **recipes**, quantities are for six people unless otherwise stated.*

*There are descriptions of **traditional produce**, such as wine, salumi, olive oil, and cheese.*

Wild produce traditionally picked by local people in Tuscany includes truffles, mushrooms, herbs, and various wild fruits.

Each entry *for a place of interest gives the address, phone number, opening and closing days. It is advisable to telephone before stopping by a farm, vineyard, or agriturismo.*

Places of interest are marked with a symbol (see inside back cover for key to symbols) to indicate the kind of produce available, and they are listed in alphabetical order by place.

Each restaurant entry *gives the address, telephone number, and weekly closing day.*

Price categories for a three-course meal including a bottle of wine:

€ under €25
€€ €25–€36
€€€ €36–€46
€€€€ €46–€60
€€€€€ over €60

The restaurant entries assess quality, comfort, traditional food, service, and value for money.

Tuscany Throughout the Year

SPRING

T USCAN SPRING can come as early as
March, especially along the coast.
In the hedgerows and thickets, you
can find the young, tender wild
shoots known locally as "asparagus,"
such as butcher's broom or even the
sweet young tips of wild hops. Waste
ground is studded with borage
flowers – one of the most valuable
of wild herbs – looking like little blue
stars. Coastal pine woods and the
inland woods on hills and mountains
conceal magnificent morel
mushrooms, while richly scented St.
George's mushrooms form circles
around sloe trees which are sprinkled
with white blossom. Specially trained
hounds nose out white truffles under
the pine woods that stretch along
the coast from Cecina to Argentario.

Spring is when Tuscan extra-virgin
olive oil reaches peak quality,
shedding the bitter, pungent taste it
has when newly pressed. This is the
ideal time to visit the olive groves
and presses to buy oil. Northwest
Tuscany has some of the finest
chocolate confectioners in Italy –
Europe even – and spring is the
perfect time to sample their wares
in the form of chocolate eggs, the
traditional Easter gift. Another
Tuscan springtime tradition is the
Easter lamb or kid: those raised in the
Garfagnana or the Casentino are
particularly famous. This is also a
good time to sample some of the
seafood specialities: local mullet and
swordfish cooked Livorno-style,
cuttlefish in sauce, and grilled eels
from Orbetello are tasty in April.

SUMMER

S UMMER IS THE time for wandering
through Tuscany's mountain
woods or exploring the coast, but this
time of year is a mixed blessing for
gourmets. In June the coast offers a
wealth of wonderful fish, but July
and August bring hordes of
vacationers from the towns, and there
is not enough fish caught in the local
seas to go around. Then there is the
breeding period when fishing is
banned and only a fortunate few are
able to buy from the small boats
exempt from the ban. Shellfish are at
their finest in the summer, but make
sure you buy from reputable sources.

For those who prefer not to risk the
seafood, the hinterland compensates
with an abundance of flavorful
vegetables: taste the *bruschetta*
(bread rubbed with garlic, toasted
and topped with ripe tomato) or
panzanella (moist bread seasoned
with oil, vinegar, and herbs). In June
and early July the small artichokes on
sale are perfect for preserving in oil.
Peaches, yellow in Tuscany, white on
Elba, are especially good if bought at
orchards where they are allowed to
ripen on the tree. Summer brings
thyme, oregano, and other herbs that
color and scent the dry meadows,
while the woods on the Apennine
ridges provide juicy bilberries,
raspberries, and wild strawberries. In
the mountains there are mushrooms,
but the season is short. Generally,
high summer is too dry for them, and
you have to wait until late September,
when they are plentiful.

FALL

FOR GOURMETS, this is Tuscany's prime season. At San Miniato, Volterra, the Sienese Crete, around Arezzo and many other small villages, the white truffles are ripening. In the Garfagnana and the Casentino there are very fine porcini (cèpe mushrooms), while other parts of Tuscany have an abundance of different mushrooms, which sometimes linger until after Christmas. They include numerous varieties that are essential to the peasant dishes of the region – sauces with fresh pasta and thick seasonal soups like *acquacotta* (tomatoes, mushrooms, vegetables, eggs, and bread). This is the season for sweet chestnuts, a staple of the cuisine of areas like the Lunigiana, Amiata, and the Mugello, and for the renowned wild boar of Maremma, which adorns tables in both homes and restaurants. Game birds are traditional throughout the region, with wood pigeons a particular favorite.

At Chiusi, and above all Torre del Lago, this is the season for the famed local dish of coot cooked *alla Puccini* and wild duck. Game dishes go well with Brunello and the region's other fine red wines. In the fall the ban on fishing is lifted, and this is the time to eat the young squid and mullet, skillfully prepared by the chefs of Viareggio or San Vincenzo, plus the larger fish passing through local waters at this time, especially the amberjack *(ricciola)*.

WINTER

IN MEDITERRANEAN REGIONS like Tuscany, outdoor life continues through the mild winter months, and both the local cuisine and the natural setting are tempting for the gourmet tourist. Nature is still active: there are lots of evergreen herbs, all kinds of

tasty mushrooms and fruits there for the picking in the woods, hedgerows, and meadows. The typical Tuscan meal, with a choice of meats roasted on a spit over the fire, and the rustic cooking found in farmhouses and simple *trattorie* all over the region, serving up traditional thick soups and full-bodied red wines, seem designed to warm up the diners gathered convivially around a large table.

The first mild days are traditionally enjoyed among the crowds at the famous carnival of Viareggio in February. This is the chance to sample the excellent local shellfish, especially scampi and mantis shrimp. Nature is particularly generous in certain localities dotted across Tuscany where the valuable black truffle is found. Not far from the sea there are market gardens producing early artichokes and black cabbage, an important ingredient in *ribollita* (vegetable soup). This is the time when the pig is killed, after a fall spent grazing in the woods on the chestnuts and acorns, giving its flesh a rich flavor. Now, homemade *salumi* (preserved meats) begin their long slow curing, lasting up to two years for a *prosciutto crudo*.

Wines

Tuscany is one of italy's prime wine regions, producing great red wines. The rather folksy image of Chianti in its straw-lined flask has given way in recent years to designer bottles of fine wine that rival the best French reds. This is not the result of some invention of modern marketing but the rightful success of a deep-rooted local tradition, as illustrated by the ancient farmhouses that stand amid the vines. The changeover from a patrician, but antiquated, management of the estates to a bold modern business approach is recent.

Despite the miracles worked by technology, Tuscany will never become a region of great white wines because the French vines planted here produce wines lacking in local character, and the traditional Trebbiano and Malvasia vines are limited by the soil. There are three exceptions: Vernaccia di San Gimignano, Montecarlo, and the whites of the islands, all of which show great potential. Dessert wines also show great promise – if the Vin Santo (Tuscany's traditional "holy wine") lacks the noble flavor of the great French dessert wines, here too the Tuscans are learning to exploit the potential of their yeasts to obtain outstanding wines made from grapes that have been semidried on racks.

A Choice Selection of Tuscan Wines

To accompany the full range of the typical cuisine of the region you need a choice selection of Tuscan wines, which should include the following:

♦ Vermentino from the Luni hills, Apuan Alps, or hills of Lucca (a light summer aperitif).
♦ Vernaccia di San Gimignano, aged (as a general table wine and as an accompaniment to white meats).
♦ Montecarlo Bianco (good with seafood).
♦ Young Vernaccia di San Gimignano (with fish, summery first courses, savory toast).
♦ Young Chianti (with *cacciucco* – Livornese fish soup; for dining al fresco; with *salumi* – cured meats; and with *crostini* and *bruschetta* – savory toasts).
♦ Chianti, medium-aged reds of Montalcino and Montepulciano, Morellino of Sansano (traditional first courses, main courses with white meat).
♦ Chianti Classico or Rufina, Brunello di Montalcino, Vino Nobile di Montepulciano, (roasted or stewed red meat).
♦ Brunello di Montalcino cru, fully aged, Sassicaia (well-aged *pecorino* cheese).
♦ Vin Santo (*cantucci* cookies).
♦ Ansedonia Passito or Moscadello (various desserts)
♦ Aleatico (for desserts and social drinking).

THE RIGHT GLASS

The shape of a wine glass is designed to reduce contact between the hand holding the glass and the wine itself. Its form reduces possible interference from any odors or the heat of the hand. The glass should be held by the stem, between the goblet that holds the wine and the foot of the glass. Modern designers produce wine glasses that are both beautiful and practical. Wine glasses should be perfectly transparent so you can appreciate the wine's color and also check its state of health (for example, too few bubbles or too large bubbles in a spumante *metodo classico*, or an orangey color in a young red wine, which is a symptom of early aging). The best glasses are made of crystal.

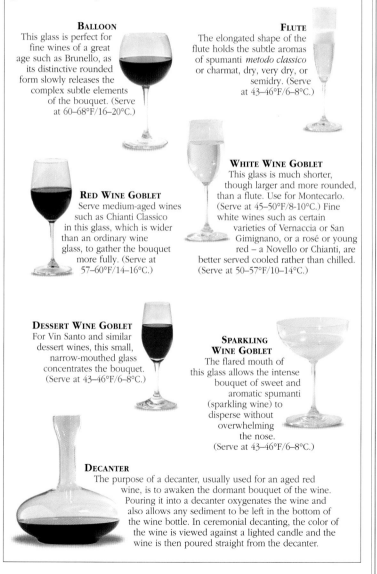

BALLOON
This glass is perfect for fine wines of a great age such as Brunello, as its distinctive rounded form slowly releases the complex subtle elements of the bouquet. (Serve at 60–68°F/16–20°C.)

FLUTE
The elongated shape of the flute holds the subtle aromas of spumanti *metodo classico* or charmat, dry, very dry, or semidry. (Serve at 43–46°F/6–8°C.)

RED WINE GOBLET
Serve medium-aged wines such as Chianti Classico in this glass, which is wider than an ordinary wine glass, to gather the bouquet more fully. (Serve at 57–60°F/14–16°C.)

WHITE WINE GOBLET
This glass is much shorter, though larger and more rounded, than a flute. Use for Montecarlo. (Serve at 45–50°F/8-10°C.) Fine white wines such as certain varieties of Vernaccia or San Gimignano, or a rosé or young red – a Novello or Chianti, are better served cooled rather than chilled. (Serve at 50–57°F/10–14°C.)

DESSERT WINE GOBLET
For Vin Santo and similar dessert wines, this small, narrow-mouthed glass concentrates the bouquet. (Serve at 43–46°F/6–8°C.)

SPARKLING WINE GOBLET
The flared mouth of this glass allows the intense bouquet of sweet and aromatic spumanti (sparkling wine) to disperse without overwhelming the nose. (Serve at 43–46°F/6–8°C.)

DECANTER
The purpose of a decanter, usually used for an aged red wine, is to awaken the dormant bouquet of the wine. Pouring it into a decanter oxygenates the wine and also allows any sediment to be left in the bottom of the wine bottle. In ceremonial decanting, the color of the wine is viewed against a lighted candle and the wine is then poured straight from the decanter.

Olive Growing in Tuscany

TUSCANY IS A FAMOUS olive-growing region and the olive groves on the wooded hillsides are a characteristic feature of the Tuscan landscape, though some areas are more favorable than others. Olive groves are usually small, so the local crop is not large but produces very fine olive oil. The traditional business skills of the region and the expertise of olive growers have played an important role in the success of Italian olive oil worldwide, providing a model for other olive oil producers.

Olive growing in Italy goes all the way back to the Etruscans of the 6th century BC, and it was further developed by the Romans. With the fall of the Roman empire the vast organization for growing and marketing olives fell into disarray. Monasteries were the first to tend the great olive groves again before the medieval city states started to foster olive growing once more. The trade in olive oil grew in economic importance until it became a formidable instrument of political power in the 14th century. Today, olive oil remains an essential ingredient of Tuscan cuisine, a vital flavoring in cooked dishes and salads.

THE ORIGINS OF OLIVE GROWING
The Medici (a powerful political family in the 15th, 16th, and 17th centuries) fostered the growing of olives. They gave wooded hillsides to the municipalities on the condition that they were leased cheaply for planting olive groves and vineyards. Growing olives became one of the main economic resources of the region, resulting in the distinctive Tuscan landscape of today.

THE FLAVOR OF TUSCAN OLIVE OIL
Tuscany produces some of the finest olive oils in Italy and, although they vary in much the same way that wines do, generally they have a strong aromatic scent. Tuscan olives are harvested well before they ripen, to produce oils richer in antioxidants and other nutritious substances. The early harvesting, combined with the soil, climate, and the local olive varieties, results in peppery, slightly bitter oils with a rich color.

OLIVE OIL
Tuscany's extra-virgin olive oil is so renowned that it is a favorite target of counterfeiters. In spite of its fame and quality, however, this oil has received only a recognition of IGP (Protected Geographic Indication), as opposed to a generic Tuscan DOP (Denomination of Protected Origin). This decision was made in Brussels, on account of the large range of different oils produced in various areas of Tuscany. Soon, though, several local DOPs will be approved, joining the existing ones of Terre di Siena and Chianti Classico.

OLIVE VARIETIES

With its long olive-producing history and the diversity of soil and climate within the region, Tuscany has developed numerous cultivated varieties (cultivars) of the olive tree, including 106 that have been classified, some of which are of great importance. In addition to the varieties described below, other important ones include **Pendolino**, a type which is widespread, hardy, and produces abundant oil of reasonable quality; **Maurino**, a variety typical of the area between Monte Albano and Lucchesia, with a medium-sized tree bearing fruits that ripen early and produce fine oil; **Santa Caterina**, a large vigorous tree that produces bright green olives that are usually harvested in September for immediate eating. Other common varieties are **Corniolo, Craputea, Lavagnino, Leucarpa, Manzanilla, Nebbio, Ogliarola, Passola, Piangente, Ravece, San Francesco,** and **Taggiasca**.

MORAIOLO

This variety originated in Tuscany but is widely grown in other parts of Italy, especially Umbria, and in other Mediterranean countries. It has a good resistance to wind but not to intense, prolonged cold. It produces an abundance of olives, which ripen over a medium-to-long period of time, and have a good oil yield. The oil is very fine, without marked aromatic notes but with excellent texture and a distinctly bitter and pungent flavor.

CORREGGIOLO

A self-pollinator similar to Frantoio, this variety's fruit ripens late and over a long period. The trees are fairly vigorous, with drooping branches and the fruits borne on thin, supple canes. The olive yield is high and consistent, producing an oil that is particularly aromatic, full-bodied, and flavorsome.

MAREMMANA

A vigorous plant with large, intensely green, spear-shaped leaves. It produces a good oil with somewhat muted bitter notes.

LECCINO

Grown in nearly all olive-producing regions both in Italy and worldwide, this variety is well-known for its resistance to inclement weather, cold, and disease. A consistent high-yielding variety, the olives ripen early and uniformly. Its oil is not particularly aromatic.

FRANTOIO

A Tuscan original, this variety has spread throughout Italy and nearly all olive-growing areas of the world, a testimony to its consistently high yields and the notable quality of its oil, which is fine, aromatic, and flavorsome. The variety is not resistant to bad weather and is very sensitive to cold.

Fish and Seafood

UNLIKE THE LIGURIAN COAST, the Tuscan coastline is not studded with little fishing harbors, but its larger ports, notably Viareggio and Livorno, provide fine fish. The waters of Gorgona and other islands, the shallows of Vada, and the Formiche of Grosseto offer an excellent range of fish, including scampi and crayfish, delivered live to the counters of the fish shops. The lagoon of Orbetello, with its modern fish farms, is particularly productive, but this is not always reflected in the restaurants. Inland there are not that many restaurants specializing in fish cuisine, although fish is commonly eaten on a Friday thoughout Tuscany. The best fish restaurants are found mainly along the coast.

RICCIOLA SERIOLA DUMERILI (AMBERJACK)

Amberjack, which grow to a large size, are found in schools in deep water around rocky headlands and steep cliffs. They abound in the Tuscan archipelago and are prized for their firm, flavorsome white flesh. They are usually eaten as fish steaks or grilled whole.

PESCE SPADA (SWORDFISH)

The white close-grained flesh of this fish is delicious provided it is not overcooked and it remains moist. Swordfish is found particularly in the port of Livorno, usually sold as steaks.

CALAMARETTI (YOUNG SQUID)

The fry of squid are one of the delicacies of Tuscan cuisine. They need to be cooked only a few seconds by steaming or tossing in a pan with vegetables. Their delicate flavor provides great scope for many delicious dishes.

CALAMARO (SQUID)

The squid is the most prized and costly of cephalopods (soft-bodied shellfish). Its sweet flesh is delicious cut into rings and fried. It is also very good poached, stuffed, and baked or served cold in a mixed *antipasto di mare*, or seafood salad.

VONGOLA VERACE OR ARSELLA NERA (CLAMS)

This very common shellfish is usually cooked but may be served raw like oysters. Though somewhat expensive, clams are found in numerous modern Tuscan seafood dishes as well as the traditional *cacciucco* (fish soup). Called *vongole veraci* or *arselle* in Italian, in Viareggio they are known as *nicchi*.

MISTO DI SCOGLIO (MIXED SEA FISH)

The fish referred to as *misto di scoglio* include small bream, wrasse, young scorpion fish and rainbow wrasse, gurnard, sea perch, and hake. Delicious but too small to grill or fry on their own, they are essential for an authentic *cacciucco* and a variety of other fish soups.

PAGRO (PORGY)

This is a white fish typical of the Tyrrhenian coast and is highly prized in Tuscany, especially when it is baked. Sea bream (called *pagelli* in Italian, *paraghi* in the Tuscan dialect) is similar but has a flatter snout and pinkish markings. Larger specimens are called *occhialone* or *fragolino*.

SARDINA

A common and very economical fish, the sardine is tasty and very nourishing. It is ideal fried, grilled, made into fish cakes, or preserved in oil.

SPARNOCCHIA OR MAZZANCOLLA (MANTIS SHRIMP)

The mantis shrimp is common in Tuscan waters, especially around the island of Gorgona. It is popular for grilling and steaming and is also an ingredient in more expensive versions of *cacciucco* (fish soup). Mantis shrimp are sold live at the market at Viareggio – always avoid those sold headless.

Porcini Mushrooms

T̲USCAN CUISINE REGULARLY FEATURES *porcini* mushrooms, which are also
known as cèpes, from the French. *Porcini* are distinguished from other
Boletus mushrooms – a family which has tiny tubes under the cap instead of
gills – by four features: strong smell, sweet taste, a netlike pattern covering the
stalk, and by the white flesh, which does not discolor when cut. They are
found all over the region, fresh, dried, or preserved in oil, in homes and all
types of restaurant, from the humblest *trattoria* to the grandest *ristorante*.
Dishes featuring *porcini* do not vary greatly, and the mushrooms are eaten in
quite simple ways, in *risotto*, or in *ravioli,* for example. In certain areas of
Tuscany, including Lunigiana, Garfagnana, and Casentino, you can find the
world's finest examples of *porcini,* judged on aroma, flavor, and texture. In
other areas, such as Monte Amiata, the Maremma Grossetana, Colline Metallifere,
the hinterland of Livorno, the Mediterranean scrublands, and the woods of Siena
and Arezzo, the quality is not as high but they are more abundant.

PORCINO D'AUTUNNO
(*Boletus edulis*)
The fall *porcino* shuns the heat, so in
summer it is found only in the mountains
and in the depths of woods; in fall it
appears on hillsides, but prefers cool
areas. The mushroom's stalk is usually
white and the cap appears in various
shades of brown, sometimes almost
white, under beech trees, and is slimy
in wet weather. The most flavorsome
examples are found growing under
chestnut trees, the firmest examples
among fir and beech trees; those in
oak woods are much less prized.

PORCINO DEL FREDDO
(*Boletus pinicola*)
This species grows between May and
November but rarely during the hottest
months. It is found under chestnut,
beech, pine, or fir trees, especially with
bilberries or heather. It has unusual
red coloring and is the largest of
all the *porcini*. It is best suited to
preserving in oil because it is generally
very hardy, not particularly aromatic,
and the color is very striking.

FIORONE OR PORCINO D'ESTATE
(*Boletus reticulatus*)
This summer *porcino* starts growing
in May and is rarely found after
September. It grows throughout
the region at all altitudes but only
in grassy glades and in sunny areas.
This is the most richly scented and
flavorsome of the *porcini* but it is
vulnerable to parasites. The cap is
velvety and slightly cracked, the stalk
is beige with a raised netlike pattern,
and the flesh has a very light texture.

MORECCIO OR PORCINO NERO
(Boletus aereus)
This black *porcini* mushroom is most common along the coast and on warm hillsides. It grows almost exclusively in the fall, usually under holm oaks, deciduous oaks, and chestnut trees. It has a dark brown cap marbled with ocher and an ocher-colored stalk. It is full-flavored and aromatic when picked but the scent and taste soon fade. The flesh remains snowy white when dried, making it ideal for keeping in this way.

PORCINI IN OIL
Jars of *porcini* preserved in oil are a feature of the region's farmhouses and traditional *trattorie*. In keeping with tradition, the oil is usually extra-virgin olive oil. Jars should be stored in a cool dark place and kept no later than the spring after the season of picking.

DRIED PORCINI
Porcini secchi, or dried *porcini*, are even more common throughout Tuscany than fresh ones. The local varieties are prized over those from other regions, although the latter have flooded the market. If possible, buy unpackaged dried mushrooms directly from the pickers or at small shops in areas where they are found locally. Store them either in the freezer or at least place them there from time to time to kill the eggs of potential parasites.

Truffles

Tuscany is one huge truffle patch with many areas producing black truffles and even the prized white variety. Numerous fairs and festivals celebrate this wonderful gift of nature, especially in the areas that are lucky enough to produce white truffles, such as the Sienese Crete and San Miniato. Truffles are seasonal but, fortunately, Tuscany has a truffle for every month of the year, so there are always fresh ones available. Always buy truffles in season when they are very fresh and clearly identifiable. Be wary of various speciality foods described as "truffle flavored" *(al tartufo)*: in reality, they may be perfumed with a synthetic aroma. The high prices these truffles command and the strong international demand for them have led to some cases of fraud. The most common type of swindle is to import flavorless truffles from abroad, bought cheaply (sometimes less than 50 cents for two pounds), and then artificially perfume them with a synthetic aroma. Tasteless unripe truffles are sometimes gathered – seriously damaging the truffle patches – and these are likewise flavored artificially.

TARTUFO BIANCO PREGIATO
(Tuber magnatum)
The white truffle is actually a light hazel color if found growing under oak, almost whitish if under poplar or willow, or with reddish tones if under linden (lime) trees. It is identifiable by its strong and distinctive aroma and fine, densely veined flesh – marked veining is the first sign of proper ripeness. It ripens from October to December and by law it can only be gathered in these three months. Its flavor is best appreciated when added raw to hot dishes. Areas where it is found are San Miniato, the Sienese Crete, Volterra, and there are some small patches near Arezzo.

BIANCHETTO OR MARZOLO
(Tuber borchii)
The perfume of this March truffle is strong and very garlicky but it lasts only a few hours after picking and then begins to fade. It adds an excellent flavor to soups. Picking is permitted from January 15 to April 30. It is found in many parts of Tuscany, and is abundant in the coastal pine woods.

The March truffle differs from the prized white truffle by the coarse loose veining and domed shape.

The wrinkled gray surface of this truffle has dark reddish tints.

TUBER MACROSPORUM
This truffle occasionally turns up among batches of summer black truffles. It is often mistakenly sold at the same price even though it is far more highly prized because its perfume is almost identical to that of the white truffle. Sadly, it is very rare. Harvesting is permitted from September to December.

The flesh is gray with fine reddish veins, which are often not evident because they darken on contact with the air.

Hazel-colored flesh has white veining.

SCORZONE
(Tuber aestivum)

The summer black truffle is the most common truffle in Tuscany, found all over the region. It is excellent when fresh, though not as good as the black truffle *(see below)*, but it usually costs about one-tenth of the price of the white truffle. Its flavor is heightened in stuffings and in baked dishes. Harvesting is allowed from May to December.

Black surface is knobbly.

Surface is rough but not knobbly.

TARTUFO NERO PREGIATO
(Tuber melanosporum)

The prized black truffle is usually found in oak woods where the sun can penetrate. This is the *diamant noir* (black diamond) of the French; in Italy it also called *nero di Norcia* (black truffle of Norcia). It has a delicious scent of ripening fruit with a whiff of garlic. It blends well with other foods, and it will enhance the flavor of hot sauces and stuffings, terrines, and pâtés. It is at its best at the end of January, but it can be harvested from November 15 to March 15 and costs about half as much as the white truffle. It grows in scattered patches across the region.

Grayish flesh with sparse, thick veins.

Flesh is black with fine white, translucent veining.

TARTUFO D'INVERNO
(Tuber brumale)

Hazel trees rather than oak are preferred by the winter black truffle, though it is sometimes found together with the prized black truffle. At the market (and in the kitchen) it is somewhat less valuable than the summer black and the prized black (its perfume is less delicate and persistent), but its gastronomic uses are the same. Harvesting is permitted from November 15 to March 15.

Black grainy surface.

OTHER TRUFFLES

There are various small truffles that are very similar to the March truffle. These can be distinguished only with a microscope but they ripen at different times from the March truffle. These include the *Tuber puberulum, Tuber dryophilum,* and *Tuber maculatum.* While the law does not allow their sale, the law is not enforced. A black truffle called *Tuber mesentericum* is sometimes found in the Tuscany region. Unfortunately, it has an unpleasant smell of carbolic acid and is not worth buying.

Florence,
Arezzo,
and
Casentino

Florence, Arezzo, and Casentino

GEOGRAPHICALLY AND GASTRONOMICALLY, this area is the most varied part of Tuscany. Visitors from all over the world arrive in Florence and the city seems able to accept their customs and habits while still preserving its own distinctive character. Pratomagno and the Apennine ridge are covered by extensive forests, created and protected for centuries by the Camaldolesi monks. The Mugello developed a whole way of life based on the chestnut tree, and the Val di Chiana is famed for its excellent beef. The climate is Mediterranean, water is abundant, and the food and wine are part of an ancient culture and the result of centuries of prosperity. Life here is very good.

Firenzuo

Scarperia

San Pietro a Sieve

Borg San Lore

Montemurlo

Bivigliano

PRATO

Calenzano

Carmignano

Sesto Fiorentino

Lastra a Signa

Fiesole

FLORENCE

Arno

Capraia a Limite

Montelupo Fiorentino

Scandicci

Pontassi

Fucecchio

EMPOLI

BISCOTTI (PRATO COOKIES)
These traditional Tuscan cookies are believed to have come from Prato originally. Known as *biscotti di Prato*, or *cantucci*, they are usually eaten after dipping into Vin Santo *(see p34)*.

Florentine wineries are a mix of innovation and tradition. The stainless steel containers of modern technology exist alongside small new oak *barriques* as well as great old wooden barrels used to age the traditional wines *(see pp24–7)*.

Enoteca Ristorante Pinchiorri in Florence is one of Italy's top restaurants, known for the excellent quality of the food and the extensive wine list. The cellar is one of the most prestigious in Europe.

◁ **Dome of Florence cathedral viewed from the hills outside the city**

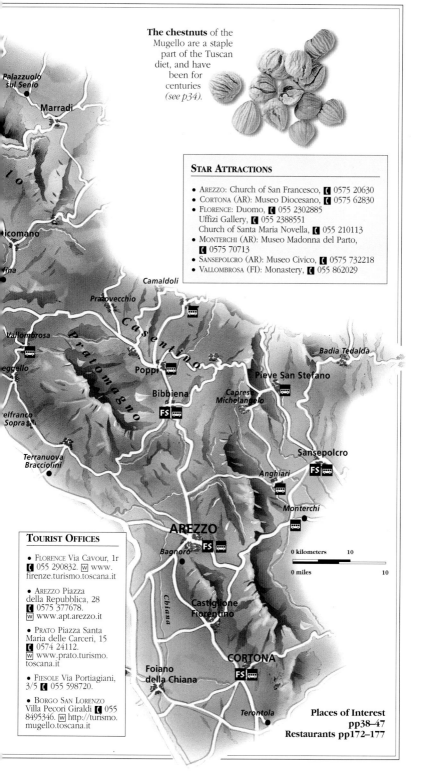

The chestnuts of the Mugello are a staple part of the Tuscan diet, and have been for centuries *(see p34)*.

STAR ATTRACTIONS

- AREZZO: Church of San Francesco, C 0575 20630
- CORTONA (AR): Museo Diocesano, C 0575 62830
- FLORENCE: Duomo, C 055 2302885
  Uffizi Gallery, C 055 2388551
  Church of Santa Maria Novella, C 055 210113
- MONTERCHI (AR): Museo Madonna del Parto, C 0575 70713
- SANSEPOLCRO (AR): Museo Civico, C 0575 732218
- VALLOMBROSA (FI): Monastery, C 055 862029

Palazzuolo sul Senio

Marradi

icomano

fina

Camaldoli

Pratovecchio

Vallombrosa

Casentino

Pratomagno

eggello

Poppi

Bibbiena

Badia Tedalda

Pieve San Stefano

Capreše Michelangelo

elfranco Sopra

Terranuova Bracciolini

Sansepolcro

Anghiari

Monterchi

FS

TOURIST OFFICES

- FLORENCE Via Cavour, 1r
  C 055 290832. W www.firenze.turismo.toscana.it

- AREZZO Piazza della Repubblica, 28
  C 0575 377678.
  W www.apt.arezzo.it

- PRATO Piazza Santa Maria delle Carceri, 15
  C 0574 24112.
  W www.prato.turismo.toscana.it

- FIESOLE Via Portiagiani, 3/5 C 055 598720.

- BORGO SAN LORENZO Villa Pecori Giraldi C 055 8495346. W http://turismo.mugello.toscana.it

AREZZO

Bagnoro

Castiglione Fiorentino

Chiana

CORTONA

Foiano della Chiana

Terontola

0 kilometers 10

0 miles 10

Places of Interest pp38–47
Restaurants pp172–177

Wines

FLORENTINE WINES WERE FAMOUS as long ago as the early Middle Ages. At the start of the 18th century the Grand Duke of Florence identified a number of localities that were famed for their vineyards, including Carmignano, Pomino and Valdarno di Sopra. (The Chianti area was not included because at that time it was limited to the territory of Siena and only later extended to the hills around Florence.)

In the Florence area, which lends itself to producing fine reds, the prince of the vines is the Sangiovese, which has gained a good reputation following recent modifications in Chianti-making. Sangiovese provides 75–100 percent of the grapes, Canaiolo Nero up to 10 percent, Trebbiano Toscano, Malvasia del Chianti, and other red grapes up to 10 percent). Its potential is still being studied, but Sangiovese is producing wines of great character. Other vines producing red grapes in this area are Canaiolo Nero, Cabernet Franc, Cabernet Sauvignon, and Merlot. Among white grape vines, the traditional Malvasia del Chianti and Trebbiano Toscano are now second-string grapes, while Pinot Bianco and Chardonnay are increasingly used blended or as single varieties.

CHIANTI COLLI FIORENTINI

This is the Chianti of the subzone south of Florence as far as Impruneta; to the east and west the zone stretches south along the banks of the Arno and between the Pesa and Elsa valleys to Barberino. The terrain to the east, with a warm, dry climate and sandier soils, yields wines of less body and greater saltiness. The soils to the east, on wooded hillsides, have a damper, cooler climate that yields finer perfumes and a longer life.

Chianti Colli Fiorentini is well suited to flavorsome dishes like cacciucco (fish soup) and first courses of pulses and cereals such as zuppa di farro (grain soup). The Superiore, which is stronger, and the Riserva, which is aged longer, are more suited to robust first courses with meat sauces, meat grilled or cooked on the spit, and game.

CHIANTI RÙFINA

This is considered the most refined of the various types of Chianti. The territory stretches northeast from Florence. The wine is born fairly rich in tannins, ensuring it ages well – it will keep for up to 40 years or more – but it is also slightly tingling to the palate. For this reason the wine needs to be allowed to mellow slowly.

A well-balanced wine with good body, particularly suited to dishes with a strong flavour, such as trippa alla fiorentina (Florentine-style tripe), red meat, and mature cheeses.

MAIALE UBRIACO

6 pork chops • 2 cloves garlic, chopped • 1 teaspoon fennel seeds • 2 glasses Chianti • salt • pepper

Heat a nonstick pan over a medium heat. Season the pork chops with plenty of salt and pepper and place them in the hot pan. Add the chopped garlic and the fennel seeds and cook over a high heat until the chops are golden on both sides. Pour in the red wine and continue cooking until most of the wine has evaporated.

CHIANTI MONTALBANO

This Chianti area covers some of the provinces of Florence to the west of the city and also Pistoia to the northwest. The wines produced around Vinci and Lamporecchio were already renowned in the 18th century, as was noted by the Grand Duke Cosimo III. At that time it was a robust wine with a high alcohol content. The current trend is for a red wine with a more elegant structure and less alcohol.

Generally Chianti Montalbano is light and fresh and makes pleasant drinking. It is very versatile, complementing both red and white meat.

CARMIGNANO

Production of this wine is restricted to hillsides in the municipal areas of Carmignano and Poggio a Caiano. It differs from other local reds because of the use of Cabernet Franc and Cabernet Sauvignon grapes, which give it a quite distinctive character. These grapes were already in use in the 18th century, when they were known as *uva francesca*. The DOCG label is reserved for Rosso and Rosso Riserva.

The rosé labelled Carmignano followed by the letters DOC is often called Vin Ruspo.

Carmignano DOC also appears on the label of various kinds of Vin Santo: dry, semi-sweet (also Reserve) and Occhio di Pernice (ordinary or Reserve).

BARCO REALE ROSSO

This wine is the young version of Carmignano, made from the same grapes but aged for a shorter period. Fresh and mellow, it is ideal as an all-purpose table wine. The name comes from a wall, called the Barco Reale, 31 miles (50 km) long. It was erected for Cosimo I, the Grand Duke of Tuscany in the 1570s, to separate his farmland from his game reserve. Barco Reale is also Rosato, Vin Santo, and Vin Santo Occhio di Pernice.

A Reserve red is also produced and the Pomino line is completed with a white and a red Vin Santo, both especially good wines.

POMINO

The zone of production for Pomino wine is very small and forms part of the municipal territory of Rùfina. A feature is the presence of French vines, introduced in the early 19th century, which found a suitable microclimate in the high altitudes (1600–2400 feet/500–800 m) above sea level. White wine is produced from Pinot Bianco and Chardonnay grapes and red from Sangiovese, Canaiolo, Cabernet Franc, and Cabernet Sauvignon grapes.

CHIANTI COLLI ARETINI

Chianti from the Colli Aretini is lighter-bodied and has a lower alcohol content than other Tuscan Chianti. Chianti Colli Aretini is ideal for general use as a table wine and is also well suited to first courses with meat sauces and also to pork and veal dishes, even those with well-seasoned sauces.

BIANCO VERGINE VALDICHIANA

This white wine is produced either still, lightly sparkling, or fully sparkling in eight communes of the province of Arezzo and roughly half the province of Siena. It goes well with delicate *antipasti*, soups, vegetable dishes, and unsalted fish.

The basic grape is Trebbiano Toscano, comprising at least 60 percent, blended with other white grapes, especially Malvasia.

WINE TYPE	GOOD VINTAGES	GOOD PRODUCERS	WINE TYPE	GOOD VINTAGES	GOOD PRODUCERS
Red Wine			**Red Wine**		
Chianti Rùfina	97, 95, 90	Frescobaldi di Firenze, Fattoria di Basciano a Rùfina	Carmignano	97, 95, 90	Tenuta Capezzana di Carmignano
Super Tuscans *(see p130)*	98, 97, 95, 90	Antinori di Firenze, D'Alessandro di Cortona, Frescobaldi di Firenze, Ruffino di Pontassieve	Chianti	97, 90	Antinori di Firenze

Salumi

Tuscany has a quite different approach to *salumi* (cured meats) from the rest of Italy, preferring a dry, highly seasoned product with plenty of pepper (often whole black peppercorns), made for eating with the unsalted local bread. These preserved meat products reflect a taste developed over many centuries. In Tuscany, pigs were not fed on swill, scraps, and cereals but were raised wild, free to graze and root about in the woods where they ate acorns, sweet chestnuts, truffles, and other tubers, which in turn made their flesh firm and flavorsome and naturally produced hams and salami with these tasty qualities. Because of the warm Tuscan climate, the meat products were then salted abundantly to ensure they kept well.

Natural casing.

TUSCAN SALAMI

This salami (cured sausage) is eaten uncooked. It is made of ground lean pork and lardons of hard fat chopped with a knife. It has a firm texture and is extremely tasty, with a marked flavor of black pepper.

Filling is a mixture of beef and pork.

Pure pork filling.

RIGATINO

In Tuscany this *pancetta* (cured pork belly) is always rather dry and well seasoned. Sometimes chilli is added to give it a spicy flavor.

SPALLA (SHOULDER)

Shoulder of pork is often cured to produce ham, but not on all estates since it may also be used for salami. This is "poor man's *prosciutto* (cured ham)," the fare of people who work on the land. Compared with the leg, the shoulder tastes more salty, peppery, and fatty. It must be stored in cool, dry conditions.

PIEDUCCI (PIG'S FEET)
Pig's feet are seasoned with salt, vinegar, garlic, and rosemary, then dried. They are used to flavor soups.

ZUPPA DI FAGIOLI CON I PIEDUCCI

1 pig's foot • 1 lb (450 g) dried zolfini *beans*

Soak the pig's foot in cold water for 48 hours to remove the salt. After 24 hours, add the beans to soak with the pig's foot. The next day, drain the meat and beans and put them in an earthenware pot or large saucepan. Cover with water, bring to the boil, then cover and simmer over a low heat for 2 hours. Remove some of the beans with a slotted spoon and mash them. Break up the meat and return it to the pot with the mashed beans. Reheat. Serve the soup with *bruschetta* rubbed with garlic and drizzled with olive oil, or use it as stock for soups made with grains or cabbage.

Traditionally, Florentine salami with fennel (finocchiona) *is a fairly large size.*

Meat is finely ground for a soft texture.

This medium-sized type of salami is usually less garlicky. It is often found at small traditional delicatessens.

SBRICIOLONA OR FINOCCHIONA
These salamis are flavored with fennel seed and, frequently, with plenty of garlic as well.

Thick layers of fat are streaked with lean meat.

GUANCIALE (PIG'S CHEEK)
The cheek of the pig is salted, seasoned with pepper, and matured. *Guanciale* is very tasty but is usually used as a flavoring ingredient in other dishes rather than eaten on its own.

SALSICCIA

This classic sausage is made from different cuts of pork, finely ground, seasoned with salt, pepper, and a little garlic, and stuffed into a thin natural casing. Sausages are best eaten straight from the grill. Cured sausage, which may contain spices, liver, fennel, or red wine, can be sliced and eaten on *crostini* (toasted Tuscan bread).

SOPPRESSATA OR COPPA (PIG'S HEAD SAUSAGE)

This sausage is prepared using all parts of the pig's head. The head is boiled with herbs and spices, chopped coarsely, and flavored with garlic and pepper. Parsley and chilli may also be added.

This sausage has a firm, gelatinous, spongy texture.

Tuscan prosciutto crudo should be sliced very thinly.

TUSCAN PROSCIUTTO CRUDO (CURED HAM)

Cheaper hams are saltier and smell mainly of pepper. A fine *prosciutto crudo* has a delicate aroma, and, while it is more salty than classic Parma ham and San Daniele from the Veneto, it is not excessively so. The texture is firm and it has a definite, lingering meaty flavor, spiced with pepper. The quality depends on the ingredients and the skill of the producer, and no two hams taste exactly the same.

OTHER PORK SPECIALITIES WORTH TRYING

Sanguignaccio or **buristo** (blood sausage) is made of pork blood and cartilage and may come in a sausage shape such as *buristo di Cinta (see p104)* or in a large piece such as the *buristo* of Montalcino *(see p137)*. Other cured meats made from lean cuts of pork – fillet, loin, or the collar – are common. **Capocollo** (cured neck of pork) is similar to the *coppa* from Lombardy and Emilia-Romagna, but is much drier and more peppery. Some producers flavor small spicy salamis by adding chilli to them. **Lardo** (lard), flavored mainly with rosemary, is another very popular delicacy in Tuscany.

Extra-Virgin Olive Oil

FLORENCE IS RINGED with olive groves, and all the lower ridges of the Valdarno and its tributaries are dotted with olive trees. The types of oil produced in the area differ greatly, not so much through tradition – because nearly everywhere the tendency is to harvest early and produce fruity oils – but because of differences in soil and the choice of different varieties of olive tree. Most olive-growing estates in the region are small or medium-sized and the majority aim for high quality. Nearly all the estates combine olive oil production with wine-making or, in areas unsuited to growing vines, with other types of agriculture such as growing grain or vegetables.

RÙFINA OLIVE OIL
This oil is produced in an area north of Florence comprising the communes of Rùfina, Dicomano, and Londa. The oil is fruity with a marked scent of herbs, strong, very full-bodied and flavorsome.

OIL FROM PRATOMAGNO
This oil is produced in the territory east of Florence in the bend of the upper Valdarno lying between the provinces of Florence and Arezzo. The territory includes the communes of Reggello (FI), Castelfranco di Sopra, and Loro Ciuffenna (AR). The oil is very similar to that of the Colli Fiorentini, but generally more intense.

OIL FROM THE COLLI FIORENTINI
Inland south of Florence is the area that produces this oil. The territory covers Bagno a Ripoli, Fiesole, Scandicci, Impruneta, Incisa, and San Casciano, stretching as far as Poggibonsi and San Gimignano. The oil is medium-bodied with a full, smooth, fruity flavor which has a vegetable aftertaste and some slightly bitter, pungent notes.

OIL FROM MONTE ALBANO

East of Lucca, between the province of Pistoia and the northern part of the province of Florence, is the area producing this olive oil, especially at Vinci, Carmignano, Artimino, and Montelupo Fiorentino. The oil is generally medium-light and fruity with herbal scents and a balanced flavor. This flavor varies in intensity from season to season.

OIL FROM THE COLLI ARETINI

Produced in the territory south of Arezzo, covering various communes including Castiglione Fiorentino and Cortona, this is a medium-bodied fruity oil, fresh and aromatic. Body and fluidity is average. It has a harmonious taste with slightly bitter and pungent notes and a hint of artichoke.

PUTTANAIO

3–4 tablespoons virgin olive oil • 3 onions, sliced • 2 sprigs rosemary, chopped • 3 cloves garlic, crushed • 2 stalks celery, sliced • 3 potatoes, diced • about 2 lb (800 g) green peppers, seeded and diced • 3 eggplants, diced • 2 carrots, diced • 2 zucchinis, diced • 18 lb (8 kg) ripe tomatoes, chopped • 3 tablespoons chopped fresh basil, thyme, and parsley • salt

Heat the oil in a large pan, add the onions, rosemary, and garlic; fry until soft. Add the diced vegetables and tomatoes. Season and simmer until the vegetables are cooked. Garnish with the chopped herbs before serving the soup.

The olive tree breaks the monotony of great fields of grain.

LAUDEMIO OLIVE OIL

This was originally the finest oil – the one that the sharecropper was required to reserve for the landowner – it was referred to as "the master's oil." Today, Laudemio is a brand name given to the produce of a consortium of estates, all of which use the same bottle design. The denomination does not represent a traditional area or specific properties or quality, and the regulations are vague about some essential factors. They cover a very broad area of membership (central Tuscany), best-by dates, harvesting by December 15 (normal for Tuscany, weather permitting), and rather vaguely defined production techniques. In other words, the quality from different estates may vary.

Chianina Beef

THE CELEBRATED DISH *Bistecca alla Fiorentina* (Florentine T-bone steak), traditionally cooked over hot wood embers, is best when made with beef from pedigree Chianina cattle, which is generally rated as of superior quality. Chianina cattle are traditionally reared in the Val di Chiana, particularly around Cortona. The distinctive, white-coated breed – one of the oldest breeds in existence – only produces high quality meat if it has been raised in exactly the right conditions, however. While other breeds of cattle are rarely temperamental, Chianina cattle are unusually sensitive and their state of well-being influences the quality of the meat – if the animal is high-strung, the meat is tough. The Chianina cow flourishes when looked after by the same person. It objects to sharing its stall with other cattle, and the calf has to be raised alongside its mother. There is debate as to whether the quality of beef is better when the cattle graze freely outdoors or when they are kept in a stall and fed on a mixture of fresh grass and hay.

For Chianina beef to be first-rate, the animal should be mature – this means over 16–18 months old – and it should have grown to over 1,760 lb (800 kilos), yielding 1,100 lb (500 kilos) of meat.

BISTECCA ALLA FIORENTINA
This is a T-bone steak (rib steak with the fillet steak still attached). Its total weight varies from 1 lb 2 oz–2 lb 4 oz (500 g–1 kg) and it is usually sliced thickly, up to about 2 inches (5 cm).

An essential feature of Chianina beef is the very firm flesh which is tender but never dry, despite the small amount of surface fat and marbling. The flavor is quite distinctive.

BISTECCA ALLA FIORENTINA

1 T-bone steak, about 2 lb 4 oz (1 kg) in weight and including the fillet steak, rib, and under-rib • extra-virgin olive oil • salt • pepper

Heat the grill or light the barbecue. Sprinkle both sides of the steak with pepper and lay it on the grill, keeping it some distance from the embers, if cooking on a barbecue. Cook for 5 minutes, then turn over and season the cooked side with salt. Cook the second side for 5 minutes (or longer, if preferred) and season with salt. Remove from the grill and brush with olive oil (season the oil with garlic and herbs, if preferred).

BISTECCA (CHOP)
This is the ordinary rib steak without the fillet. It is often used as part of a plate of assorted roast meats for a typical Tuscan meal.

For the thickness to be just right for perfect cooking, there has to be both the rib and the under-rib.

POLZO
This is the cut under the shoulder,
good for *stracotto* (braising), boiling,
and, above all, *scottiglia* (stew).

*This small fat-free joint is
suitable for machine slicing
for* carpaccio *(steak sliced
very thin and eaten raw).*

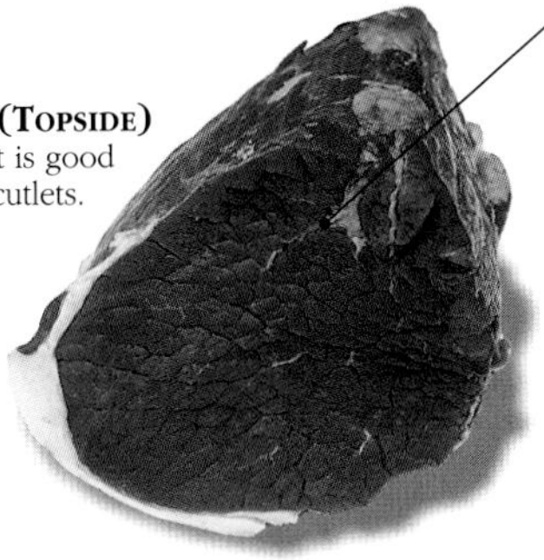

GIRELLO (TOPSIDE)
This lean cut is good
for roasting and for cutlets.

*The layers of lean beef alternating
with fat and bone make a
tasty broth when boiled.*

SPICCHIO DI PETTO (MIDDLE BRISKET)
This is called *biancostato* in the rest of
Italy and is typically used for making
boiled beef. It is also used for *scottiglia*
(stew) after part of the fat has been
removed.

*This lean cut is very
popular because it
is easy to cook.*

NOCE (RUMP)
This lean part of the leg is
used for scallops, breaded
cutlets, and small steaks.

OTHER CHIANINA CUTS
Because the Chianina breed is mainly associated with the T-bone steak, other cuts
tend to be neglected. However, the superiority of Chianina beef is obvious in all cuts,
from forequarter to rump. In Tuscany it is particularly important to use Chianina beef
for traditional dishes, recipes devised for that type of very tender beef. For *stracotto
alla fiorentina* (Florentine braised beef), for example, the best cuts, in addition to
polzo, are **scannello** (sirloin) and **cappello del prete**; for *scottiglia* ask for **reale**.

Traditional Produce

A DEEP-SEATED LOVE of tradition ensures the continuing popularity of all kinds of local produce. A traditional meal in this region will never stray far from a long-standing pattern: *crostini (see p36), prosciutto (see p29), pappardelle* (a type of ribbon pasta) with hare, and mixed roast meats. The mild Tuscan climate and the exacting demands of producers and consumers mean that you can still find free-range chickens, *salumi (see p27)* made with local ingredients, local varieties of vegetables, traditional cakes, and freshly baked breads.

CHESTNUTS

The quality of a chestnut is determined by the size and the number of nuts in a single husk. Chestnut trees may produce fruit with a single large nut in each husk or several small ones. The larger varieties with a single nut are much prized by confectioners for their fine flavor and also for their appearance because the inside shell does not press into the kernel. Larger nuts are also easier to work with.

CHESTNUT FLOUR

A staple in mountain areas since ancient times, chestnut flour *(farina di castagne)* is the basic ingredient of *castagnaccio* (chestnut cake). The flour becomes stale very quickly so it should not be stored for too long.

ZOLFINI BEANS FROM PRATOMAGNO

These small, pale yellowish beans, which are now very rare, are exclusive to Pratomagno. The thin-skinned beans have a dense texture and a good flavor. They are easily digested and particularly rich in iron and fiber.

Small zolfini beans are a pale yellow color.

These sweet almond cookies are traditionally eaten after dinner, dipped in sweet Vin Santo.

ZUCCOTTO

This cream and sponge-cake dessert is a Florentine speciality, now seen all over Italy. A mold of sponge is filled with whipped cream, confectioner's custard, and chocolate. The chilled *zuccotto* is turned out to serve.

BISCOTTINI DI PRATO

These almond cookies, which come from Prato, are also called *cantuccini*. They are made from flour, eggs, sugar, almonds, and pine nuts. The dough is shaped into a long loaf and baked, then it is sliced and baked again until the slices are crunchy.

SUGO DI PECORA

2 lb 4 oz (1 kg) boned shoulder or leg of mutton, trimmed of excess fat and cubed • olive oil for frying • 2 onions, chopped • 3 cloves garlic, finely chopped • 1–2 sprigs of rosemary • 1 sprig of sage • 8 oz (200 g) ground lean mutton • 4 oz (100 g) chopped prosciutto crudo • the zest of ¹/₂ a lemon • pinch of freshly grated nutmeg • 1 tablespoon tomato paste diluted in a little warm water • 1 lb 2 oz (500 g) tomatoes, peeled • salt • pepper

Heat a frying pan, add the cubed mutton, and fry for 1–2 minutes to seal the meat. Heat a little oil in a saucepan, add the onions, garlic, rosemary, and sage and fry until softened. Add the ground mutton and ham, stirring well. Add the cubed mutton, nutmeg, lemon zest, and diluted tomato paste. Cook over a moderate heat until the water has evaporated. Add the tomatoes and season. Cook over a low heat for about 1 hour, until the meat is tender, adding extra hot water, if necessary. Serve the mutton sauce with pasta.

MUTTON

Pecora (mutton), which is meat from the adult sheep, is widely eaten in the Campi Bisenzio area. Shepherds used to move their flocks seasonally and customarily paid their way in kind. They handed over the weaker sheep exhausted by traveling the Passo dei Pecorai before they made their descent to marshy plains that were difficult for sheep to cross.

PANE SCIOCCO (UNSALTED BREAD)

When it comes to bread, Tuscans are great traditionalists. The large loaves, elongated or rounded, above all unsalted, have a fairly heavy texture well suited for making the popular *crostoni* (toasted bread), for mopping up sauces, or as a base for soups.

GEMMA D'ABETO

The monks of Monte Senario produce this aromatic liqueur from herbs and fir cone seeds.

VALDARNO CAPONS

These free-range capons with yellow legs and a bright red crest are typical of certain villages in the Valdarno. They have firm, flavorsome flesh and are especially delicious in casseroles.

WHAT TO SAMPLE

Cantucci all'anice are sweet crunchy cookies flavored with aniseed. They are usually dunked in red wine before eating. They are made in Prato by the same firm that makes *cantuccini (see p34)*. Various **herbal liqueurs** are produced by the monks of Monte Senario and Camaldoli, who also sell **honey**, **candies**, and **chocolate**. The Sieve and other rivers yield very fine **trout**. In the Casentino in particular, many shepherds make cheese, and some of their **pecorino** and **ricotta** is as good as that produced in the Crete region, a popular cheese-making region to the south of Siena. **Schiaccioni** are a local large white bean worth trying. The Mugello, the pretty area to the north and east of Florence, has black truffles, and the Valdarno region has white as well. The Empoli area produces fine vegetables, including **white asparagus**.

Wild Produce

PINAROLO
(Boletus luteus)
Winter *porcini* has a distinctive cap covered with a skin that comes away easily (the skin has to be removed before eating). Its skin is very slimy and brownish in color, while the stalk has a broad ring. Found only in pine woods, it is one of the best *porcini* for preserving in oil as well as being excellent deviled fresh.

PORTENTOSO
(Tricholoma portentosum)
This silky gray mushroom is very common in the late fall and can be found in the stands of fir or pine trees mostly in Vallombrosa and Lunigiana. It is excellent preserved in oil or deviled, and is ideal in stews.

CROSTINI CON I CIMBALLI

1¼ lb (600 g) caps of cimballi *(funnel-cap mushrooms), chopped coarsely • 3 cloves garlic, chopped • pinch of chilli powder • extra-virgin olive oil • 1 dessertspoon chopped tomatoes • 1 sprig of parsley, chopped • salt • Tuscan bread*

Place the mushrooms in a saucepan with the garlic and chilli, plenty of oil, and salt. Cook over a high heat until the mushrooms shed their moisture, then lower the heat and cook until the moisture evaporates completely. Add the tomato pulp and parsley, and continue cooking for another 10 minutes. Toast slices of Tuscan bread, spread with olive oil, and top with the mushrooms.

CIMBALLO
(Clitocybe geotropa)
In its early stages this mushroom – sometimes known as the Ridestone funnel-cap mushroom – looks like a large nail, then it grows into a tall, scented, coffee-colored funnel. It grows in the mountains and meadows, in coastal areas under hedges, on heaths, and in scrub where it forms zigzag lines. The cap is exquisite; the dried stem is ground into a powder.

DORMIENTE
(Hygrophorus marzuolus)
This spring mushroom – sometimes known as silvery snowbank mushroom – is found in the mountains of Vallombrosa when the snow thaws, and around Siena and Arezzo in February and March. It is protected – only mushrooms larger than ¾ inch (2 cm) can be picked. It has a mild flavor and is excellent fresh, cooked in cream sauces or in flans, or preserved in oil.

CHIOCCIOLE ALLA NEPITELLA (SNAILS WITH CALAMINT LEAVES)

1 large onion • 1 stalk celery • 1 carrot • 1 chile • 2 cloves garlic • extra-virgin olive oil • 1¼ lb (500 g) peeled tomatoes • calamint leaves • 4½ lb (2 kg) small white snails, ready cleaned • 8 fl oz (200 ml) red wine • meat stock • salt • pepper

Chop the vegetables, chile, and garlic and fry in a large pan with plenty of oil. When the vegetables have softened, add the tomatoes, calamint, salt, and pepper. Lower the heat and simmer gently for about 10 minutes. Stir in the snails and sprinkle the wine over them. Simmer gently for 1½ hours, adding stock if necessary to prevent it from drying out.

NEPITELLA
(Calamintha nepeta)
Gathered from early spring until the first frosts, calamint is found from the coast to the hills in Tuscany. It flowers in June and July. In Tuscan cooking it is used with mushrooms, snails, artichokes, or lamb. It must be used in very small quantities otherwise the dish will taste of caramel. It is often confused with mint, but the perfume is sweeter and heavier. Use calamint sparingly because it can cause sleeplessness and palpitations.

PIMPINELLA
(Sanguisorba minor)
A curious and unmistakable salad herb, *pimpinella* smells rather like melon peel. It is common at all altitudes, especially on the edges of pathways and vegetable patches. Use it raw in salads or add it to white wine for an intriguing aperitif.

PEPOLINO
(Thymus serpyllum and other varieties*)*
Wild thyme is the most common wild herb at all altitudes and latitudes. It is a tender plant that covers walls, stumps of trees, and banks between woodland and pasture. The flowered tips are picked between May and October. It is excellent fresh or dried, for roasts, stews, and meat sauces. Fresh thyme can be added to salads.

MORA DI ROVO
(Rubus species)
In Tuscany an abundance of blackberries can be found on the edge of thickets. They have large, flavorsome fruits, especially those growing on the Apennine range. They are ideal for jams and syrups, and children enjoy picking and eating fresh blackberries.

Places of Interest

FLORENCE, AREZZO, AND CASENTINO form a zone that runs the whole length of Tuscany and embraces a large city, cool, shady mountains along the crest of the Apennines, the forests of Casentino, and the Mediterranean coast of the Basso Aretino. Its cuisine is a showcase for the region's food and drink, with outlets of notable quality in the Arezzo area – especially the butchers' shops. In the summer many stores close on Saturday afternoons.

ANGHIARI (AR)

 Valledimezzo

località Toppole 25
☎ 0575 788103

This goat farm set amid woods and olive groves offers organically produced goat's-milk cheeses and yogurts. Fresh milk is also for sale.

AREZZO

🐂 **Luca Macelleria**

Palazzo del Pero, 62/a
☎ 0575 369519
● Wed pm

In 2002 Corrado Falcinelli, the heir to three generations of butchers and producers of salumi, sold his business to a "complete-cycle" farmer, that is one who feeds his animals cereals and hay of his own production. In the first few months after the sale, Falcinelli stayed on as a consultant to ensure continuity of quality. Chianina and beef from other breeds are available, as well as typical Tuscan all-pork salumi completely free from preservatives.

🐂 **Pollo San Marco**

frazione San Marco,
via dei Frati, 12
☎ 0575 901601
● Sat pm

Here you will find beef, pork, lamb, an assortment of game birds and animals, plus a variety of other local produce, including Chianina beef, the firm's own salumi, free-range, yellow-legged chickens from Valdarno (see p35), and ready-to-cook dishes, such as collo ripieno (stuffed neck of beef).

 Tavanti

borgo Santa Croce, 15
☎ 0575 352354
● Wed pm

Bread sold here is made in the traditional way and then baked in a wood-fired oven.

🍇 **Torre di Gnicche**

piaggia San Martino, 8
☎ 0575 352035
● Wed

This wine shop, bar, and restaurant has a very good selection of Italian wines from all regions and a fine choice of Tuscan produce. Try the salumi and cheese or sample hot or cold dishes cooked traditionally. The cakes are homemade. Open from noon to 3:00PM and from 6:00PM until late.

BADIA TEDALDA (AR)

 Piegai

piazza Bonafede, 23
☎ 0575 714246
● Wed pm

You can buy Chianina beef from cattle that grazed on the company's farm at Caprile, an "agriturismo" (a place for farm or wine estate vacations). Likewise, the pork is from pigs from a nearby farm. Other specialties include pork and wild boar sausages.

BIVIGLIANO (FI)

🍁 **Convento di Monte Senario**

☎ 055 406441
● Fri

As well as their famous Gemma d'Abeto liqueur, the monks produce Elixir di China, Amaro Borghini, and Alkermes from an ancient recipe.

PANZANELLA

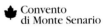

12 slices stale bread • 2 teaspoons white wine vinegar • 12 anchovy fillets, chopped • 6 tomatoes, cut into wedges • 3 onions, sliced • fresh basil leaves, roughly torn • extra-virgin olive oil • salt • pepper

Soften the bread by soaking it in cold water with the vinegar added. Squeeze it dry and divide it between six plates or bowls. Cover each slice of bread with some of the chopped anchovy, tomato wedges, onion slices, and torn basil leaves. Drizzle olive oil over the top, season with salt and pepper, then repeat to make a second layer.

STRACOTTO ALLA FIORENTINA

2 lb (1 kg) braising steak or brisket in a single piece tied with string • 1 pint (500 ml) Chianti wine • sprigs of rosemary and sage • 1–2 bay leaves • 4 cloves garlic, chopped • 2 onions, chopped • 3 sticks celery, chopped • 3 carrots, chopped • extra-virgin olive oil • 1 lb (500 g) plum tomatoes, chopped • salt • pepper

Put the beef in a bowl with the wine, herbs, and all the vegetables except the tomatoes. Leave to marinate in a cool place for 24 hours. Drain the meat and pat dry. Heat the oil in a flameproof casserole, add the meat and brown all over to seal it. Remove the vegetables from the marinade with a slotted spoon and brown them in a little oil in a second pan, then add to the beef. Pour in the wine from the marinade, add the tomatoes, and simmer for 30 minutes. Remove the vegetables, purée them, and pour the purée back into the pan. Simmer for a further 4 hours, adding water if necessary (but keep the gravy thick). Season with salt and pepper. Untie the meat and serve cut into thick slices, accompanied by the gravy.

CALENZANO (FI)

🌾 **La Pasta di Anna Paola**

via Puccini, 237
📞 055 8879505 ⬤ Mon

Here you will find a wide variety of flat and stuffed pasta specialties made from good quality fresh ingredients. The extensive selection varies according to the season and the produce available.

CAMALDOLI (AR)

🍁 **Antica Farmacia dei Monaci Camaldolesi**

via Camaldoli
📞 0575 556143
⬤ Wed, Nov 1–Easter

The Carthusian monks at the monastery produce various liqueurs flavored with different herbs, an aperitif, a dessert liqueur made from fir cones, candies (such as pine, barley, honey, and fruit drops), and a wide variety of honey (with forest honey the local specialty). The monks also make chocolate from their own special recipe.

CAPRAIA A LIMITE (FI)

🍇 **Tenuta Cantagallo**

località Capraia Fiorentina, via Valicarda, 35
📞 0571 910078 ⬤ Sat

This family-run farm is located in the Park of Montalbano. The proprietors also own two other farms: Le Farnete in Carmignano and Del Podere Matroneo in Greve in Chianti. As well as wine and oil, it is possible to taste other produce (though not all of it is of the high quality one would expect from this area). Alongside the production of the classic Chianti di Montalbano and Carmignano (both regular and Reserve), Carleto (from Rhine Riesling grapes) is also made here.

CARMIGNANO (PO)

🍇 **Fattoria Ambra**

via Lombarda, 85
📞 055 8719049

This estate's wine-making technique is based on a policy of separating the different varieties of grape so the wine-makers have more control over the combinations of grapes and are better able to harmonize the final blend. Much of the production is devoted to producing the estate's top wines, Carmignano Vigna Santa Cristina in Pilli and two Reserves: Le Vigne Alte Montalbiolo and Elzana, all with good structure and a velvety texture.

🍇 **Fattoria di Artimino**

via della Nave, 6
📞 055 8751424

With about 173 acres (70 hectares) of vineyards and twice this area under olive groves, Fattoria di Artimino is one of the most beautiful and interesting Tuscan estates. The Medici villa complex houses a four-star hotel (Hotel Paggeria Medicea) and two restaurants (Biagio Pignatta and Le Cantine del Redi). The vineyard's leading wines are Carmignano and Carmignano Riserva Villa Medicea, as well as Barco Reale and Villa dell'Iris.

Fattoria Ambra at Carmignano

FAGIOLI AL FIASCO (BEANS IN A FLASK)

*1 lb (450 g) dried cannellini beans • 1 sprig of sage •
2 cloves garlic, crushed • extra-virgin olive oil •
pepper • salt*

Soak the beans in cold water overnight. The
next day, drain them and put in a pan with all
the other ingredients, adding plenty of oil.
Add enough water to cover, bring to
the boil and simmer for 1–2
hours. In Tuscany, the
beans are cooked in a
Chianti flask placed in
the embers of a fire.
Use fresh Sorana
beans instead, if
available *(see p61)*.

🍇 Tenuta Capezzana

via Capezzana, 100
☎ 055 8706005
⬤ Mon; Sun (winter)

*This is the largest farm in
Carmignano, with about
222 acres (90 hectares) of
vineyards and 370 acres
(150 hectares) of olives
around a 15th-century
Medici villa. There is a fee
for tastings. Among the
wines with the Carmignano
label are the excellent
Villa di Capezzana and
Barco Reale. Worthy of a
special mention are the
Chardonnay, the Trefiano
(made from organic
Sangiovese, Cabernet
Sauvignon, Cabernet
Franc, and Canaiolo
grapes), and a rosé, Vin
Ruspo. The extra-virgin
olive oil is excellent, as is the
grappa. Accommodation
is also available.*

🍇 Il Poggiolo

via Pistoiese, 90
☎ 055 8711242
⬤ Sat pm

*The vineyards here are
scattered over the heart
of the commune and the
estate focuses on the whole
line of Carmignano wines.
This includes a traditional
red (a reserve; a rosé
called Vin Ruspo; and
a younger Barco Reale)
and Vin Santo based on*

*Trebbiano grapes. These
wines offer very good
quality at reasonable
prices.*

CASTIGLION FIORENTINO (AR)

🫒 Frantoio Amatucci

località Noceta, 41/b
☎ 0575 657129

*This olive mill produces
and sells the traditional
extra-virgin olive oil of
the Colli Aretini. The oil
is ideal for classic Tuscan
soups and all dishes
finished with a drizzle
of good-quality olive oil.*

CORTONA (AR)

🍇 Baldetti Mario

località
Pietraia-Terontola, 21
☎ 0575 67143

*This estate is situated in
a historic building dating
from 1780. From here
it is possible to enjoy
beautiful panoramic
views all the way to
Lake Trasimeno. The
surrounding vineyards
are organically cultivated.
Among the wines on offer:
Bianco Val di Chiana
(Trebbiano, Chardonnay,
Malvasia), Sangiovese,
Pietraia (Chardonnay,
Grechetto, Malvasia),
and Grechetto Cortona.*

FLORENCE

🍇 Enoteca Alessi

via delle Oche, 27/29/31 r
☎ 055 214966
⬤ Sat in July

*This large wine shop is
located on two levels.
The lower floor contains
over 2,000 of the very
finest Italian wines,
subdivided by region and
commune. The serving
counter is on the upper
floor, where you can find
Tuscan and house
specialties, particularly
confectionery, as well
as a choice selection of
liquors and liqueurs.*

Il Poggiolo at Carmignano

Boutique dei Dolci

via Fabroni, 18 r
C 055 499503
○ Mon

An original confectionery shop founded and run by an Italian-American. The recipes are American, English, French, and Dutch, all prepared with organically grown ingredients. The theme cakes for kids, made with original American cake molds of Disney and Warner Brothers cartoon characters, are one of the shop's specialties, as is the classic cheesecake. Another selling point is located in Via dei Servi, 43 r.

Salumeria Del Panta

via Sant'Antonio, 49 r
C 055 216889
○ Mon

This shop features a vast assortment of traditional Tuscan salumi *and cheeses, some of them almost impossible to find elsewhere. It also offers excellent international specialties. Here you will find the finest preserved fish – anchovies, sardines, herrings, dried or salted cod. There are all kinds of pickles, preserves in oil, flour, pulses, and cereals, including some very unusual ones, plus different kinds of rice, and spices sold loose.*

✿ Dolci e Dolcezze

piazza Beccaria 8 r
C 055 2345458
● Mon, Sun (summer)

This confectioner's and café is renowned for its very imaginative pastries and cakes, as well as some interesting savories. All ingredients are carefully chosen from natural produce and artificial or chemical products are rigorously excluded.

Traditional Florentine dishes

🍴 Fernando Primizie

via Don Minzoni, 38 r
C 055 587540
● Wed pm

Here you will find a good variety of vegetables and fruit, organically grown or from small local market gardens. There are also cheeses and preserves and a fine selection of wines, though Tuscans dominate.

🍴 Fratelli Vettori

borgo san Jacopo, 63 r
C 055 212797
● Wed pm

This grocery offers high-quality fruit and vegetables, as well as a selection of spring produce. The prices are a little steep, on account of both the quality on offer and the well-deserved reputation of the shop. There is also a range of Tuscan wines.

🍇 Enoteca Romano Gambi

via Senese, 21 r
C 055 222525
● Sun

All the names that count among local and Italian wines, plus wines from France and the US, can be found here. There is also a good selection of whisky and grappa and a variety of confectioneries, cakes,

and snacks. Salumi *and cheese are sold at Christmas. Book for a tasting. A second shop is in the town center at Via Borgo SS. Apostoli, 21-23 r (055 292646).*

❄ Gelateria Giorgio

via Duccio da Boninsegna, 36
C 055 710849
○ Mon, Sun pm

This shop is celebrated throughout Tuscany for its quality ice cream and the torta millefoglie *(vanilla slice) and Florentine* schiacciata *(bread).*

🍵 Hemingway

piazza Piattellina, 9 r
C 055 284781
● Mon

This bar-cum-tea house is renowned for its wide selection of teas and even more for the range of excellent handmade chocolates and derivates (pralines, cakes, hot chocolates etc). Sunday brunch is available.

LAMPREDOTTO E TRIPPA IN ZIMINO

extra-virgin olive oil • 3 cloves garlic, chopped • 1 lb (500 g) tomatoes, peeled • 1 chile, deseeded and chopped • 2 lb (1 kg) beet leaves, cut into strips • 2 lb (1 kg) plain tripe (see below), cut into strips • salt • pepper

Heat some oil in a pan, cook the garlic briefly, then add the tomatoes and cook for about 10 minutes. Add the greens and cook for 3 minutes. Add the tripe, season, and cook for 40–45 minutes. In Italy this dish is made with half plain tripe and half *millefoglie* tripe (which looks like the leaves of a book).

Pastificio Moretti

via Datini, 22 r
055 685607

*On offer here is a wide
variety of pasta, and also
ready-cooked food.*

Gastronomia Palmieri

via Manni, 48 r
055 602081
● Sat pm (summer)

*The variety and quality
of its products make this
one of Italy's most
interesting cheese shops.
This fine delicatessen
offers an excellent choice
of delicacies – caviar,
pâté de foie gras, bread
baked in a wood-fired
oven, preserves, extra-
virgin olive oil, salumi,
and much more. There is
a well-stocked enoteca
(wine cellar) with some
foreign wines, and there
is an excellent selection
of ready-made dishes
on sale.*

Gastronomia Pegna

via dello Studio, 26 r
055 282701
● Wed pm

*Pegna has been a
household name in
Florence for 140 years.
The products on offer
at this delicatessen are
skillfully selected from Italy
and abroad and include
a choice of salumi, cheese,
preserves, spices, terrines,
and confectioneries.*

Pitti Gola e Cantina

piazza Pitti, 16
055 212704 ● Mon

*Close to Palazzo Pitti,
this wine shop boasts a
clientèle of Florentine
connoisseurs who enjoy
the wide range of wines,*

BACCALÀ ALLA FIORENTINA

***extra-virgin olive oil • 3 cloves garlic, chopped • 1 onion,
chopped • 1 lb (450 g) tomatoes, peeled • 2 lb (1 kg) salt
cod, presoaked • 1–2 tablespoons chopped fresh parsley
• flour • salt • pepper • parsley, to garnish***

Heat some oil in a pan, add the garlic and onion, and
cook until lightly browned. Add the tomatoes and season
with salt and pepper. Meanwhile,
bone the cod, leaving the skin on,
and cut it into largish squares.
Heat plenty of oil in a pan,
Flour the pieces of cod, add
them to the hot oil, and fry
until golden. Remove the
fish from the pan, drain on
paper towels, and add it to
the tomato sauce. Stir in the
chopped parsley, and serve
garnished with extra parsley.

---

*spirits, preserves, and
pickles, all strictly Tuscan
produce. Visitors can
browse through cookbooks,
and there is an area for
wine tasting.*

Forno di Marcello Pugi

viale De Amicis, 49 r
055 669666
● Fri pm

*This bakery is famous
in Florence and the
surrounding area for its
delicious schiacciata
all'olio (olive oil bread)
and pizza slices. The
excellent bread is made
using fresh yeast.*

Bar Pasticceria Robiglio

via dei Servi, 112 r
055 212784

*For almost 75 years,
Robiglio has delighted
gourmets with its
traditional confectioneries
and excellent coffee. There
are three other branches,
one in via Tosinghi, 11 r
(055 215013), one in
viale Lavagnini, 18 r (055
490886), and the other in
Viale dei Mille, 12 r (055
585856). There is also an
ice-cream parlor in Viale*

---

*Strozzi, 8 r (055 495939).
Pralines and snacks are
available at the bar.*

Salumificio Senese

via Ugnano, 10
055 751611
● Wed pm

*This firm produces
excellent fresh meat from
pigs raised on its own
farm at Lastra a Signa
and by other local
breeders. They make their
own salumi, including the
Tuscan classics, and serve
aromatic sausages from
other regions. They do
roast suckling pig and
cooked meats to order.*

Macelleria Soderi Paolo

interno Mercato Centrale
San Lorenzo
055 2398496 ● pm

*Exceptionally good beef
(sometimes Chianina),
fine Fanano pork, lamb
from the mountains of
Pistoia, and various
ready-to-cook cuts of meat
plus about 30 types of
ground beef are sold here.
Follow their instructions
for grilling the meat.*

🍁 Sugar Blues

via XXVII Aprile, 46/48 r
📞 055 483666
🕐 Wed pm

Sugar Blues specializes in macrobiotic foods. Gourmets looking for wholesome, organically grown produce, and both fresh and preserved specialties will find this shop worth a visit. A selection of natural essences is also sold.

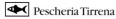 Pescheria Tirrena

via dei Cerchi, 20 r
📞 055 216602
🕐 pm

The owner of this shop is a real expert. Every day he selects the pick of the catch, especially shellfish and top-quality white fish.

❋ Gelateria Vivoli

via Isola delle Stinche, 7 r
📞 055 292334
🕐 Mon

The same family still oversees the high quality of the ingredients used in this ice-cream parlor, which has been famous in Florence for 70 years. Nowadays there are more than 40 delicious ice-cream flavors to choose from. The classics – cream, chocolate, lemon, and torroncino (nougat) – are based on recipes that go back to the 1920s. In the café, the breads and desserts are made from natural ingredients.

🍇 Le Volpi e l'Uva

piazza De Rossi, 1
📞 055 2398132

This wine shop is located 131 feet (40 meters) from Ponte Vecchio, in a 15th-century building. It has a quick turnover of around 130 Italian and French labels, exclusively from small or little-known wineries. Many wines can be bought by the glass, matched with a selection of Italian and French raw-milk cheeses, salumi, and other gastronomic delights.

🐂 Macelleria Zagli

via Valori, 6 r
📞 055 587571
🕐 Wed pm

This butcher's shop stakes its name on high-quality Tuscan produce such as Chianina beef (and not just the rib steaks but also the less prized cuts), free-range Valdarno chickens, and pork from Tuscan pigs. Various ready-to-cook dishes are also sold.

FOIANO DELLA CHIANA (AR)

🍇 Fattoria Santa Vittoria

località Pozzo,
via Piana, 43
📞 0575 66807;
0575 966026
🕐 Sat pm

This 19th-century cellar displays agricultural machinery from times gone by. There are two types of tasting to choose from: a small tasting, which is free of charge, or a tasting combined with a guided tour. Please note that there is a charge for the latter option, and it should be booked well in advance. Small, self-catering apartments are also available for visitors to rent. Among the wines on offer: Valdichiana Grechetto and Poggio al Tempio (a blend of Sangiovese, Merlot, and Cabernet Sauvignon grapes). Oil is also produced here.

MONTELUPO FIORENTINO (FI)

🐦 San Vito in Fior di Selva

località Malmantile
📞 0571 51411

This estate, surrounded by woods, is set in a wonderful panoramic position just 12 miles (20 km) from Florence. The land is farmed organically and produces Vin Santo, spumante, and grappa. San Vito also produces good extra-virgin olive oil as well as honey. The estate is one of many agriturismo farms, and vacation apartments are available for visitors to rent.

CASTAGNACCIO (CHESTNUT CAKE)

*1lb (400 g) chestnut flour • 4 walnuts, crushed
• 3 oz (75 g) pine nuts • 2 oz (50 g) raisins
•1 sprig of rosemary • extra-virgin olive oil • salt*

Preheat the oven to 400°F (200°C). Put the flour and a pinch of salt into a mixing bowl. Whisk in enough warm water to make a paste. Pour into a greased 8 inch (20 cm) cake pan, and bake in the oven for 5–6 minutes. Scatter the walnuts, pine nuts, raisins, and rosemary leaves over the top and sprinkle with oil. Bake for a further 20 minutes.

MONTEMURLO (PO)

Marchesi Pancrazi Tenuta di Bagnolo

località Bagnolo,
via Montalese, 156
📞 0574 652439 ⬤ Sat

This 16th-century estate belongs to the Marquis Pancrazi, who inherited it from the Strozzi family of Montemurlo. The estate is well-known for its Villa di Bagnolo extra-virgin olive oil. It also produces good-quality wine, which is bottled after two months of storage in oak barriques to soften it a little. The wine is made from Pinot Nero grapes. These vines were first planted here when they were mistakenly sold as Sangiovese in the 1970s. The Casaglia extra-virgin olive oil from another family estate at Calamanco is excellent.

PALAZZUOLO SUL SENIO (FI)

Dispensa della Locanda

via Borgo dell'Oro, 1
📞 055 8046019
⬤ Mon–Wed (Oct–May)

Among the firm's own specialities are prosciutto and salame from Cinta pigs – these differ from the standard Cinta Senese breed because they have developed features that help them adapt to high altitudes. The firm also produces cocktail onions preserved in oil, quince jam, liqueurs from fruits and wild herbs, chestnut honey, and various other local delicacies.

Azienda Agricola Lozzole

frazione Quadalto
Lozzole 📞 055 8043505

CROSTINI ALLA TOSCANA

extra-virgin olive oil • ½ an onion, finely chopped • 12 oz (350 g) chicken livers • 1 oz (30 g) capers • 2 anchovy fillets • ¾ oz (20 g) butter • 1 glass white wine • meat stock • 4 slices Tuscan bread • chopped tomatoes and herbs (optional) • salt • pepper

Heat some oil in a pan, add the onion and cook until softened. Add the livers, pour in the wine, and cook for 5 minutes. Drain the livers and purée with the anchovies and capers. Return to the pan, stir and add enough stock to make a creamy mixture. Season with salt and pepper. Remove the pan from the heat and stir in the butter. Toast the bread, spread with paté and cut each slice into several pieces. Top with chopped tomatoes and herbs.

A large number of goats, sheep, and pigs that graze freely in chestnut woods are bred here. The estate sells a range of fresh and mature pecorino and caprino (goat's milk) cheeses, some scented with herbs, and chestnuts in season. The farm has not yet received a permit to butcher its own meat, however.

PIEVE AL BAGNORO (AR)

Villa Cilnia

località Montoncello, 27
📞 0575 365017

This medium-sized wine estate in the Aretine Hills offers a good Chianti Colli Aretini and Chianti Riserva. It also produces Mecenate, made from Chardonnay and Sauvignon Blanc grapes, and Vocato made from Sangiovese and Cabernet Sauvignon grapes.

PONTASSIEVE (FI)

Castello del Trebbio

via Santa Brigida, 9
📞 055 8304900
⬤ Mon am

This estate is located in a 12th-century castle that once belonged to the families Pazzi and Medici. A coat of arms sculpted by Donatello can be found in the courtyard, while the chapel boasts a fresco by Andrea del Castagno. The cellar's structure and flooring are 12th-century originals. There is a fee for the tasting, which includes wine-and-food matchings. Agriturismo facilities are on offer. Oil, grappa, jams, and saffron can be bought here, as well as wines such as Bianco della Congiura (Chardonnay), Chianti Rùfina Riserva Lastricato, and Pazzesco (Sangiovese, Syrah, Merlot).

🍇 Fattoria di Galiga e Vetrice

località Montebonello
via Vetrice, 5
📞 055 8397008

This estate is among the main producers of Chianti Rùfina and makes good-quality wines. They also produce Vin Santo and an excellent extra-virgin olive oil called "Il Lastro."

❄️ Gelateria Sottani

località San Francesco,
via Forlivese, 93
📞 055 8368092
⬤ Wed pm

The owner of this ice-cream parlor boasts that only natural products – in particular, good-quality fresh milk from the Mugello – go into the ice creams. There is an extraordinary variety of flavors – all the classics plus intuffato al Vin Santo. Whatever fruit is in the market – including exotic varieties and wild fruit – is included in their sorbets.

🍇 Tenuta di Bossi

via dello Stracchino, 32
📞 055 8317830

This winery is housed in a building that has been part of the estate since 1592. A section is being turned into an agricultural museum. The wines include Chianti

Fattoria di Galiga e Vetrice at Pontassieve

Rùfina Riserva Villa Bossi, Mazzaferrata (Cabernet Sauvignon), Vin Santo del Chianti Rùfina Riserva Marchese Gondi, and Chianti Rùfina San Giuliano. Oil and grappa are also made. As well as producing wine, Tenuta di Bossi offers agriturismo-style accommodation.

PRATO

🍽️ Gastronomia Barni

via Ferrucci, 24
📞 0574 607845
⬤ Wed pm

Carefully selected Italian and French cheeses and fine Tuscan salumi are sold here. The wine shop sells wines from around the world and a selection of dessert wines. The ready-made dishes are excellent.

🎂 Luca Mannori

via Lazzerini, 2
📞 0574 21628
⬤ Tue

Owned by one of Italy's top pastry chefs, this shop offers numerous delectable specialties, including an Italian celebration cake. The pralines are superb, as is the whole chocolate range, especially the highly artistic, hand-painted eggs for Easter.

🍪 Biscottificio Mattei

via Ricasoli, 20/22
📞 0574 25756
⬤ Mon, Sun pm;
Sun (Jul–Aug)

Since 1858, this has been the place to buy cookies in Prato. Sample the delicious cantuccini and cantucci all'anice cookies.

Oak barrels holding Tuscan Chianti

Oil store at the Frantoio di Santa Tea

50 acres of olive groves. The focus is on red wines, with Chianti Rùfina in a standard version and Reserve, and two blends kept in new oak barriques for 12 months: I Pini, made with equal quantities of Cabernet Sauvignon and Sangiovese, and Il Corto, with a higher proportion of Sangiovese.

Pasticceria Nuovo Mondo

via Garibaldi, 23
0574 27765
Mon

Paolo Sacchetti is a top confectioner. He makes international specialties, and at Christmas, although he is not Milanese or even from Lombardy, he makes one of the very finest panettoni *(a Milanese cake) you can find anywhere.*

Primizie di Renato Palermo

via Gobetti, 18
0574 30713
Wed pm

This shop offers fruits and vegetables selected for their quality. The emphasis is on organically grown produce, and trusted market gardeners are favored more than official certificates. As far as possible the produce is Tuscan, but Renato Palermo also looks further afield to other regions where the produce is fresh, in season, and of the finest quality. The same policy guides the selection of various other delicacies: dried pasta, preserves in extra-virgin olive oil, traditional candies, and cakes. Note the local big white beans called schiaccioni *and the selection of exotic and dried fruits.*

Vannucchi Ortofrutta

via Vincenzo da Filicaia, 2
(angolo via Strozzi)
0574 36382
Wed pm

Local produce is sold here in season; a variety of spring vegetables and exotic fruits from leading producers further afield is also available. Local varieties of beans include capponi *and* schiaccioni.

REGGELLO (FI)

Frantoio di Santa Tea

località Santa Tea,
frazione Cascia,
055 868117
Sat am

The firm's olive oil has an intensely fresh, fruity bouquet and an aroma of newly mown grass. The flavor is strong and bitter, with an aftertaste of the salad leaf arugula.

RÙFINA (FI)

Fattoria di Basciano

viale Duca della Vittoria, 159
055 8397034
Easter–Oct

The estate has about 50 acres (20 hectares) of vines and another

Azienda Agricola Colognòle

via del Palagio, 15
055 8319870   Sat

This family-run firm has always been linked with carefully balanced wines that age well, and so the wines marketed are usually a vintage older than average. The grapes from individual vineyards are vinified separately and then blended

---

CIBREO

2 lb 4 oz (1 kg) *chicken livers, hearts, testicles, and rooster's combs or crests*
• *extra-virgin olive oil*
• *1 onion, chopped* • *2 cloves garlic* • *2 oz (50 g) salted anchovies, chopped* • *6 oz (150 g) peeled, plum tomatoes*
• *4 egg yolks* • *juice of 1 lemon* • *1–2 tablespoons chopped fresh parsley*
• *salt* • *pepper*

Clean and cut up the giblets. Heat plenty of oil in a pan and fry the onion, garlic, and anchovies for a few minutes. Add all the giblets and cook until lightly browned. Add the tomatoes and salt and pepper and simmer for 2–3 minutes. Meanwhile, whisk the egg yolks, lemon juice, and parsley with a little warm water in a bowl. Remove the pan from the heat. Still whisking, pour the egg mixture into the pan. Serve the mixture hot with rice or polenta.

---

to make Chianti Rùfina and Chianti Rùfina Riserva del Don. A single white, Quattro Chiacchere, is made from Chardonnay alone. The estate also produces olive oil of excellent quality and offers agriturismo vacation facilities.

Fattoria Selvapiana

località
Selvapiana, 43
☎ 055 8369848

From a solid family tradition anchored in the land come some of the area's finest Chianti Rùfina. The two single-vineyard wines, Bucerchiale and Fornace, both Chianti Rùfina Riserva, are excellent. Fornace contains a small proportion of Cabernet Sauvignon. The extra virgin olive oil is fabulous, and there is also a delicious range of honey.

SANSEPOLCRO (AR)

Erboristeria di Aboca

via Aggiunti
☎ 0575 7461 ● Mon

This is the sales outlet for one of Europe's most important herbalists, Valentino Mercati. Although the firm's current policy favors herbal cures over foodstuffs, in this wonderful old shop you will find essences (sweet and bitter orange) useful in cooking, plus naturally farmed dried herbs, and herbal teas that are ideal for the end of a meal.

Gelateria Creperia Ghignoni

via Tiberina Sud, 850
☎ 0575 741900
● Tue (winter)

Not to be missed; the owner, Palmiro Bruschi,

TRIPPA ALLA FIORENTINA

extra-virgin olive oil • 2 stalks celery, finely chopped • 2 carrots, finely chopped • 1 onion, finely chopped • 2½ lb (1 kg) tripe, cut into strips • ¾ lb (300 g) tomatoes, peeled and chopped • 4 oz (100 g) Parmesan cheese, grated • salt • pepper

Heat some oil in a pan, add the celery, carrots, and onion and fry until they have softened a little. Add the tripe and cook it for a few minutes. Add the chopped tomatoes, season to taste with salt and pepper and simmer for 25–30 minutes. Stir in the grated Parmesan cheese and serve at once.

---

won the Italian ice-cream championship. In addition to assorted ice creams, there are delicious crêpes and mousses to try.

Martini Aldo

via XX Settembre, 95
☎ 0573 742310

Beef (Chianina and other breeds) and pork organically reared in local farms are available here. Also for sale are excellent porchetta and sausages in oil. The duck sauce (only in season) is unmissable, as is the pigeon's paté for crostini.

SCANDICCI (FI)

Fattoria Baggiolino

località La Romola,
via della Poggiona, 4
☎ 055 768916
○ Fri pm, Sat am

This firm produces an excellent extra-virgin olive oil. It is bottled as Laudemio and is one of the best sold under this name. They also sell wines: Chianti dei Colli Fiorentini Riserva, Poggio Brandi, Borro dell'Ermellino, Vin Santo, and grappa.

TERRANUOVA BRACCIOLINI (AR)

Associazione Fagiolo Zolfino

frazione Penna, 123b
☎ 055 970 5039

This is the ideal place to buy Zolfini beans from Pratomagno (see p34). Book them in advance.

VINCI (FI)

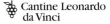

Cantine Leonardo da Vinci

via Provinciale
di Mercatale, 291
☎ 0571 902444

This winery stands in open countryside, on a road linking Empoli and Vinci. It is about 2.5 miles (4 km) from Cerreto Guidi, home of the Villa Medicea, and about 3 miles (5 km) from Vinci and its Museo Leonardiano. As well as free tastings, it is possible to book a guided tasting. There is a fee for this option. Try Chianti Leonardo, San Zio, and Sant'Ippolito (Syrah and Merlot). The underground cellar holds 400 barriques and 600 tonneaux to age some of the wines.

LUNIGIANA, GARFAGNANA, AND VERSILIA

Lunigiana, Garfagnana, and Versilia

Running from the coast to the highest peaks of the Apennine ridge, this area has something for everyone. Versilia has a long tradition of excellent dishes made with fresh local fish. The Garfagnana offers a very rustic way of life. The Lunigiana has a cuisine that takes elements from the three bordering regions: Tuscany, Liguria, and Emilia-Romagna. In this area farming and the food industry provide the greatest variety of gourmet pleasures. The area also shows great inventiveness in the choice of vines for wine, and it is unrivaled in Italy (or the world) for *porcini* (cèpe mushrooms). Mushrooms are not the only woodland food to play a part in the area's cuisine – chestnuts, bilberries, and raspberries are all widely used. Finally, there is Pescia, not only the center of Italian flower culture but also right in the middle of an area producing wonderful fruits and vegetables.

Passo della Cisa

Pontremoli

Villafranca in Lunigiana

Licciana Nardi

Tresana

Fivizzano

Podenzana *Aulla*

Fosdinovo

CARRARA

MASSA

Montignoso

Forte dei Marmi *Pietrasanta*

Lido di Camaiore

VIAREGGIO

TOURIST OFFICES

• Pistoia Piazza Duomo, 4 ☎ 0573 21622. ⓦ www.pistoia.turismo.toscana.it

• Lucca Piazza S. Maria, 35 ☎ 0583 919931.

• Viareggio Piazza Mazzini, Palazzo delle Muse ☎ 0584 48881. ⓦ www.versilia.turismo.toscana.it

• Montecatini Terme Viale Verdi, 66 ☎ 0572 772244.

The area around Lucca is the most important **wine-making zone** in this region, producing the excellent Montecarlo and other wines. Left, grapes are being harvested for Rosso delle Colline Lucchesi *(see pp52–3)*.

PORCINI

The *porcini* at Garfagnana are among the world's finest, especially those from wooded mountain slopes. They are usually sold from September to November.

◁ **Drying grapes for the "governo" (fortifying) of wine**

Agriturismo (farmhouse vacations) in the Garfagnana are very popular with visitors. The area is dotted with lovely old farmhouses, each with a fascinating history.

Viareggio is not simply a fashionable seaside resort, it is also a very active fishing harbor where a splendid variety of **fresh fish and shellfish** *(see pp54–7)* is landed.

Tuscany's fresh **vegetables** are particularly fine, and they are a vital part of the region's cuisine. Market gardens sweep from the mountains to the coast, giving the area an enormous variety of growing conditions.

STAR ATTRACTIONS

- CAPANNORI (LU): Villa Torrigiani, 0583 928008
- CASTELNUOVO DI GARFAGNANA (LU): National Park of the Apuan Alps, 0583 644354
  National Park of Orecchiella, 0583 619098
- COLLODI (LU): Villa Garzoni, 0572 429590
- LUCCA: Cathedral, 0583 957068
- PISTOIA: Cathedral, 0573 21622

0 kilometers   10

0 miles   10

Abetone
Cutigliano
astelnuovo Garfagnana
FS
Barga
San Marcello Pistoiese
Bagni di Lucca
Borgo a Mozzano
PISTOIA
FS
Agliana
Ponte a Moriano   Collodi   Pescia   Pieve a Nievole
FS
Uzzano   Montecatini   Monsummano Terme
Montecarlo   Terme
LUCCA   Capannori
Lamporecchio
o di ssaciuccoli   FS
Altopascio
Balbano

Places of Interest pp66–73
Restaurants pp177–180

Wines

Tᴴᴇ ᴀʟᴘɪ ᴀᴘᴜᴀɴᴇ (ᴀᴘᴜᴀɴ ᴀʟᴘs), which run parallel with a stretch of
the Tyrrhenian coast between Massa, Carrara, and Viareggio, corral
the warm sea breezes and create an ideal climate for vineyards. The
same breezes flow up the lower part of the Arno Valley, creating
equally good conditions for vines at Lucca. Further inland, toward
Pistoia, the influence of the sea wanes, but the Apennine ridge gives
shelter from the colder influences of the north and helps to provide
a favorable climate for growing flowers. This area produces very
respectable white wines from vines like Vermentino and Albarola, a
link with nearby Liguria, as well as Trebbiano Toscano, Greco, Grechetto,
and Malvasia del Chianti vines. Certain French varieties have long been
grown locally and are used in some of the DOC wines, such as Pinot,
Sémillon, Sauvignon, and Roussanne. The same is true of reds: alongside
Sangiovese, Canaiolo, and rare vines like Ciliegiolo, Colorino, Malvasia
Nera, and Pollera Nera are Syrah, Cabernet, and Merlot.

Cᴀɴᴅɪᴀ ᴅᴇɪ Cᴏʟʟɪ Aᴘᴜᴀɴɪ

This white wine is made
in a tiny area at the foot of
the Apuan Alps above
Massa and Carrara, so
production is limited.
Made from two Ligurian
vines, Vermentino and
Albarola, the wine is
straw-colored with a
fine scent and low
alcohol content. It is
perfect with *frittelline di
cieche* (made with the
fry of eels) and delicate
fish dishes. There is also
a Vin Santo version.

*White Colli di Luni is based
on Vermentino with some
Trebbiano Toscano and
other white grapes. It is
perfect with fish antipasti
and vegetable soups.*

Cᴏʟʟɪ ᴅɪ Lᴜɴɪ

This is a recent
denomination.
Its production
straddles the two
regions of Liguria
and Tuscany.

Sᴄᴀʟᴏᴘᴘɪɴᴇ ᴀɪ ᴘᴏʀᴄɪɴɪ

*1¹/₂ lb (600 g) porcini caps (cèpe mushrooms), sliced •
2 cloves garlic • extra-virgin olive oil • 2 oz (50 g) butter
• 1 small onion, chopped • 6 veal scallops • white wine
• 1 sprig calamint or mint • meat stock • salt • pepper*

Fry the mushrooms in a shallow pan with one of the
cloves of garlic, some oil, and salt over a high heat until
their moisture evaporates. In a separate pan, heat the
butter with a little oil. Chop the second garlic clove and
lightly fry with the onion in the butter. Add the scallops
and cook until browned on both sides. Season with salt
and pepper, and moisten with a little white wine. Cook
until the meat is almost tender, then cover it with the
mushrooms. Add a little stock and the calamint leaves
and cook together for 1 minute before serving.

*Red Colli di Luni is based on
Sangiovese with other black
grapes and up to 10 percent
Cabernet. It is excellent with
roasts and other meat dishes.*

COLLINE LUCCHESI

This denomination applies to wines produced on the hills around Lucca. In addition to the generic whites, rosés, and reds, it includes varietals (wines made from single grape varieties): Vermentino and Sauvignon grapes for whites, Sangiovese and Merlot for the reds which have the Riserva label. The grapes for table wines are also used to make white Vin Santo and Occhio di Pernice.

The rosé and red are both made from Sangiovese and Canaiolo Nero. The red resembles a young, very drinkable Chianti and is perfect with suckling pig, fried chicken, or roast rabbit.

CIONCIA

• 2 lb 4 oz (1 kg) veal (traditionally flesh from the head, cheeks, tail, but use ready diced pie veal, if necessary) • extra-virgin olive oil • 3 stalks celery, chopped • 3 carrots, chopped • 1 onion, chopped • 8 oz (200 g) peeled, plum tomatoes • chopped fresh parsley • chopped fresh basil • black olives • 1 glass white wine • chilli powder • salt

Trim and wash the veal and and cut into small pieces. Place in a pan, cover with water, and simmer for about 30 minutes, then drain well. Heat some oil and fry the meat lightly, then add the chopped vegetables and tomatoes, herbs, olives, and wine. Season with chilli powder and salt and simmer for 3 hours.

The white is made from seven varieties of white grapes, creating a wine with a subtle delicate perfume that is well-suited to soups and vegetable omelettes.

The white (Trebbiano Sémillon, Pinot Grigio and Bianco, Vermentino, Sauvignon. and Roussanne) goes with delicate pastasciutte (pasta) and fried fish.

MONTECARLO

This wine is made from traditional Tuscan grapes together with some French ones, which give it a finer perfume and a well-balanced flavor. There is also a Vin Santo version.

Red Montecarlo (made from Sangiovese and Canaiolo, Syrah, Cabernet, and Merlot) goes with spelt or mushroom dishes.

OTHER WINES WORTH TRYING

In the province of Pistoia you will find DOC **Colli dell'Etruria Centrale** and also DOC **Chianti**, some of which is made using the "*governo*" technique of adding dried grapes or must to the fermented wine to soften it.

WINE TYPE	GOOD VINTAGES	GOOD PRODUCERS
Red Wine		
Super Tuscans (see p130)	98, 97, 95, 90	Moretti, Le Murelle di Lucca
Colline Lucchesi	99, 97	Valgiano di Capannori, La Badiola di Capannori
White Wine		
Montecarlo	00, 99	Fattoria del Buonamico Fattoria del Teso

Fish and Seafood

IT IS A PLEASURE to visit the outdoor market at the popular coastal resort of Viareggio when the sea is calm and the fishing boats have been out. With both rocky and sandy seabeds close at hand, and the seas around the island of Gorgona rich with fish, the catch is varied. There are excellent inexpensive fish on sale, as well as the seasonal ones that pass through these waters – fish that are hard to find even in the big city markets. The shellfish are nearly always sold still alive at the market. Viareggio has the same varieties of fish found in other Tuscan seaports: those typical of Livorno's cuisine are described on *pp78–9*, others on *pp14–5* and *p161*. The local cuisine is noteworthy for its use of fewer spices than other regions – the fish is so fresh it does not need to be disguised with sauces or other artifice.

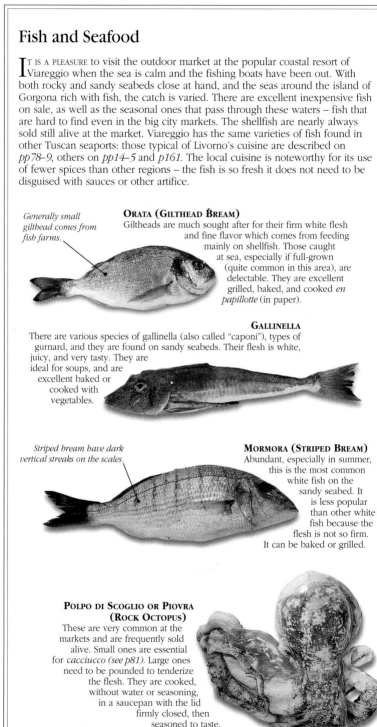

Generally small gilthead comes from fish farms.

ORATA (GILTHEAD BREAM)
Giltheads are much sought after for their firm white flesh and fine flavor which comes from feeding mainly on shellfish. Those caught at sea, especially if full-grown (quite common in this area), are delectable. They are excellent grilled, baked, and cooked *en papillotte* (in paper).

GALLINELLA
There are various species of gallinella (also called "caponi"), types of gurnard, and they are found on sandy seabeds. Their flesh is white, juicy, and very tasty. They are ideal for soups, and are excellent baked or cooked with vegetables.

Striped bream have dark vertical streaks on the scales.

MORMORA (STRIPED BREAM)
Abundant, especially in summer, this is the most common white fish on the sandy seabed. It is less popular than other white fish because the flesh is not so firm. It can be baked or grilled.

POLPO DI SCOGLIO OR PIOVRA (ROCK OCTOPUS)
These are very common at the markets and are frequently sold alive. Small ones are essential for *cacciucco (see p81)*. Large ones need to be pounded to tenderize the flesh. They are cooked, without water or seasoning, in a saucepan with the lid firmly closed, then seasoned to taste.

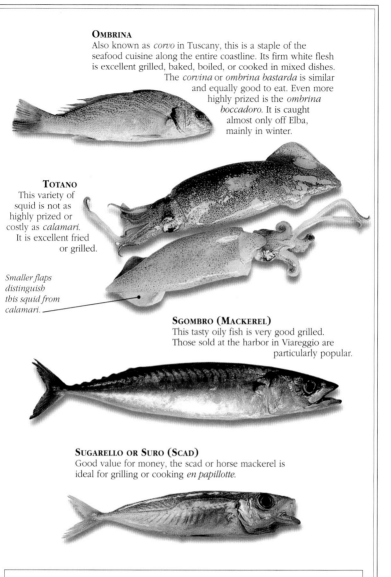

OMBRINA
Also known as *corvo* in Tuscany, this is a staple of the seafood cuisine along the entire coastline. Its firm white flesh is excellent grilled, baked, boiled, or cooked in mixed dishes. The *corvina* or *ombrina bastarda* is similar and equally good to eat. Even more highly prized is the *ombrina boccadoro*. It is caught almost only off Elba, mainly in winter.

TOTANO
This variety of squid is not as highly prized or costly as *calamari*. It is excellent fried or grilled.

Smaller flaps distinguish this squid from calamari.

SGOMBRO (MACKEREL)
This tasty oily fish is very good grilled. Those sold at the harbor in Viareggio are particularly popular.

SUGARELLO OR SURO (SCAD)
Good value for money, the scad or horse mackerel is ideal for grilling or cooking *en papillotte*.

OTHER MOLLUSCS WORTH TRYING
Moscardini (small squid) are valued for sauces, especially the fall fry called **fragolini**. There are numerous kinds of shellfish. The finest **cozze** (mussels) are farmed at nearby La Spezia. **Coltellacci** or **cannolicchi** or **cannelli** (razor clams), much appreciated in Versilia, have a long shell which contains a sweet, fleshy mollusc. **Telline** and **arselle** are important in Viareggio's cuisine, but these smooth wedge-shaped clams are very rare. The clams called **vongola grigia** or **cappa gallina** are used in pasta sauces. The **tartufo di mare** (Venus clam), which is very expensive, is sometimes eaten raw. The little cockles called **cuori**, picked up by children on the beaches, have grooved shells and contain a hard red mollusc which is tasty when cooked in seafood sauces. **Capesante** or **pellegrine** (scallops) are good but most are imported. Also popular are the sea snails (**chioccioline di mare**) called **maruzzelle**.

TRACINA OR PESCE RAGNO (WEEVER)

This fish is found on the sandy seabed. The flesh is white, tasty, and ideal for soups. It is very common and good value. The fish must be handled carefully because it has poisonous spines.

CICALA OR CANOCCHIA (MANTIS SHRIMP)

This common crustacean is inexpensive, with sweet flesh. It is excellent boiled and served in salads and is essential for soups, including *cacciucco*.

The mantis shrimp is best when bought alive.

SCAMPO (SCAMPI)

Scampi from Gorgona reach the Tuscan ports alive. They are delicious, with sweet firm flesh. Excellent raw and in myriad classic recipes, or for creative cooking.

Buy scampi alive if you can.

OTHER CRUSTACEANS WORTH TRYING

Gamberetti grigi (brown shrimp) are common at the markets: they are fried and eaten, shell and all. **Astici** (lobsters) are widely eaten but are not caught locally. **Aragoste** (crayfish) are caught off the islands and Argentario, but at the markets you will find mostly fine Sardinian ones. The big red crabs and granseola crabs are more typical of Italy's east coast, while here you find dark **granchi** (crabs) used in soups.

ALICE OR ACCIUGA (ANCHOVY)

These small blue fish are very tasty when freshly caught. In Tuscany, they are eaten fried, marinated raw, or baked in fishcakes, much as elsewhere in Italy. Salted, preserved anchovies are delicious with unsalted Tuscan bread.

Anchovies are more slender than sardines.

ROMBO (TURBOT)

This flatfish is found on the sandy seabed. The white flesh is tasty and firm, and cooks quickly. It is suited to all kinds of recipes. The ones caught in Tuscan waters are very popular.

BRANZINO OR SPIGOLA (SEA BASS)

Sea bass is the most sought-after fish on the market. Actively farmed, it is always excellent, but those caught with a hook and line, especially large ones, are definitely the finest. It is cooked *en papillotte*, baked, or grilled. Tuscans like to cook it with wild fennel.

OTHER FISH WORTH TRYING

Dentice (dentex) are often caught with depth lines. **Occhiata** (saddled bream), which live in schools along the coast, are good grilled. **Tonnetti** (small tunny fish) are sliced and grilled or stewed. **John Dory** (**sanpietro**, in Tuscany, but also **pesce gallo**) has delectable flesh. **Soglioline** (sole) caught along the coast are better than imported ones. **Cernie** (grouper) and **cerniole** (wreckfish) are caught off the islands, as are large fish such as **leccia** (amberjack) and **pesce castagna** (Ray's bream).

Game Birds

Game birds are an important part of Tuscany's gourmet tradition, and the marshlands near Torre del Lago ensure that this is an area rich in birds. The area offers unique recipes using ingredients that are not easy to find elsewhere, such as coot, mallard, and small marsh ducks. In the market at Viareggio, and the ones in other cities in the area, you can buy all kinds of game birds which in other parts of Tuscany can only be found in specialty shops supplying the catering industry.

Tordo (Thrush)
Songbirds such as song thrush, rock thrush, mistle thrush, and fieldfare are appreciated for their tender, aromatic flesh, especially when the birds have been feeding on the sweet-smelling berries that grow wild. The birds are cooked on a spit, or in casseroles with olives, grapes, and juniper berries, or they are made into pâtés.

Wild duck goes well with fruit, as in this dish of duck breasts with raspberries and vinegar.

This thrush and blackbird terrine includes both the liver and the giblets. Black truffles add extra flavor to the dish.

Germano (Mallard)
Mallard is the most common wild duck in Tuscany. Its flesh is much firmer than that of farm-bred duck, and it has a better flavor, but the birds are interchangeable in recipes.

Little bustard is cooked in a casserole with a sweet-and-sour pickle of sorb apples.

Merlo (Blackbird)
Although blackbirds are widely hunted, they are not as popular as thrushes. They have a good flavor from feeding on berries, but the flesh is tough. The flavor comes out best in *pâtés* and dishes that require lengthy cooking.

Fagiano (Pheasant)
The pheasant is the hunters' favorite prey. It is unlikely to be a wild bird, since pheasants are bred for the game reserves. When newly released their flesh is pretty tasteless, but after living in the wild and feeding freely for some time they acquire a gamey flavor. Pheasants are roasted, cooked in casseroles with cream, truffles, and fruit, or in traditional *salmi*, and are made into countless pâtés and terrines.

FOLAGA (COOT)

This water bird is very popular at Torre del Lago. It must be plucked and skinned as soon as it is killed. The coot has a distinctive, slightly fishy flavor and is used to make the classic recipe *folaga alla Puccini*, which dates back to the days of the Italian composer.

Wood pigeon is cooked slowly in a rich gravy with wild cherries, which enhance the flavor of the meat.

COLOMBACCIO (WOOD PIGEON)

The wood pigeon has firm, aromatic, and well-flavored flesh. The bird is widely hunted in Tuscany, where one of the favorite ways of cooking it is in a casserole with olives.

FOLAGA ALLA PUCCINI

- *1 coot* • *juice of 1 lemon* • *extra-virgin olive oil* • *1 carrot, finely chopped* • *2 onions, finely chopped* • *1 stalk celery, finely chopped* • *4 bay leaves* • *1 sprig of thyme* • *1 fresh chile, finely chopped* • *a few leaves of calamint (or mint)* • *1 salted anchovy, boned* • *red wine* • *meat stock* • *1 dessertspoon flour* • *1 sprig of basil* • *salt* • *pepper*

Pluck and skin the coot, then soak it for about 2 hours in cold water mixed with the lemon juice. Cut the bird into pieces, discarding the head, wing tips, and the cone of the rump with the tail feathers attached. Heat some oil and fry the carrot, onion, celery, and bay leaves until the vegetables have softened. Add the coot flesh, thyme, chile, calamint, and anchovy. Brown the meat, then season with salt and pepper. Cover and cook slowly, moistening if necessary first with the wine and then the stock. When the coot is almost cooked, uncover the pan, add a ladleful of stock mixed with the flour, and allow to thicken. Stir in the basil and serve.

BECCACCIA (WOODCOCK)

The woodcock is the most prized of the game birds. It is becoming increasingly rare and is hardly ever seen in any market. It is cooked undrawn and the entrails (apart from the crop) are eaten. There are many regional and international recipes for this bird, but the most popular dish is roasted woodcock with the entrails spread on toast.

OTHER GAME BIRDS WORTH TRYING

Other wild ducks shot in the marshy areas include **alzavola** (teal), **moriglione** (pochard), **fischione** (widgeon), and **codone** (pintail). The **tortora** (turtle dove) is appreciated for its delicate, tender flesh. Partridges are also hunted in Tuscany, both the common gray partridge **(pernice)** and the rock partridge **(coturnice)**, but they are becoming increasingly rare. Wild **quaglia** (quail) are are much tastier than the farm-bred ones usually found in shops. **Beccaccino** (snipe) are smaller than woodcock, but just as tasty, and they can be used in the same recipes.

Traditional Produce

THIS AREA OF northern Tuscany has wonderfully varied landscapes: there are mountains with lakes and woods, and then hills that slope gently to the plains and the sea. The numerous delicacies are closely bound up with these natural settings and the climate, and the produce ranges from Mediterranean olives to spelt (a traditional type of grain) from the mountains. The popularity of the local produce has spread through a mixture of factors: a general concern for traditional qualities, the growth of *agriturismo,* and specialty shops supported by a clientele capable of recognizing quality. It is worth finding trusted stores that specialize in good quality foods.

FILETTO DELLA LUNIGIANA
This dried pork fillet is seasoned with salt and pepper. It combines both Tuscan and Emilian traditions, being less dry and having less salt and pepper than other specialty meats of the region.

LASAGNE BASTARDE
These are *tagliatelle* and *pappardelle all'uovo* made with a mixture of white flour and chestnut flour for extra flavor. They are found in restaurants and on sale in small pasta shops, mainly in Lunigiana and around Monte Amiata.

TORTA DI PEPE
A specialty of Camaiore, this savory pie is made with a *brisée* pastry and filled with beet leaves, rice, eggs, *ricotta, pecorino,* Parmesan, and breadcrumbs, all seasoned with plenty of freshly ground pepper *(pepe).*

BUCCELLATO
Lucca's traditional cake is sold by all *pasticcerie* and bakers in the city. It is a very simple cake, made with flour, sugar, muscatel raisins, and aniseed. Traditionally it was a round loaf, but long shapes are now more common.

PANE DI ALTOPASCIO
This is one of the most prized Tuscan breads and is sold outside the area, reaching supermarkets in northern Italy. Loaves sold locally are normally round; when exported it is usually sold in long broad loaves.

LUCCA OLIVE OIL

The area producing Lucca oil includes the coastal area of Versilia, above all around Carrara, the area north of Lucca along the Serchio, and other smaller zones near Camaiore and Ponte a Moriano. These oils are very fine and fruity. The flavor is of average intensity, full and balanced, sweetish though slightly peppery, with a lingering taste.

CANNELLINI DI SORANA

These white beans are common in Tuscan cooking. Sorana, north of Pescia, produces beans of slightly smaller than average size and these are much sought-after.

DRIED CHESTNUTS

Once a staple ingredient of traditional cooking in many mountain areas, dried chestnuts *(castagne secche)* are now a delicacy used in sweet and savory dishes.

TESTAROLI

A wholewheat flour and water dough is cooked in earthenware pans with lids called *testi*. The dough forms thick sheets which are boiled and served with pesto or tomato and mushroom sauce.

CHESTNUT FLOUR

Chestnut flour *(farina di castagne)* is produced in various areas, including Lunigiana, the Mugello, the Casentino, and Amiata and is an ingredient of many traditional recipes.

NECCI CON LA RICOTTA

1 lb (450 g) chestnut flour • sugar • chestnut leaves
• 1 lb (450 g) fresh ricotta cheese • salt

Mix the flour with a pinch of salt and sugar to taste. Knead in enough water to form a thick but not solid dough. Heat several earthenware *testi* until sizzling hot, then place a chestnut leaf on each one. Spread with a ladleful of paste, then alternate leaves and paste to form layers. Leave to cool. Remove and serve with the cheese and sugar.

PECORINO FROM GARFAGNANA AND LUNIGIANA

This *pecorino* is generally drier than the similar cheese from the Crete to the south. It has a strong milky scent and a distinctive flavor from the mountain grasses the sheep feed on, quite different from that of cheese from the more arid coastal areas.

RICOTTINE DELLA LUNIGIANA

This cheese is eaten very fresh. It is also a traditional cheese for making desserts, especially with chestnuts.

FARRO (SPELT) FROM GARFAGNANA

Spelt is a very ancient cereal which has been cultivated in the Garfagnana for over 7,000 years. Equally ancient is the gastronomic tradition of spelt soup *(minestrone di farro* or *zuppa di farro)*, a trademark of this area.

MINESTRONE DI FARRO

8 oz (200 g) dried borlotti beans • ¾ lb (300 g) spelt • 2 oz (50 g) pancetta, chopped • 1 onion, chopped • 1 stalk celery, chopped • 1 carrot, chopped • ¼ of a Savoy cabbage, cut into strips • tomato purée • extra-virgin olive oil • salt • pepper

Soak the beans in cold water overnight. The next day, drain them, put in a pan, and cover with fresh water. Bring to the boil and simmer for 1½ hours. Drain the beans and set aside a quarter of them. Mash the rest with the cooking water, return to the pan, add the spelt, and cook for about 1 hour. Sauté the pancetta, onion, celery, and carrot in some oil. Add the cabbage, the tomato purée diluted in a little water, then the spelt and the whole beans and simmer for 15 minutes. Season and drizzle a little oil over the soup before serving.

TROUT

The Serchio river is celebrated for its fish, which is less commonly eaten now that the number of fishermen has declined. However, the tradition of using the excellent trout from the mountain streams remains strong.

AGNELLO AL TESTO

*1 leg of lamb • 4 oz (100 g) lardo
(lard) • sage • rosemary • garlic
• 2 lb (1 kg) potatoes • extra-virgin
olive oil • salt • pepper*

Make incisions in the
leg of lamb with the
tip of a knife. Make
a paste with the
lard, herbs, and
garlic and push it
into the incisions.
Season with salt and
pepper. Put the lamb
in a *testo* (earthenware
pan with a lid) and cover with
plenty of oil. Sink the pan into hot
wood embers; heap them over the
lid. Cook for 45 minutes, renewing
the hot embers frequently.

*Rosemary and garlic are
often used in curing* lardo.

LARDO FROM COLONNATA
Among the pinnacles of Tuscan
gastronomy, this *lardo* (lard) is
highly rated. The lard is matured
in tubs of marble from nearby
Carrara. Once removed, it quickly
loses its flavor, so it is cut only
when needed. It may be used in
cooking or thinly sliced and eaten
sprinkled with pepper.

ROLLED PANCETTA
FROM LUNIGIANA
A combination of the
Tuscan style mixed with
the traditional styles of the
nearby valleys of Parma
and Piacenza produces
this *pancetta* (bacon
cured from belly of pork).
Tuscan custom is reflected
in the use of herbs,
especially rosemary, while
the Emilian influence is the
technique of rolling the bacon and
salting it only lightly, to keep it moist.

WHAT TO SAMPLE
Black-headed lambs, a breed called **Massese** from the Garfagnana and the Lunigiana,
are much appreciated and sought-after outside the region. In the Pescia district there is
excellent **asparagus** and **fruit** such as **cherries**. Some producers have begun to
specialize in herbs. There are a number of **soft fruit** farms. Pistoia has its traditional
cakes and **candies**, such as **sugared almonds**, **brigidini** (aniseed-flavored wafers),
and **berlingozzi** (carnival cakes). The Garfagnana has **truffles**, black and white.
Around Abetone there are locally produced **aromatic grappas** scented with berries
and herbs. The **table olives** are excellent; many types are small and a brownish-black
color, rather like Ligurian *taggiasca* olives. **Biroldo** is a blood sausage, its more
authentic versions containing raisins and pine nuts, which is eaten raw if very fresh.

Wild Produce

PRUGNOLO
(Lyophyllum georgii)
Even in antiquity this spring mushroom was prized. Now it is protected and it is forbidden to pick any under ¾ inch (2 cm) high. Whitish with tender flesh and an intense scent of fresh flour, it is sliced and eaten raw on risotto or pasta or cooked quickly in white sauces. It forms circles in mountain meadows or under thorn bushes in the hills.

GRIFOLA
(Polyporus frondosus)
This is a giant fungus that can weigh up to 110 lb (50 kg). From a single stalk growing at the foot of broadleaf trees, it fans out into numerous branches forming a kind of dense bush. When young, it is good preserved in oil.

COLOMBINA
(Russula cyanoxantha)
Easily found, even at markets, this mushroom has distinctive white gills, and is firm and springy to the touch. Commonly known as "the charcoal burner," it grows in woods, especially beech, and is excellent grilled, baked with potatoes, or in deviled dishes.

COCCORA
(Amanita caesarea)
The most expensive mushroom on the market, also known as *ovolo*, grows in broadleaf woods and is protected by a ban on picking specimens under 1½ inches (4 cm). When closed it forms a white ball. If this is cut open, it reveals embryo mushrooms with orange cap, yellow stalk, and gills. They are not tastier when closed (they should be left in the woods to allow the spores to mature); open ones have more flavor, whether raw or cooked.

COCCORA IN INSALATA (MUSHROOM SALAD)

1 clove garlic • 1 lb (450 g) coccore or ovoli, thinly sliced • juice of 1 lemon • extra-virgin olive oil • salt • pepper

Cut the garlic clove in half and rub the individual serving plates with the cut surfaces. Arrange the mushrooms on the plates. Mix together the lemon juice, oil and salt. Season with pepper, pour the dressing over the mushrooms, and serve at once.

MINESTRA DI CECI

1lb (450 g) chickpeas • 1 small onion, chopped • 1 small carrot, chopped • 1 small celery stalk, chopped • 2 cloves garlic, chopped • 1 sprig of rosemary • 1 sprig of winter savory • extra-virgin olive oil • grated parmesan cheese (if preferred, mix it with some mature pecorino) • 1 piece of the cotenna (skin) from a prosciutto • salt • black pepper

Rinse the chickpeas, then soak in water for 24 hours. The next day, heat some oil and lightly fry the onion, carrot, celery, garlic, and rosemary leaves. Drain the chickpeas, reserving the liquid, and stir them into the vegetables with the cotenna. Strain the soaking water and add enough to the pan to cover the beans. Cover the pan and simmer until the chickpeas are tender. Remove the cotenna and purée the soup in a blender. Return it to the pan and add the savory; season and simmer for 10 minutes. Serve with the cheese and extra oil to drizzle.

SANTOREGGIA (WINTER SAVORY)
(Satureja montana)
Commonly found on dry, stony slopes, this herb is similar to thyme but has different spear-shaped leaves. It has long been noted for its supposed aphrodisiac qualities. Santoreggia is excellent fresh or dried with sauces, braised, roasted, or grilled meat, pulses, and snails.

MIRTILLO NERO (BILBERRY)
(Vaccinium myrtillus)
This summer berry, also called a huckleberry, is abundant on the Apennine ridges in high-altitude woods of beech or chestnut. It can be eaten fresh – it has a high vitamin C content – or used in jams and liqueurs.

OLIVELLO SPINOSO (SEA-BUCKTHORN)
(Hippophae rhamnoides)
Wear gloves if you want to pick these orange berries as there are plenty of thorns concealed among the blue-green leaves. However, they are definitely worth the trouble, being rich in vitamin C, and they make exquisite jam. The plants are found in the Apennines on open ground and along escarpments and waterways.

TIMO (THYME)
(Thymus communis)
Thyme is found all over Tuscany and is used a great deal in cooking – in fact, it is a staple of numerous traditional recipes. The flowering sprigs are better than the leaves alone. It is excellent fresh or dried.

Places of Interest

THIS IS A GOOD area for shopping, though prices at Versilia are often inflated because it is such a fashionable tourist spot. The shopkeepers are accustomed to catering to a clientele in search of traditional specialty foods, and many are very knowledgeable. In addition to the addresses given below, the outdoor market at Viareggio is definitely worth a visit.

ABETONE (PT)

🍁 Il Baggiolo

via Brennero, 55/57
☎ 0573 606838 ⬤ Tue

Specializing in wild bilberries (huckleberries), which are picked in the local woods, Il Baggiolo sells jams, liqueurs, and juices. They also sell products derived from other berries, both wild and organically farmed.

AGLIANA (PT)

Ⓖ Arte del Cioccolato di Catinari

via Provinciale, 378
☎ 0574 718506 ⬤ Mon

Roberto Catinari is one of the great Italian and European pastry chefs.

BERLINGOZZO

*3½ oz (100 g) butter •
14 oz (400 g) plain flour
• 2 eggs • 2 egg yolks •
7 oz (200 g) sugar •
grated zest of 1 lemon •
3½ fl oz (100 ml) whole
milk • 1 teaspoon baking
powder • salt*

Preheat the oven to 350°F (180°C). Grease and flour an 8 in (20 cm) cake pan with ¾ oz (20 g) each of the butter and flour. In a bowl, vigorously mix the rest of the flour and butter, eggs and yolks, sugar, zest, milk, baking powder, and a pinch of salt. Pour into the pan and bake for 40 minutes.

At his shop you will find 120 types of delicious chocolates, such as ones with liqueur centers (grappa, Vin Santo, whisky, Gemma d'abeto, amaretto liqueur, and coffee), or wrapped chocolates weighing 1 oz (30 g) each. The gianduia tortine (chocolate cream cakes) are excellent. Numerous trainees come here from as far away as the US, and Catinari has produced creations to order for famous designers like Armani.

🍇 Enoteca Lavuri

via Provinciale, 154/g
☎ 0574 751125
⬤ Tue am

This wine store has a wide selection of the most significant Tuscan wines. Its guiding policy is to comb the region for new products, provided they have a good pedigree. There are also interesting Italian and foreign wines. Lavuri also offers a fine selection of cheeses, coffees, and liquors, including some collector's items.

🏭 Marini

località Ferruccia,
via Selva, 313
☎ 0574 718119
⬤ Wed pm
◻ in summer: only am

Marini is a delicatessen and butcher's shop, family run since 1904, selling Chianina beef and local salumi, which includes traditional specialties no longer found elsewhere.

BORGO A MOZZANO (LU)

🐟 Ittica la Macchia

frazione Valdottavo,
località La Macchia,
via Lodovica
☎ 0583 835088

This fish farm with agriturismo facilities sells the fry of mountain and rainbow trout, sturgeon, eels (including the much prized large female eels called capitoni), freshwater crayfish, and small trout for frying.

CAMAIORE (LU)

🏭 Bonuccelli Salumi

via Vittorio Emanuele, 9
☎ 0584 989680
⬤ Wed pm

Here you can find traditional salumi, both local and Tuscan (and some made with wild boar's meat). Particularly interesting products include salt ham, lardo, and biroldo (a Tuscan blood sausage). There is a range of Italian and imported cheeses and a selection of fine wines. The butcher specializes in pork and ham.

🌳 Gastronomia Claudio

via Provinciale, 45
☎ 0584 989069
⬤ Wed pm

Angelo Torciliani is an enthusiast for cheeses, scouring Italy for them from Val d'Aosta to Sicily. He makes a point of stocking many fine cheeses produced by traditional dairies in different regions. The delicatessen also stocks ready-made delicacies (try the torta di pepe and the ravioli), plus various specialties of Torciliani's own, such as the quite

PATTONA AL TESTO

dry chestnut leaves
• 1 lb (450 g) sweetened
chestnut flour • salt

Soak the leaves in warm water for 10 minutes. In a mixing bowl, mix the flour with a little salt and enough water to make a paste. Drain the leaves and pat dry. Pour 2 dessertspoons of the mix onto the smooth surface of two overlapping leaves. Fold the leaves over the mixture and place in an earthenware *testo*. Repeat until the mix is all used up. Cover the *testo* and bake the discs for 30 minutes under smoking embers.

---

remarkable cantucci, *as well as much local produce (olives, oil, flour) and delicacies from other regions. Everything is chosen with knowledge and passion. The selection of wines is also excellent.*

CAMPORGIANO (LU)

Mulin del Rancone

località Rancone
C 0583 618670
O Mar–Nov

This splendid farm, which offers agriturismo *facilities in an old converted watermill on the banks of the Serchio, rescued the local Pontremolese breed of cattle when they were on the verge of extinction. It produces and sells many traditional local products, such as lentils, conserves, spelt, and fruits and vegetables preserved in oil. Then there are the cookies:* neccini *(made from chestnut flour),* farrini *(spelt flour),* formentini *(maize flour). They also sell* salumi, *cheese, and honey which comes from the Garfagnana.*

CAPANNORI (LU)

Azienda Agricola La Badiola

località San Pancrazio,
via del Parco
C 0583 309633;
328 1510088

This estate produces an interesting red wine, Vigna Flora, which is made from Cabernet Sauvignon and Merlot grapes, and La Badiola Colline Lucchesi Bianco. The extra-virgin olive oil is not bad, if perhaps rather sweet.

Fattoria Colle Verde

località Castello
frazione Matraia
C 0583 402310

The estate aims to produce white wines with low acidity, which are well-structured and richly perfumed. A good example is the Brania del Cancello Bianco, made from equal quantities of Trebbiano and Chardonnay grapes. Another notable wine is the Colline Lucchesi Rosso Brania delle Ghiandaie, which is made from a careful selection of red grapes. The estate also produces a very fine extra-virgin olive oil.

Fattoria di Fubbiano

frazione San Gennaro,
località Fubbiano
C 0583 978011

This corner of Tuscany has an unusual microclimate and has been chosen for the grafting of experimental varieties of vines by the Regional Authority. These include a Vermentino used to produce Colline Lucchesi Vermentino. The Teroldego grape has been imported to boost the Sangiovese in making the red Pàmpini, which is aged in barriques. *The estate also makes two finer blends of the Rosso delle Colline Lucchesi, from vines with a western exposure for the Villa and a southern for the San Gennaro. The extra-virgin olive oil is excellent. There are superb* agriturismo *facilities with farmhouses available to rent.*

Fattoria Maionchi

località Tofori,
via di Tofori, 81
C 0583 978194

This late 17th-century estate offers accommodation in farmhouses that preserve their original features. Various DOC and table wines, extra-virgin olive oil, conserves from the farm's own fruit (try the pear and grappa jam), and grappas are sold here.

The Fattoria di Fubbiano at Capannori

Cooperativa del Pastore

via Sarzanese Valdera, 845
Castelvecchio
di Compito
☎ 0583 979804

*The dairy on this
estate produces
various ewe's-milk
cheeses best eaten
fresh. It also sells,
to order, the
excellent Massese
breed of black-
headed lambs.*

Tenuta di Valgiano

frazione Valgiano
☎ 0583 402271
◉ Sat

*This estate produces a
range of straightforward,
good wines: Bianco delle
Colline Lucchesi Giallo
dei Muri (from Trebbiano
and Chardonnay) and
Rosso delle Colline
Lucchesi and Rosso
dei Palistorti (Sangiovese
and Syrah). There are
also two regional classics:
a single-grape Merlot
and the Scasso dei Cesari.
The estate also produces
excellent extra-virgin
olive oil.*

CARRARA

Pescheria Elda

frazione Marina di Carrara,
viale Colombo, 9/c
☎ 0585 785060
◉ Mon pm, Sun pm

*Quality counts here, and
this depends not just on
freshness but also on the
origin of the produce.
For example, the farmed
fish comes from very
carefully selected
hatcheries: sea bass
and bream from
Portovenere, mussels
from La Spezia, and
shellfish from a select
group of producers in
the northern Adriatic.*

GRAN FARRO (SPELT AND BEAN STEW)

*1 lb (400 g) dried borlotti beans • ¾ lb (300 g) spelt
• extra-virgin olive oil • 2 cloves garlic • 1 onion • 1 stalk
celery • 3 leaves sage • 1 sprig of marjoram • 1 sprig of
rosemary • 6 oz (150 g) diced cotenna
(skin) of prosciutto • ¾ lb (300 g)
ripe tomatoes • salt • pepper*

Soak the beans in water for 12
hours. Drain the beans, put in a
pan and cover with fresh water,
then simmer until tender. Drain,
reserving the cooking water.
Press the beans through a sieve
to purée them. Heat some oil in
a pan, add the vegetables, herbs,
tomatoes, and cotenna. Season to
taste and fry for a few minutes. Add
bean purée and the spelt. Simmer for
40 minutes, adding some of the bean cooking
water, as necessary. Drizzle with olive oil before serving.

---

*The fresh fish is all local,
coming from Viareggio
and La Spezia.*

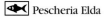

Pasta e Gastronomia di Grandi Patrizia

via Santa Maria, 1
☎ 0585 72195
◉ Tue

*Here you can buy take-
out dishes, most of
them typical of Carrara,
such as marinated salt
cod, stockfish, taglierini
ai fagioli (pasta with
beans), rice cakes, plus
fresh pasta, especially
tordelli, and seasonal
specialties including
fish. On Sunday an
interesting, complete
menu is offered, from
antipasto to dessert, at
very reasonable prices.*

Lardo di Colonnata di Giannarelli Marino

frazione Codena,
piazza Fratelli Rosselli, 10
☎ 0585 777329

*This is a specialty
producer of the typical
local lardo (cured pork
fat), which is processed
here but then matured*

---

*at Colonnata, its place
of origin. It is sold at the
firm's butcher's shop at
number 11 on the piazza.*

FIVIZZANO (MS)

Azienda Agricola Arcobaleno

località Rosare di Sopra
☎ 0585 92508

*Organic strawberries,
woodland berries, and
vegetables are produced
here. They are sold fresh
or made into liqueurs
and conserves.*

Farmacia Clementi

via Roma, 109
☎ 0585 92056
◉ Wed pm

*This pharmacy, with its
fine furnishings from
the late 19th century,
is well worth visiting even
if you are not in search
of medicine. The Elixir
di China is made to a
recipe belonging to the
great-grandfather of the
present owner, and the
fruit syrups are made of
berries cultivated on the
firm's own soft fruit farm.*

 Azienda Agricola il Pino

località Pastena
di Ceserano
[C] 0585 982355

*This farm grows and
sells organic strawberries.*

FOSDINOVO (MS)

🐦 Barbero Nanni

località Fravizzola
[C] 0187 68410

This agriturismo *offers
accommodation in five
bedrooms, in a hillside
setting. The owner selects
a clone of the Vermentino
grape for the Colli di Luni
Vermentino di Fravizzola
and puts Mammolo grapes
to use in the Colli di Luni
Rosso del Fornello.*

LAMPORECCHIO (PT)

✹ Pasticceria Carli - da Pioppino

piazza Berni, 20
[C] 0573 82177
[●] Wed

*For well over a century
now, this confectionery
shop has been making
authentic* brigidini *and*

berlingozzi *to the same
traditional recipe.*

LICCIANA NARDI (MS)

⛰ Apicoltura Dell'Amico e Amorfini

località Amola
[C] 0187 471502

*Local honey – aromatic
chestnut, dandelion,
acacia, honeydew, and
meadow – is produced
and sold here, along with
jars of local dried fruit
preserved in honey.*

🐦 Montagna Verde

località Apella
[C] 0187 421203

This is an agriturismo
*where refreshments are
available. Chestnuts,
chestnut flour, honey,
pecorino cheese, and
mushrooms (from the
estate's woods) are sold.*

LIDO DI CAMAIORE (LU)

🏺 Casanova di Chiatri

località Chiatri Puccini,
strada per Casanova
[C] 0583 356356

*This modern
establishment was
built next to an old-
fashioned olive press
that produces excellent-
quality extra-virgin
olive oil. Visitors can
purchase this in handy
75-cl bottles. Casanova
di Chiatri belongs
to the prestigious
Corporazione Mastri
Oleari (the guild of
oil-makers).*

Gastronomia Giannoni

viale Colombo, 444
[C] 0584 617332
[●] Wed pm

*Ready-to-eat dishes
made only from fresh
produce, including fish,
can be found here.
There is a fine selection
of salumi, including
well-matured prosciutto
di Langhirano.*

LUCCA

🌾 Antica Bottega di Prospero

via Santa Lucia, 13
[●] Wed pm

*This 200-year-old
shop sells all kinds of
different beans, spelt,
and other cereals, as
well as pulses and
chestnut flour.*

♣ La Cacioteca

via Fillungo, 242
[C] 0583 496346
[●] Wed pm

*On sale here is a wide
range of Tuscan
pecorino, especially
from the Garfagnana,
some of it matured by
the owner Aldo Pieracci
by storing in caves and
barrels. There is also
a selection of Tuscan
salumi, oil, and wine
from around Lucca,
and cheeses from all
over Italy.*

TORDELLI LUCCHESI

**2 lb 4 oz (1 kg) plain flour • 7 eggs • ¾ lb (300 g) loin of
pork • rosemary • 1 lb 2 oz (500 g) rump steak • 6 oz
(150 g) veal brain • 4 oz (100 g) beet leaves • thyme • 1
slice Tuscan bread • meat stock • grated nutmeg • grated
Parmesan cheese • extra-virgin olive oil • pepper • salt**

Preheat the oven to 350°F (180°C). Make incisions in the
pork and insert rosemary leaves. Place the pork and the
steak in a roasting pan, brush with a little oil, and season.
Roast for 30 minutes, basting with stock, if necessary.
Meanwhile, steam the beet leaves and brains until
cooked. Soak the bread in some meat stock. Dice all the
meat and the leaves. Mix with the bread, 1 egg, the
cheese, thyme, and nutmeg. Season. Mix the flour,
6 eggs, and salt, knead the dough and roll it out. Fill with
the meat to form large ravioli. Cook in boiling salted
water for 4 minutes. Serve with butter and cheese.

Piazza del Mercato in Lucca, once a Roman amphitheatre

Delicatezze di Isola

via San Giorgio, 5
0583 492633
Wed pm

A wide range of delicacies, some typical of Lucca and others from all over the world, including cheese and some unusual salumi (made from game and turkey), smoked fish, and wines are sold here.

Tenuta di Forci

via per Pieve Santo Stefano, 7165
0583 349001
Fri pm, Sat

This 14th-century farm offers its fine extra-virgin olive oil under the label Olio dell'Antico Frantoio di Forci.

Lucca in Tavola

via San Paolino, 130/132
0583 581022
Mon (Jan–Mar)

At this delicatessen you will find all the specialties of the Lucca area, chosen

by the owner, a sommelier and oil taster, including wines, oils, spelt and spelt products, honey, preserves, and olives.

Taddeucci

piazza San Michele, 34
0583 494933
Thu

This pasticceria has been in the same family for 120 years. Specialties include buccellato (typical Lucca cake, which looks more like bread than cake), cantucci, and traditional vegetable pies (spicy but sweet, made with beet leaves).

Enoteca Vanni Giulietta

piazza San Salvatore, 7
0583 491902
Mon am

Within the stone walls and vaulted ceilings of this shop is stocked an extensive choice of local and other Italian wines. One section is devoted to whisky (including collector's items) and grappas. Book in advance for a tasting. Lucca olive oil is also sold.

Polleria Fratelli Volpi

via San Paolino, 42
0583 56689
Wed pm

Free-range chickens, ducks, and pigeons, wild game, rabbits from the Garfagnana, Pratomagno hams, pork sausages, wild boar, goose, and game from small local producers can all be found here. There are also various poultry and game dishes prepared, ready for cooking in the oven.

ZUPPA FRANTOIANA (BEAN SOUP)

1¼ lb (600 g) dried cannellini beans • 3 cloves garlic • sprigs of sage • extra-virgin olive oil • 1 onion, sliced • 4 oz (100 g) rigatino (bacon), sliced • 1 lb (400 g) black cabbage (cavolo nero), sliced • 2 potatoes, chopped • 2 carrots, chopped • 1 stalk celery, chopped • 8 oz (200 g) pumpkin, chopped • 1 head chicory, chopped • 1 bunch of mixed herbs, chopped • 6 slices crusty bread • salt • pepper

Soak the beans in water overnight. The next day, drain and place in a pan with 2 garlic cloves and the sage. Cover with water and simmer for 2 hours. Drain the beans and reserve the water. Heat some oil in a pan, add the onion and bacon and fry until browned. Add the vegetables and the bean water and cook for 30 minutes. Crush half the cooked beans and add the crushed and the whole beans to the soup. Season with salt and pepper. Rub the bread with the remaining garlic and sprinkle with oil. Place the slices in a tureen and pour the soup on top.

MASSA

 Gelateria Eugenio

località Ronchi,
Marina di Massa,
via Pisa
☎ 0585 240369
● Mon (winter)

*This ice-cream parlor
is famed for the excellent
quality and the sheer
variety of its many ice
creams, some of them
sublime.*

Podere
Scurtarola

via dell'Uva, 3
☎ 0585 831560

*This is one of the few
producers that still bottles
the rare white wine
Candia dei Colli Apuani
in both the dry and the
semisweet versions.
The Scurtarola Rosso
is made from almost-local
vines such as Massaretta
and Buonamico, plus
Ciliegiolo and a fair
proportion of Sangiovese.
It is drunk young. A small
quantity of Vermentino
Rosso wine is made from
local grapes. The farm
also sells two different
kinds of honey (chestnut
and acacia flavors) and
olive oil.*

Drogheria
Caffè gli Svizzeri

via Cairoli, 53
☎ 0585 43092
● Wed pm

*This long-established
grocery store has two
main sections: one
provides a choice selection
of local produce from the
land – spelt, testaroli
(pasta disks like
pancakes), chestnut flour,
ricotta cheese. The other,
in response to consumer
demand, offers an
extensive choice of pulses
and cereals. They also
sell teas and spices.*

TORTA DI ERBE (HERB PIE)

*4½ lb (2 kg) mixed green leaves and herbs • 2 oz
(50 g) cured pork fat (lardo) • 2 oz (50 g) mortadella
(or local salami) • 2 oz (50 g) pecorino cheese • 4 fl oz
(100 ml) extra-virgin olive oil • 8 oz (200 g) flour •
pepper • salt*

Preheat the oven to 400°F (200°C). Cook the leaves and
herbs in boiling water until tender. Squeeze dry and chop
with the pork fat and mortadella. Mix in the cheese and
oil and season. Mix the flour, water, a
little oil, and salt into a dough.
Line a pie pan with half the
dough, add the cooked
leaves and herbs, and
cover with the rest
of the dough. Bake for
10 minutes then lower
the temperature to
350°F (180°C) and cook
for a further 20 minutes.
Serve warm.

MONSUMMANO TERME (PT)

© **Slitti Caffè
e Cioccolato**

via Francesca sud, 1268
☎ 0572 640240
● Sun

*In Italy, chocolate
confectioners are rare,
but Monsummano has a
world champion. Andrea
Slitti has won many
awards in recognition of
the taste and appearance
of his creations, which
are true works of art.
This shop and café has
wonderfully luscious and
imaginative chocolates,
chocolate bars, Arabian
coffee beans swathed in
chocolate, chocolate
teaspoons for stirring
coffee, creamy spreads,
and chocolate sculptures.*

MONTECARLO (LU)

 **Fattoria
del Buonamico**

località Cercatoia,
via Provinciale di
Montecarlo, 43
☎ 0583 22038
● Sat pm

*This is a leading producer
of Montecarlo Bianco and
Rosso, backed up by a
white, Vasario, from
Pinot Bianco fermented
in wood and aged in
barriques. There are also
two reds: Cercatoia, with
a good proportion of
Sangiovese Grosso
followed by Cabernet
Sauvignon, Merlot, and
a little Syrah; and
Il Fortino, from pure
Syrah grapes from a
30-year-old vineyard.*

Carmignani

località Cercatoia
via della Tinaia, 7
☎ 0583 22381

*This family-run estate
produces Montecarlo
Rosso Sassonero, For
Duke (from a blend
of Syrah and Merlot
grapes), and Il Merlo-T
della Topanera (from
Merlot). A good extra-
virgin olive oil is also
available. From March
to November agriturismo
accommodation and
restaurant facilities are
in place. The restaurant
is a favorite spot for
music-lovers and poets.*

🍇 Fattoria del Teso

località Teso,
via Poltroniera
☎ 0583 286288

*This winery is located
in an 18th-century villa,
and wine-making has
been practiced here since
the 1500s. The cellar
features a large tasting
room where lunches
and dinners can be
organized upon request.
A fee is payable for a
guided visit, which
includes a tasting with
food. It is also possible
to visit the Vinsantaia,
where Vin Santo is made
and where two types of
barrels are used. Among
the wines produced
here are Anfidiamante
Montecarlo Rosso
Riserva, Montecarlo
Bianco and Rosso, Stella
del Teso (a blend of
Roussanne, Sauvignon,
Chardonnay and
Vermentino grapes),
and Vin Santo del Teso
(Trebbiano Toscano,
Colombana). The extra-
virgin olive oil and
grappa are also of
good quality.*

MONTIGNOSO (MS)

🍽 La Bottega di Adò

via Vecchia
Romana Est, 66
☎ 0585 348315
⬤ Wed pm

*The traditional Tuscan
hams and sausages of
this long-established*

salame *producer have a
slightly sweet flavor, in
the Emilian style. The
company pursues a
policy of high quality
and is best known for its
sausages, made to the
highest standards. They
should be eaten fresh and
raw. Note also the firm's
salamis – traditional soft
Tuscan* mortadella, *its*
biroldo *(a blood sausage
similar to* buristo*),*
soppressata, *excellent*
cotechini *plus, of course,*
lardo di Colonnata.

🍇 La Caloma

località Zamparina
☎ 0585 348110;
335 6615704

*This wine estate is located
in a 15th-century family
villa in the center of the
village. The traditional
period cellar is tiny, but
it contains the latest
equipment. Among the
wines produced here
are Candia dei Colli
Apuani Calomina
Bianco and Caloma
Nero (Vermentino Nero,
Merlot, Balzaglina).
Grappa is also available.*

🍽 Gastronomia Osvaldo

località Cinquale,
via Gramsci, 32
☎ 0585 309193
⬤ Wed pm (exc summer),
Sun pm

*Here you can find a well-
chosen line of often very
exclusive delicacies from
every corner of Tuscany.*

*There are wonderful
specialties, like the*
salumi *and* pecorino
*cheeses, always of the
very highest quality.*

PISTOIA

 Panetteria Capecchi

via Dalmazia, 445
☎ 0573 400208
⬤ Wed pm

*This firm claims that a
brick oven using gas, not
wood, bakes the best cakes
and bread, and sampling
their wares it is impossible
to disagree. The Tuscan
bread and other types of
traditional Italian bread
are excellent, as is the*
schiacciata *baked on the
floor of the oven. The*
cantucci, *made with
natural ingredients of high
quality, are exceptional.
The range of foods is
completed with various
Italian cheeses and* salumi.

🛒 Primizie e Funghi Sauro e Assunta

piazza della Sala, 11
☎ 0573 21663
⬤ Wed pm

*Excellent local fruit and
vegetables are stocked
by this grocer, plus best-
quality produce from
further afield, including
an unusual range of
exotic fruits. In addition,
all kinds of dry fruit, a
large assortment of pulses,
cereals, flour, mushrooms
from Abetone, and a
selection of gastronomic
specialties are sold. In
season, truffles from San
Miniato and Acqualagna
are also available.*

TRESANA (MS)

Tomà Rita

località Groppo, via Bola, 41
☎ 0187 477946
☐ Oct–Dec

The Fattoria del Teso at Montecarlo

This is the place for fresh chestnuts in season, plus dried chestnuts and chestnut flour.

VIAREGGIO

Forno Benzio e Pancaccini

via Mazzini, 75
0584 962439
Wed pm

Many excellent kinds of bread are sold at this bakery, especially pane brutto *(the Tuscan name for oddly shaped loaves),* ciabatta *(loaves containing lard), and* ciabatta polesana *(loaves made with a flour that can be left to rise for a long time). Cookies like* anicini *and* pratolini *are also available.*

Rolando Bonini

via Mazzini, 181
0584 44175
Wed pm

Seemingly a small, unassuming butcher's shop opposite the celebrated Ristorante Romano, but in reality this is a shop run by a

Il Puntodivino wine store

great game expert. He sells game caught by various hunters in this area and also in the Maremma, and has contracts (contratti) *with the forestry guards. As well as fresh game birds and animals (plus all cuts of free-range Hungarian geese), the shop offers a selection of dry meats and bottled sauces based on game.*

Gelateria Mario

via Petrolini, 1
0584 961349
Mon (exc summer)

The specialties of this ice-cream parlor are whipped ices and fresh

fruit sorbets. It also sells fruit that is filled with ice cream flavored with the same fruit. A second shop located in via dei Lecci, 132 sells semi-freddi *(ice cream and sponge desserts) and cakes.*

Il Puntodivino

via Mazzini, 229
0584 31046
Mon

This is a particularly charming wine shop with a tasting counter and an excellent restaurant run by Roberto and Cristina Franceschini. It stocks 500 wines and liquors from all over the world. It also has very fine extra-virgin olive oil. Snacks made with lardo di Colonnata are served with the wines.

 Volpe Giuseppe

via San Martino, 104
0584 48800
Sun pm

At the well-stocked fish market of Viareggio this is the most interesting fishmonger. Volpe supplies scampi from Gorgona, Sardinian crayfish, local red shrimps sold live, and all the fish you need to make a real cacciucco *(fish soup).*

VILLAFRANCA IN LUNIGIANA (MS)

Antica Lunigiana

località Filetto,
via San Genesio, 21
0187 495124
Wed pm

This bakery is the place to buy real testaroli *(pasta disks like pancakes),* torta d'erbe *(herb pie), and, above all,* Carsenta *flat peasant bread cooked on chestnut leaves in a* testo.

CACCIUCCO ALLA VIAREGGINA

extra-virgin olive oil • 4 cloves garlic • 1 fresh chile, seeded and chopped • 1lb (500 g) octopus • 1 lb (500 g) cuttlefish • 1 glass red wine • 1½lb (800 g) ripe tomatoes, chopped • 1½lb (800 g) mixed fish (scorpion fish, gurnard, hake, weever, white bream, small ombrine) • 1¼lb (600 g) shark steaks and conger eel • 10 razor clams • slices of bread • 1–2 tablespoons chopped fresh parsley • salt

Heat some oil in a pan. Chop two of the garlic cloves and lightly fry with the chile. Cut the octopus and cuttlefish into largish pieces and stir into the pan. Add the wine and cook over a low heat until the wine has evaporated. Add the tomatoes; cook for 15 minutes. Add all the other fish, cutting up the large ones so they cook uniformly. Cover with hot water and simmer without stirring. When the fish is nearly cooked, add the razor clams and cook until all the fish is tender. Season with salt. Toast the bread, rub with the remaining garlic, and use to line a tureen. Pour in the soup, garnish with parsley and serve.

PISA
AND
LIVORNO

Pisa and Livorno

THE PROVINCES OF Pisa and Livorno are strongly influenced by the sea, for better or for worse. On the plus side is the fact that Livorno (which is still known by its anglicized name of Leghorn in many tourist brochures) is one of the most important fishing harbors on the Tyrrhenian and that means plenty of fresh fish. It owes its prosperity to Cosimo I, who chose Livorno – a tiny fishing village in 1571 – as the site for Tuscany's new port when Pisa's harbor silted up. The other plus is that the sea air suits some types of vegetables and fruits. On the minus side, the salt air has an unfavorable effect on the quality of the extra-virgin olive oil produced along the coast. However, the benefits of the sea are felt further inland where the warm air from the sea, the hilly ground, and the quality of the soil make for good growing conditions. The flourishing undergrowth in the extensive woodlands along the coast and inland is rich in scents and wildlife, as well as mushrooms and berries. This is an area where agriculture, food production, and gastronomic tradition reflect a marriage of land and sea and a balance between agriculture and nature.

There is a plentiful supply of excellent **fish** at Livorno thanks to the good quality of the water and the sheer abundance of fish in the seas of Vada, Formiche Grosseto, Gorgona, and the other islands (see pp78–79).

TOURIST OFFICES

• PISA Piazza del Duomo
050 560464. W www. pisa.turismo.toscana.it

• LIVORNO
Piazza Cavour, 6
0586 204611. W www. livorno.turismo.toscana.it

• VOLTERRA Piazza dei Priori, 20 0588 86099.
W www.volterratur.it

STAR ATTRACTIONS

• PISA: tower and Cathedral, 050 560921
Baptistry and Camposanto, 050 560464
Santa Maria della Spina, 050 910510
• SAN MINIATO (PI): Cathedral, 0571 42745
• SAN PIERO A GRADO (PI): church of San Piero
• TENUTA DI SAN ROSSORE (PI): nature park,
050 525500
• VOLTERRA (PI): Museo Etrusco Guarnacci,
0588 86347
Roman amphitheater, 0588 86150
Gallery and civic museum, 0588 87580

◁ **Drop nets at Bocca d'Arno**

The village of **Bolgheri**, to the
south of Livorno, is dominated by
the castle of the della Gherardesca
family and surrounded by large
estates. Bolgheri is most famous to
gourmets as the place where the
Sassicaia vineyards are *(see p81)*.

San Miniato is one of
the main centers for
the **white truffle**,
due to the quality and
quantity of truffles
found here. A truffle
festival is held on the
last three weekends
of November.

PINOLI (PINE NUTS)

Coastal and near-coastal areas are shaded
by magnificent umbrella pines. Their pine
nuts, which can only be
harvested from mature
trees, are a popular
ingredient in the
cuisine of
Tuscany and
nearby Liguria.

0 kilometers   10

0 miles   10

Places of Interest pp88–95
Restaurants pp180–185

Fish

Fresh fish is landed at Livorno harbor from all types of fishing grounds nearby – the sandy shallows, especially those at Vada, and the deep waters with seabeds of stone or gravel off the islands. But Livorno is not the only fishing harbor on this part of the coast: fishing is also an important industry in the islands. The waters around Elba, in particular, contain many rare fish in season, such as ombine meagers and amberjack. Piombino also has a busy fishing harbor, and some small boats call in along the Riviera degli Etruschi.

PALOMBO OR NICCIOLO (SMOOTH-HOUND SHARK)
This shark has delicate flesh which is always tasty and firm, and Italians consider it suitable for children. *Palombo* is a basic ingredient in the local *cacciucco* (fish soup). It is sold ready-skinned. Often other sharks are passed off for *palombo*, which is acceptable in the case of *spinarolo* (spur dog) or *smeriglio* (porbeagle shark) because they are also tasty, but the *gattuccio* (lesser spotted dogfish) is far inferior.

RAZZA OR ARZILLA (SKATE)
Various kinds of skate are caught in these waters. Only the wings are eaten. Some regional recipes suggest boiling the fish and serving it with a sauce or stewing it.

GRONGO (CONGER EEL)
This typical coastal fish is similar to the ordinary eel but it is bonier and the flesh is less fatty. It grows to an enormous size and is used in soups and sauces.

CODA DI ROSPO OR RANA PESCATRICE (MONKFISH)
Fierce-looking *(see lower part of the photograph)* but delicious, this is one of the most versatile fish in the kitchen. Usually only the tail end is sold in slices, which is a pity since it makes a splendid soup when cooked whole. The liver is regarded as a delicacy.

STRIGLIA DI SCOGLIO (RED MULLET)

This fish is a prime ingredient of Tuscan fish cuisine. Freshly caught and lightly cooked, smaller red mullet are always cooked whole. Larger red mullet are excellent grilled or baked in paper; or they may be fried or filleted as an *antipasto* (appetizer or starter). The related, very similar *triglia di fango* is a duller color, but has a stronger flavor.

SARAGO (A TYPE OF BREAM)

This white fish is typical of the coast and is highly prized. Its flesh is very tasty. *Sarago* is usually grilled or baked.

Hake have numerous relatives. Small hake (merluzzetto) *are delicious when fried.*

NASELLO OR MERLUZZO (HAKE)

Some fine specimens of hake are sold at the markets of Viareggio and Livorno, and when the fish is that fresh, it is excellent in all kinds of recipes. Hake is a delicate fish, easy to digest.

SEPPIA (CUTTLEFISH)

The most common of the squid family, *seppie* is usually inexpensive in markets. Cuttlefish is very versatile and is used in numerous regional recipes and special-occasion dishes. It is excellent boiled and dressed for a salad, or it can be grilled or baked. Pick one with the dark outer skin intact, and avoid those already cleaned. The ink sac is used for coloring and flavoring risottos and fresh pasta, although this is not a Tuscan tradition.

SCORFANO (SCORPION FISH OR RASCASSE)

This fierce-looking fish, considered the best fish for soup, is also delicious baked with rosemary. The flesh is white, tender, and juicy.

Wines

The weather in the provinces of Pisa and Livorno is affected by the warm air currents of the Tyrrhenian Sea and, consequently, the wines produced along the coast have always been fair but not excellent, light-bodied, and rather short on bouquet. The lack of first-rate wines changed in 1968 with the creation of Sassicaia, the most influential of modern Italian red wines, and the one which paved the way for the creation of other wines based on Cabernet Sauvignon. As in most parts of Tuscany, local vines are cultivated alongside foreign vines imported in the late 19th century.

The traditional whites include Trebbiano Toscano, Vermentino, Malvasia del Chianti, and Bianco Pisano di San Torpé, with Sauvignon as an import. Among the local reds are Sangiovese, Canaiolo Nero, Malvasia Nera, and the imports Cabernet Sauvignon and Merlot. Elba with its iron-rich soil and briny breezes produces wines rich in flavor but lacking in perfume. Also, the difficulty cultivating the vines means that the wine is more expensive. Typical white grape vines grown on the island include Trebbiano Toscano (Procanico), Ansonica, and Moscato; the red grape vines include Sangioveto or Sangiovese and Aleatico.

The red (Rosso) goes well with pork chops and spare ribs; the Rosso Superiore with grilled red meats.

The whites and the rosé (Rosato) are the perfect accompaniments for first courses with light sauces.

BOLGHERI
The Bolgheri area is limited to the region of Castagneto Carducci. It produces Bianco from Trebbiano Toscano, Vermentino, and Sauvignon, with Sauvignon and Vermentino from the same vine contributing at least 80 percent; Rosato, Rosso, and Rosso Superiore from Cabernet Sauvignon, Merlot, and Sangiovese grapes; and a Vin Santo Occhio di Pernice, ordinary and Riserva, from Sangiovese and Malvasia Nera.

MONTESCUDAIO
This wine is produced in the hills, where the soil gives it a special fragrance.

The red, based on Sangiovese, is very similar to Chianti. It differs by having an intensely fruity perfume and because it is aged for only a short time, no more than about four years. Serve it with meat stews, mushrooms, and pasta with meat sauces.

The white, from Trebbiano Toscano, Malvasia, and Vermentino grapes, goes well with full-flavored fish dishes and eels.

BIANCO PISANO DI SAN TORPÉ
The Arno valley around Pisa and Livorno produces this delicately perfumed light white wine. Its name comes from a variety of Trebbiano named after the first holy martyr of Pisa. This wine is ideal as an aperitif and with vegetable dishes. The Vin Santo and Vin Santo Riserva versions are perfect with sweet cookies.

CHIANTI COLLINE PISANE
This wine is subtly perfumed with a lighter body than other Chiantis, so it makes an excellent accompaniment to a wider range of dishes, including white meats with sauces. It is also produced in Superiore and Riserva versions.

BOLGHERI SASSICAIA
This is the great wine of the Super Tuscan category. It owes its success to the Cabernet Sauvignon vine which develops an unusual bouquet and body in the soil in this area. The wine has to age at least two years in wood, of which at least 18 months is spent in small casks holding no more than 50 gallons (225 liters). It is good with *bistecca alla fiorentina*, but its perfect match is game.

CACCIUCCO ALLA LIVORNESE

extra-virgin olive oil • 2 onions, finely chopped • 1 carrot, finely chopped • 1 stalk celery, finely chopped • 4 cloves garlic • 1 handful of chopped parsley • 2½ lb (1 kg) small reef-fish suitable for soups, including a few mullet • 1 larger fish (scorpion fish, weever, gurnard, slices of conger, and palombo) • 1 lb (400 g) octopus, cut into pieces • 1 lb (400 g) cuttlefish, cut into pieces • a few scampi, cockles, and slices of squid (optional) • 1 lb (400 g) mantis shrimps • 2½ lb (1 kg) ripe tomatoes, peeled and seeded • 1 chile • 3 glasses red wine • 3 dessertspoons wine vinegar • slices of Tuscan bread • salt

Heat some oil in a large pan (preferably a terra-cotta one) and lightly fry the chopped vegetables, garlic, and parsley. Clean the small fish and add them with the chile. Fry lightly and season with salt. Add the vinegar and let it evaporate, then add the wine and the tomatoes. Simmer for 10 minutes then pass the mixture through a sieve. Heat some oil and fry the cuttlefish, octopus, and squid, if using, then add the sieved mixture and gradually all the other fish, calculating the cooking time for each (adding mantis shrimp, scampi, and cockles last). Add water, if necessary. Toast the bread and line a tureen with the slices. Pour the cooked soup over the bread and serve.

ELBA ANSONICA
Made with at least 85 percent Ansonica grapes, this is a dry white wine with a good body. It is well suited to a fish *antipasto* and delicately flavored first courses. There is also a sweet *Passito* (raisin wine) version.

ELBA BIANCO
This dry white wine, which is made chiefly from Trebbiano grapes, goes well with the island's traditional herb soups. There is also a spumante version.

ELBA ALEATICO
Considered the pearl of Elba's output – partly because of the difficulty of working the grapes – this is a pleasantly sweet red wine. Drink it with *torta ubriaca*, a fruit cake that is sprinkled with Elba Aleatico.

ELBA ROSSO AND ROSSO RISERVA
Sangiovese predominates, with small quantities of other red grapes in these wines. The young Rosso is good with white meats, especially rabbit in sauce, while the Riserva goes well with game – try it with hare.

WINE TYPE	GOOD VINTAGES	GOOD PRODUCERS	WINE TYPE	GOOD VINTAGES	GOOD PRODUCERS
Red Wine			**Red Wine**		
Bolgheri	97, 96, 90	Podere Grattammacco di Castagneto Carducci, Ornellaia di Bolgheri, Le Macchiole di Bolgheri	Montescudaio	97, 96, 90	Sorbaiano di Montecatini Val di Cecina
Bolgheri Sassicaia	97, 96, 90	Tenuta San Guido di Bolgheri	Supertuscans *(see p. 130)*	98, 97, 95, 90	Tua Rita di Suvereto, Tenuta del Terriccio di Castellina Marittima, Michele Satta di Castagneto Carducci
Chianti delle Colline Pisane	97, 90	Tenuta di Ghizzano			

Traditional Produce

Most of Tuscany grows excellent vegetables but the rural areas of Livorno and the Arno Valley between Pisa and Florence are particularly productive. One of the reasons market gardening here is so successful is the length of the growing season, which covers almost every month of the year except perhaps dry periods in high summer. The most distinctive Tuscan dishes are the soups (*minestre* and *zuppe*), and fresh vegetables are such an important ingredient in local cooking that nearly all the *trattorie* grow their own produce. The areas around San Miniato and Volterra are renowned for white truffles.

BLACK-EYED PEAS

These peas were widely used in Europe before the discovery of America. In Italy they have been replaced by *cannellini* and *borlotti* beans, but they are still grown in Tuscany, in the area around Pistoia.

ELVERS

Elvers, the fry of eels (*cée* in the local dialect), have long been caught in Tuscan river estuaries. In local recipes they are cooked quickly in a covered pan or used to make stuffed omelettes. Elvers are now protected in Italy but not in Spain, where they are called *angulas*.

CÉE ALLA PISANA

extra-virgin olive oil • 4 cloves garlic, crushed • 4 sage leaves, chopped • just over 1 lb (500 g) elvers • 1 piece of fresh chile, chopped • salt

Heat plenty of oil in a pan and sauté the chopped garlic and the sage leaves. Add the elvers and cover the pan at once, holding the lid down firmly and shaking the pan to prevent them from sticking. After a few seconds, uncover the pan and stir the elvers. Add the chile and season with salt. Re-cover the pan and cook the elvers on a low heat for a few minutes.

Cée alla pisana *is a Viareggio-style dish of elvers, cooked with garlic and sage.*

OLIVE OIL FROM THE LIVORNO MAREMMA

The area of production for this oil lies inland from the Tyrrhenian coast and comprises Castagneto Carducci, Bibbona, Sassetta, and Monteverdi Marittimo. The oil is light and fruity with floral notes and a hint of the aroma of hay. It has a balanced flavor without marked intensity.

GOBBI IN GRATELLA

2¼ lb (1 kg) cardoons
- *extra-virgin olive oil*
- *wine vinegar • salt*
- *pepper*

Cut the cardoons into
pieces about 4½
inches (12 cm) long
and cook in boiling
water until tender.
Drain and rinse under
cold running water,
then remove the strings.
Season with plenty of
oil, salt and pepper, and
a few drops of vinegar.
Leave for 2 hours and then
grill the cardoons over
very hot charcoal.

GOBBI (CARDOONS)
Cardoons with their silvery
white stalks look like prickly
celery. Those from the Arno
Valley – the area bordering the
province of Florence – are
particularly sought-after.

OIL FROM THE HILLS OF PISA
Oil from olive
groves south of Pisa
and east of Livorno
has a delicate, yet
somewhat peppery
and fruity flavor.
It has a flowery
scent and a
sweetish aftertaste
of almonds.

PASTA SECCA (DRIED PASTA)
Lari produces some of the finest
dried pasta in Italy. The pasta is
sent to specialty shops all over
the world.

Tagliatelle

Pappardelle

Tagliolini

PASTA SECCA ALL'UOVO (DRIED EGG PASTA)
Many small
producers make
different egg-
based long
pastas. Although
these pastas are
dried, they have all the
flavor of fresh pasta.

WHAT TO SAMPLE
The **wild game**, especially boar, hare, wood pigeons, and woodcock, in this area – and
especially in the Maremma around Livorno – is as fine as that found in Grosseto. Inland,
and on Elba, there are areas that are good for vegetables and for **fine fruit,** including
yellow freestone peaches, white peaches (on Elba), figs, table grapes, and cherries (on
Monte Pisano and in the Lari area). In the hill areas there is excellent **prosciutto crudo**,
ham from shoulder of pork, and **pecorino** cheese at Volterra. The **farinata di ceci**
(chickpea polenta) is a speciality of Livorno. Local confectioners make and sell marzipan
fruits. On Elba the production of **honey** and **extra-virgin olive oil** is considerable.

At the start of the season, the early artichokes do not have any spines.

CARCIOFINI SOTT'OLIO

36 artichokes (late-season ones) • 2 pints (1 liter) wine vinegar • 2 bay leaves • 1 clove • 4 juniper berries • 1 dessertspoon black peppercorns • extra-virgin olive oil • salt

Clean the artichokes, removing the tough outer leaves. Dilute the vinegar with 3 pints (1½ liters) of water and pour it into a tall saucepan. Add the spices and plenty of salt. Bring to the boil, add the artichokes, and simmer for 6–7 minutes. Drain carefully and leave to cool. Dry the artichokes and transfer to one or more clean jars. Cover with oil, taking care not to trap air bubbles inside. Store in a cool dry place.

By the time the cold weather sets in, the artichokes have developed spines.

CARCIOFI (ARTICHOKES)
Artichokes are an essential ingredient in many traditional dishes, including fish ones, in the area; *Violetto* artichokes are a traditional Tuscan variety.

CAVOLFIORE (CAULIFLOWER) FROM CASCIANA
Casciana is a spa town renowned for cultivating cauliflowers, some of which grow to a very large size.

SPINACI (SPINACH)
Inland from Livorno, tasty spinach grows all the year round. In the springtime it is eaten raw in salads; the rest of the year it is cooked in traditional dishes.

OTHER PRODUCE WORTH TRYING
All summer the vegetables in this area are full of flavor, and the **eggplant is** exceptional. Look out for **fennel**, **peas**, **potatoes** from Santa Maria a Monte, **white asparagus** from the Valle d'Arno, **zucchini**, and **celery**. Along the coast there are sweet, juicy **tomatoes**. The **basil**, both the large-leaved variety and small-leaved Ligurian basil, has a wonderful scent. Specialty producers grow **garlic**, **onions,** and **shallots**.

Wild Produce

MILK-CAP MUSHROOM
(Lactarius sanguifluus)
This mushroom is called *pineggiole* locally, but *sanguinello* in the rest of Italy. Easily recognized because the gills shed a thick, red liquid, it is an orangey color with green patches, and has chalky flesh. They are common in woods along the coast, and the best ones are found under pine trees. Excellent preserved in oil, they can also be grilled or cooked in pasta sauces.

BLACK MOREL
(Morchella conica)
When the spring flowers bloom, these mushrooms *(spugnole)* sprout along the coast under pine and heathland trees, and inland in vineyards, orchards, and wherever there have been fires in pine woods. They are exquisite, fresh or dried, in risottos, sauces, savory pies, and casseroles.

TRIPPA CON LE SPUGNOLE

extra-virgin olive oil • 18 oz (500 g) morels, sliced • 1 sprig of calamint (or mint) • 3 cloves garlic, finely chopped • 1½ lb (700 g) tripe, cut into strips • light meat stock • salt • pepper

The traditional recipe uses *porcini* (cèpe mushrooms) but morels are better. Heat plenty of oil, add the mushrooms, calamint, and garlic, and season with salt and pepper. Cook until the mushrooms shed all their water. Lower the heat, add the tripe, and cook until all the liquid has evaporated and the tripe is tender, moistening with a little meat stock, if necessary. Adjust the seasoning.

YELLOW MOREL
(Morchella esculenta)
The yellow morel *(spugnola gialla)* is highly prized in international cuisine. It is common in the coastal scrub of Tuscany in springtime, then in damp inland valleys under elm and ash trees and in vineyards. Usually sold dried at the markets, this morel is excellent in pies, risottos, soups, and with eggs or meat.

SADDLE FUNGUS
(Helvella monachella)
In spring this mushroom forms clusters under poplars where the ground is sandy, especially at the coast. It is picked along with morels. While the perfume and taste are not exceptional, it adds a pleasant flavor to sauces.

SUMMER BOLETUS
(Boletus lepidus)

Distinguished from other cèpes by its yellow stalk and scaly surface, this mushroom has rubbery yellow flesh when ripe, but turns a pinkish color when cut. It is nothing special but is picked because of the thrill of finding a cèpe in summer, when no other boletus mushrooms are to be found. If young, they are very good fried.

BORAGE
(Borago officinalis)

One of the best-known and prettiest of the wild herbs, borage *(borraggine)* grows on waste ground on the Tuscan plains. It has a pleasant taste of cucumber, and the leaves are cooked in many of the classic soups of the region and added to spinach dishes. The pretty blue flowers add a lovely splash of color to leafy salads.

CAPERS
(Capparis spinosa)

Caper plants *(capperi)* scramble over sea-facing rocks and walls. Their flower buds, salted and pickled, are one of the classic Mediterranean condiments.

PINE NUTS
(Pinus pinea)

Pinoli are found in abundance all year round in Tuscany, growing inside the cones of the majestic umbrella pines. Sadly, they are harvested by machine, which is very damaging to the undergrowth and threatens to kill off the coastal pine woods. Left on the tree, the large cones fall as they open, so the pine nuts can be picked up from the ground.

BACCALÀ IN DOLCEFORTE (SALT COD IN SWEET-AND-SOUR SAUCE)

1 glass white wine • 1 small glass wine vinegar • 2 dessertspoons pine nuts • 2 dessertspoons sugar • 1 dessertspoon sultanas • a few calamint (or mint) leaves • extra-virgin olive oil • 1¾ lb (800 g) salt cod, presoaked and cut into pieces • plain flour

Put the wine, vinegar, pine nuts, sugar, sultanas, and calamint in a pan. Bring to the boil and boil until the liquid is reduced by half. Heat the oil in a separate pan. Coat the cod pieces in flour and fry in the oil for 6–7 minutes on each side. Drain the cod and put in another pan with a little of the oil and the sauce. Sauté over brisk heat for 3–4 minutes.

Places of Interest

THE FOLLOWING PLACES sell an extensive range of foods produced in this region – fruits, vegetables, meat, fish, cheeses, pasta, honey, and preserves. They also have excellent wine-makers. In addition, it is always worth stopping wherever you see a hand-written sign outside a farm, as many farmers will sell their produce directly to visitors. You may even find some who will let you pick fruit from the trees and gather vegetables from their kitchen gardens.

ASCIANO (PI)

 Frantoio di Asciano

via Possenti, 87
C 050 855924;
02 76025678

This large estate has its own olive press, once the property of Lorenzo il Magnifico. It produces Monti Pisani Colle di Bellavista extra-virgin olive oil, one of the finest olive oils in Italy. More versatile than the classic Pisan oils, it is very good for making mayonnaise and dressing fish grilled over charcoal or poached.

BIBBONA (LI)

Fattoria Sant'Anna

località Sette Fattorie
via Aurelia Sud
C 0586 670230

The fruits and vegetables grown on the farm are used for making preserves, jams, and fruit in syrup. Sauces and soups are sold ready to heat up and serve. All the products are carefully packaged in glass jars, and they are guaranteed to keep well.

Savio

piazza Mazzini, 4
C 0586 671946
● Mon–Wed (exc summer)

This wine shop holds about 400 labels, mostly Tuscan. There is also a good selection of Sicilian wines and Champagne. All the wines are available by the glass, and can be matched with crostoni (toasted bread), a wide range of cheeses and salumi, and typical Tuscan products and desserts. The shop organizes themed evenings and wine-tasting courses. In the summer, it opens both during the day and in the evening; in the winter, it opens at 8:00PM.

CAMPIGLIA MARITTIMA (LI)

Azienda Agricola Jacopo Banti

località Citerna
C 0565 838802

The small range of red and white wines sold here includes a noteworthy Val di Cornia Bianco Il Peccato and Poggio Angelica, both made from Vermentino grapes. The olive oil comes from the olive groves dotted on the hillsides.

The gateway to Bolgheri

Rigoli

frazione Cafaggio,
via degli Ulivi, 8
C 0565 843079
● Sun pm

This estate at the foot of Mount Pitti offers a view over the Cornia Valley all the way to the Tyrrhenian sea. The cellar is new but located in a traditional farmhouse. Among the wines on sale are Val di Cornia Montepitti Bianco and Rosso, Rigoli Rosso and Testalto Rosso, and Magistro Passito (Ansonica). Oil, honey, and grappa are also available.

CAPOLIVERI – ELBA (LI)

Azienda Agricola Mola

località Mola
C 0565 958151

The cellar of a Bolgheri wine producer

This is a mixed farm, producing a range of vegetables, fruits, oil, and wine. The wines produced here are Elba Bianco Vigna degli Aiali, Elba Rosso Gelsarello, a pure Sangiovese, and two sweet wines: Elba Aleatico and Passito di Moscato.

CASALE MARITTIMO (PI)

 Camerini

via Vittorio Veneto, 31
☎ 0586 652081

Thanks to the practice of the transportation of beehives, honey from several blossoms from Garfagnana and Maremma can be purchased here.

CASTAGNETO CARDUCCI–BOLGHERI (LI)

🍇 Enoteca Il Borgo

via Vittorio Emanuele, 25/27
☎ 0565 766006
⬤ Mon

Only Italian wines – the premier wines of the Bolgheri area and the leading estates – are stocked by this wine shop. The range includes a selection of grappas and liquors and olive oil from local producers. Tastings can be organized by appointment.

🍁 Elixir China Calisaja

via Garibaldi
☎ 0565 766017
⬤ Wed pm (winter)

This is the sales outlet for a long-established firm. It imports quinine bark, which is then processed by hand in the traditional way, by pounding in a mortar

The Elixir China Calisaja shop at Castagneto Carducci

and soaking in alcohol. The resulting elixir is then stored in wood. The shop sells a wide range of local produce, including honey, preserves, and pasta, much of it organically produced. It also sells kitchen utensils.

🍇 Podere Grattamacco

località Grattamacco
☎ 0565 763840

The peak of this estate's wine production is the Bolgheri Rosso Superiore Grattamacco from Cabernet Sauvignon, Merlot, and Sangiovese grapes, followed by Bolgheri Bianco Grattamacco from Vermentino, Trebbiano, and Sauvignon. The estate produces a fine oil, one of the best in the district.

🍷 Fattoria Poggio Lamentano

località Lamentano, 138/b
☎ 0565 766008

This estate is owned by a Scot called Michael Zyw, who devotes himself to painting and the land. He produces a fine, intense, fruity extra-virgin olive oil, which is well-known abroad and appreciated by leading restaurateurs in Italy.

🍇 Azienda Agricola Michele Satta

località Vigna al Cavaliere, 61
☎ 0565 773041

Reconciling style with a commitment to quality is the goal of this estate. The Bolgheri Rosso Piastraia blends four types of grape: Merlot, Cabernet, Syrah, and Sangiovese. The red Il Cavaliere is from Sangiovese alone. Among the whites, Bolgheri Vermentino La Costa di Giulia is of note.

SEPPIE IN ZIMINO

extra-virgin olive oil
• 1 onion, chopped
• 2 stalks celery, chopped
• 2¼ lb (1 kg) beet leaves, sliced into large pieces • 2¼ lb (1 kg) cuttlefish, cut into strips
• 10 oz (300 g) peeled, plum tomatoes • chopped fresh parsley • salt • pepper

Heat some oil in a pan, add the onion and celery, and cook until softened slightly. Add the beet leaves, cover and cook for about 15 minutes. Add the cuttlefish, cook for a few minutes, and then add the tomatoes. Season with salt and pepper and simmer until the cuttlefish is tender. Garnish with the parsley.

Enoteca Tognoni

via Giulia, 6
☎ 0565 762001
⬤ Wed

*This wine store stocks
a good selection of the
great wines of Bolgheri
and Tuscany, as well
as various other Italian
wines. You can sample
and buy cheeses,
Maremma* salumi, *and
other local delicacies.
Hot and cold dishes are
served: the former include
soups made with spelt.*

CASTIGLIONCELLO (LI)

 Gelateria Dai Dai

via del Sorriso, 8
☎ 0586 753390

*Delicious ice creams
made from good-quality
ingredients are offered
here. Try the ice-cream
bricks, tartufini, cassatas,
vanilla ice cream, sorbets,
and bocconcini.*

❦ Elisabetta

località Collemezzano,
via Tronto, 10/14
☎ 0586 661096;
0586 662308

*Located near the ancient
residence of the Grand
Duke Leopold of Tuscany
and an 18th-century
church, this estate offers
visitors the chance to
stay overnight in an*
agriturismo *with a
swimming pool, tennis
courts and two
restaurants. The tasting
of basic wines is free
of charge; tastings
of local products
are possible upon
payment of a
fee. On offer
are Vermentino,
Aulo (Sangiovese,
Canaiolo,
Cabernet
Sauvignon),
Brunetti (Sangiovese,
Merlot, Cabernet*

*Sauvignon), Le Marze
Bianche (Greco di
Tufo, Fiano d'Avellino,
Chardonnay), oil, jams,
honey, and grappa.*

Mediterranea Belfiore

località La Cinquantina,
via Guerrazzi,
☎ 0586 620555

*Once a firm specializing
in processing tomato
sauces, Mediterranea
Belfiore has become a
specialist in organic
offerings. There is a
huge variety of products
on offer from several
localities, all under glass.
Tomatoes remain of
excellent quality, along
with all the sauces.*

CAVO – ELBA (LI)

🏛 Apicoltura Ballini

strada provinciale
della Parata
☎ 0565 949836

*Here is a leading breeder
of queen bees, exported
worldwide, and a*

*producer of outstanding
honey from unusual
flowers, mostly aromatic
herbs: rosemary, lavender,
cardoons, heather,
arbutus (strawberry tree),
helichrysum, eucalyptus,
sweet chestnut, and wild
flowers. There is another
shop at via Michelangelo,
11 in the village.*

CECINA (LI)

❦ Coccolino

via Leonardo da Vinci, 24
☎ 0586 680049
⬤ Mon

*This wine shop is open
from 5:00PM until 1:00AM.
It stocks about 600
wines, mostly Tuscan
but also from other
Italian regions, as well
as several international
ones. There is also a
wide choice of matching
dishes – typically Tuscan
main courses and
secondi, salumi, cheeses
from all over Italy, and
desserts. A small tasting
room is available and
themed evenings are
sometimes organized.*

BACCALÀ IN ZIMINO (SALT COD IN TOMATOES)

1¾ lb (800 g) salt cod, soaked in water for 2 days
• 1¾ lb (800 g) beet leaves • 1¼ lb (500 g) tomatoes
• extra-virgin olive oil • 3 green onions,
chopped • 2 cloves garlic, chopped • salt • pepper

Rinse the cod, remove the skin, and cut it into pieces.
Wash the beet leaves and put them in a pan with just
the water that adheres to the leaves. Cover and cook
over a low heat for about 10 minutes. Drain, squeeze out
the water, and chop coarsely. Scald the
tomatoes in boiling water, peel while
still warm, and cut into pieces. Heat
some oil in a pan and gently fry
the green onions, garlic, and
cod for 5 minutes. Using a
slotted spoon, remove the
cod and set aside. Add the
tomatoes to the pan, season
with salt and pepper, and
simmer gently for 30 minutes.
Add the greens and the pieces
of cod and stir gently for about
10 minutes. Serve piping hot.

TELLINE ALLA LIVORNESE (LIVORNO COCKLES)

extra-virgin olive oil • 1 onion, chopped • ¾ lb (350 g) tomatoes, peeled and chopped • 1 fresh chile, seeded and chopped • 2½ lb (1.2 kg) cockles (telline) • 3 eggs • chopped fresh parsley • salt • pepper

Heat some oil in a pan, add the onion, and fry until slightly softened. Add the tomatoes and chile and season with salt and pepper. Cook over a moderate heat for 10 minutes. Add the cockles in their shells and cook until they have all opened. Beat the eggs in a bowl, then add them to the pan with the parsley. Stir to mix all the ingredients and serve at once.

CRESPINA (PI)

 Bernardini

località Cenaja,
via di Lavoria, 83/85
C 050 644100
● Sat

Prosciutto crudo *and* salumi *made from pork or game are produced here. The* Boccone del Buttero *is an intriguing specialty made from strips of boar meat seasoned with olives.*

DONORATICO (LI)

 **Maestrini**

via Aurelia, 1
C 0565 775209
● Mon

A medium- to high-quality selection of Tuscan, Italian, and foreign wines, especially DOCG wines from central Tuscany, is sold here. Wines can be tasted accompanied by salumi *and cheeses in a relaxed atmosphere with background music.*

LARI (PI)

 Agriturismo Le Macchie

località Usigliano,
via delle Macchie, 2
C 0587 685327

Cinta Senese pigs graze half-wild on this farm. The meat and salumi *the farm produces are less salty and spicy to suit the taste of non-Tuscans. It has* lardo *(lard), which is processed at Colonnata in marble molds, and sausages in oil, as well as jams, preserves, and fresh vegetables. There is also a restaurant and farmhouse vacation accommodation.*

 **Martelli Artigiani Pastai**

via San Martino, 3
C 0587 684238

This family firm welcomes visitors (it is popular with Americans) and readily answers questions about its working methods. The Martelli family's pasta (in a wide range of shapes, all dried at low temperatures and extruded through bronze) is excellent, and though output is limited, it is found in leading stores on every continent.

LIVORNO

 **D.O.C. Parole e Cibi**

via Goldoni, 40/44
C 0586 887583
● Mon

An exceptional selection of wines – over 1,000 from all over the world – can be found here. There is also a wide range of grappas, whisky, and other liquors. The store has a very lively wine bar offering tasty snacks to accompany the wines, and there is a restaurant (serving in the evenings only), which is open until late.

 **Cantina Nardi**

via Leonardo Cambini, 6/8
C 0586 808006

A good selection of both Italian and Tuscan wines is sold here, with the emphasis on Val di Cornia and Bolgheri, plus the latest vintages of the "Super Tuscans." They also sell olive oil and a range of liquors. During the day they serve a small number of traditional Tuscan dishes prepared to perfection. The cacciucco *(fish soup) is very popular, and you need to order it in advance.*

Fishing boats in Livorno harbor

Azienda Agricola Cecilia at Marina di Campo on Elba

MARCIANA – ELBA (LI)

🍁 Walter Ciangherotti

località La Zanca,
via Santa Assunta, 9
📞 0565 908281

*Excellent organic honeys,
such as lavender, rosemary,
blackberry, heather, and
chestnut, are for sale here.*

BAVETTINE
SUL PESCE

¾ *lb (300 g) scampi*
*• 6 small mullet • ¾ lb
(300 g) clams • 6 mantis
shrimp • extra-virgin olive
oil • 8 oz (200 g)
monkfish • 8 oz (200 g)
small cuttlefish • 1¼ lb
(500 g) bavettine (ribbon
pasta) • 2 cloves garlic,
chopped • 1 lb (400 g)
tomatoes, chopped
• chopped fresh parsley
• salt • pepper*

Peel the scampi and
fillet the mullet. Use the
heads to make stock and
cook the shrimp and
clams in it for 5 minutes.
Strain the stock; reserve
the clams and shrimp.
Stir-fry the monkfish,
cuttlefish, fillets, scampi,
and garlic in some oil.
Add the tomatoes, salt,
pepper, and parsley and
simmer. Cook the pasta
in the stock. Add the
shrimp and clams to the
sauce and serve.

MARINA DI CAMPO – ELBA (LI)

🍇 Azienda Agricola Cecilia

località La Pila
📞 0565 977322

*The range of this firm's
Elba DOC wines includes
an outstanding Ansonica,
Rosso, and a sweet Aleatico
wine. They also produce
two grappas, one from
Ansonica grapes, the other
from a blend of Ansonica,
Moscato, and Aleatico.*

MONTECATINI VAL DI CECINA (PI)

🍇 Fattoria Sorbaiano

località Sorbaiano
📞 0588 30243

*Montepulciano d'Abruzzo
and Sangiovese are
combined with Cabernet
and Syrah in the estate's*

*Montescudaio Rosso delle
Miniere. Equally well-
balanced is the blend of
Trebbiano, Vermentino,
Chardonnay, and Riesling
for the Montescudaio
Bianco Lucestraia,
matured in* barriques. *The
estate also makes Vin Santo
and an excellent organic
extra-virgin olive oil. It
has a lively program of
farm and estate vacations.*

MONTESCUDAIO (PI)

🍇 Merlini

via delle Colline, 1
📞 0586 680354

*This fairly new estate has
all the latest technology.
There is a fee for tastings
of typical food products
matched to wines of the
Montescudaio DOC: Le
Colline Rosso, Greto delle
Ginestre Bianco, Guadi
Piani Rosso, and the
excellent Guadi Piani
Rosso Riserva. Oil and
grappa are also available.*

PECCIOLI (PI)

🍇 Tenuta di Ghizzano

Ghizzano,
via della Chiesa, 1
📞 0587 630096

*The main effort of this
estate is focused on the
extra-virgin olive oil from
its 15,000 olive trees. It is
a very active estate that
has enhanced the wine
production of the Pisan*

Delicacies from the Cioccolateria De Bondt

Azienda Agricola Acquabona

hills with a good Chianti and Veneroso, a red wine from Sangiovese, Cabernet, and Merlot grapes.

PIOMBINO (LI)

🍀 Romeo Formaggi

località Salivoli,
via dei Cavalleggeri, 5
📞 0565 44455

The region's best salumi, *as well as authentic* culatello di Zibello *and Norcia hams, are sold by this shop, which specializes in* salumi. *It also has a rich selection of cheeses from central and northern Italy:* formaggi ubriachi *from the Veneto, various types of* robiola *from the Langhe,* pecorino di fossa *from Soliano al Rubicone, and the famous Piedmontese Castelmagno.*

PISA

🍫 Cioccolateria De Bondt

via Turati, 22
📞 050 501896
⬤ Mon; Jun–Sep

About 50 types of chocolates – some made in molds while others are handcrafted like real works of art (there are even Christmas trees in season) – and 15 kinds of chocolate bars are all the work of Paul De Bondt, a skilled Dutch confectioner who settled in Pisa.

🍬 Pasticceria Salza

via Borgo Stretto, 46
📞 050 580144
⬤ Mon

A confectionery shop renowned for the freshness of its raw materials and top-of-the-line products, from chocolates to cookies, cakes, ice creams, chilled cream desserts, and traditional Sienese fruit cakes, including panforte *and* ricciarelli.

PONTEDERA (PI)

🌾 Pastificio Caponi

via Verdi, 16
📞 0587 52532 ⬤ Sat

This small, family-run firm still uses traditional methods to produce small quantities of an excellent egg pasta. It has been famous throughout Italy and Europe for 40 years for its good-quality ingredients and the care devoted to all phases of production.

🐟 Pescheria Toti

via Marconcini, 72
📞 0587 53921
⬤ Wed and Sat pm

Here you have a wide selection of excellent fresh fish, which comes mainly from the Livorno and Viareggio harbors.

PORTOFERRAIO – ELBA (LI)

🍇 Azienda Agricola Acquabona

località Acquabona
📞 0565 933013

This is one of the largest vineyards and wineries on the island, with 34 acres (14 hectares) of traditional Elba vines including Ansonica, which it produces in limited quantities. The Aleatico is interesting, with about 1,000 18-ounce (half-liter) bottles produced a year. It also produces small quantities of grappa.

🌾 La Bottega del Pane

viale Elba, 13
📞 0565 917120
⬤ Wed pm

Well-known locally for its fine focaccia *and a wide variety of modern filled rolls, this bakery also sells excellent standard white and brown bread.*

CÉE ALLA LIVORNESE (LIVORNO-STYLE EELS)

2¼ lb (1 kg) elvers • extra-virgin olive oil • 1 sprig of sage, chopped • 3 cloves garlic, chopped • 8 oz (250 g) tomatoes, peeled • chopped fresh chile • salt • pepper

Wash the elvers carefully and pat dry. Heat some oil in a pan, add the sage and garlic, and fry gently until the garlic has softened. Add the elvers to the pan and cook for 5 minutes over a moderate heat. Add the tomatoes and a small amount of chopped chile. Season with salt and pepper. Simmer for another 10 minutes before serving.

TRIPPA
ALLA LIVORNESE

extra-virgin olive oil
• *3 cloves garlic, chopped*
• *2¼ lb (1 kg) tripe,
cut into strips* • *4
dessertspoons vinegar*
• *chopped fresh parsley*
• *salt* • *pepper*

Heat some oil in a pan,
add the garlic, and fry
gently for a few minutes.
Add the tripe and cook
for 3–4 minutes. Pour in
the vinegar and a glass
of hot water. Cook until
the liquid has evaporated
and then remove from
the heat. Taste and adjust
the seasoning. Sprinkle
with the chopped parsley
and serve at once.

Azienda Agricola La Chiusa

località Magazzini, 93
☎ 0565 933046

*This estate's fine vineyards
slope down to within a few
yards of the sea. It mostly
makes Elba Bianco, but its
most interesting products
are two dessert wines, Elba
Ansonica (made from
partly dried grapes) and
Elba Aleatico. The extra-
virgin olive oil produced
by the estate merits
separate mention because
it is excellent quality and,
unhappily, there is not
enough to satisfy the very
high demand for it.*

PROCCHIO – ELBA (LI)

Macelleria Mazzarri

via delle Ginestre, 53
☎ 0565 907289
● Wed pm

*In the open season,
Mazzarri butchers local
wild boar; the rest of the
year he has excellent
meat, mostly Tuscan
(including Chianina
beef), otherwise
Piedmontese.*

RIPARBELLA (PI)

Podere La Regola

via Antonio Gramsci, 1
☎ 0586 696991;
348 5858530

*This modern estate near
the Cecina river produces
oil, grappa, and wines
of the Montescudaio
DOC: Rosso Vallino delle
Conche, Bianco Steccaia,
Rosso Ligustro, and Rosso
La Regola.*

SAN MINIATO (PI)

Frantoio Sanminiatese

località La Serra,
via Maremmana, 8
☎ 0571 460528
● Sat pm

*This estate produces superb
extra-virgin olive oil, spicy
table olives, and preserves.*

SUVERETO (LI)

Azienda Agricola Gualdo del Re

località Notri, 77
☎ 0565 829888

*The unusual DOC
Val di Cornia range of
wines – Bianco, Rosso,
and Rosso Riserva – are
the staples of this estate.
They are backed up by
other notable wines, like
the red Federico Primo
(Sangiovese and Merlot
in equal parts) and the
white Vermentino Vigna
Valentina.*

Azienda Agricola Orlando Pazzagli

via Cavour, 40
☎ 0565 829333

*With its own olive groves
and press, this estate
covers the whole cycle
of production. Its La*

TRIGLIE ALLA LIVORNESE

3¼ lb (1.5 kg) red mullet, cleaned • *4 cloves garlic, finely
chopped* • *extra-virgin olive oil* • *2¼ lb (1 kg) tomatoes,
peeled and chopped* • *1 fresh chile (misleadingly called*
zenzero *– ginger – in Tuscany), seeded and finely chopped*
• *handful of parsley, chopped* • *salt* • *pepper*

Arrange the red mullet in a single layer in a greased pan.
In a second pan, sauté the garlic in a little oil, add the
tomatoes, and simmer. When the tomatoes are half-
cooked, add the chile and season to taste with salt and
pepper. Once the sauce is well cooked, pour it over the
mullet and simmer over a low heat, taking care that the
sauce does not dry out (add a little hot water to the pan,
if necessary). When the fish are cooked, sprinkle in the
chopped parsley and serve.

Oil jars at the Azienda Agricola Orlando Pazzagli

Piastrina extra-virgin olive oil is typical of the area and is outstanding.

🍇 Petra

località
San Lorenzo Alto, 131
☎ 0565 845308;
0565 845180

This winery belongs to the Terra Moretti group and has 740 acres (300 hectares) of vineyards, olive groves, and woods. The brand-new cellar, designed by architect Mario Botta, was inaugurated at the end of 2002. The extra-virgin olive oil is excellent, and the Val di Cornia Rosso Petra and Petra Riserva are unmissable.

VICOPISANO
(PI)

🏺 Azienda Agricola
Il Frantoio

località Palazzetto, 3
☎ 050 798870

*It might be named after an old olive press (*frantoio*), but this is a technologically advanced organic farm in a valley full of olive trees. The oil is sweet with an aftertaste of*

apple, perfectly suited to shellfish. Il Frantoio is a member of the prestigious Corporazione Mastri Oleari (the guild of oil-makers).

VOLTERRA
(PI)

🐦 Agriturismo
Lischeto

località San Giusto
☎ 0588 30403

The owner of this estate is one of many Sardinians who have moved to this region; his wife is Tuscan. The estate has a milking herd of 1,000 ewes and their milk is used to

produce excellent pecorino *cheeses, both fresh and mature, and also fresh and baked* ricotta *cheeses. A second family estate not far from the coast produces excellent extra-virgin olive oil, and the honey is also outstanding. The* agriturismo *facilities on the estate include apartments to rent with meals of typical Sardinian and Tuscan dishes available.*

View of the countryside from the heights of Volterra

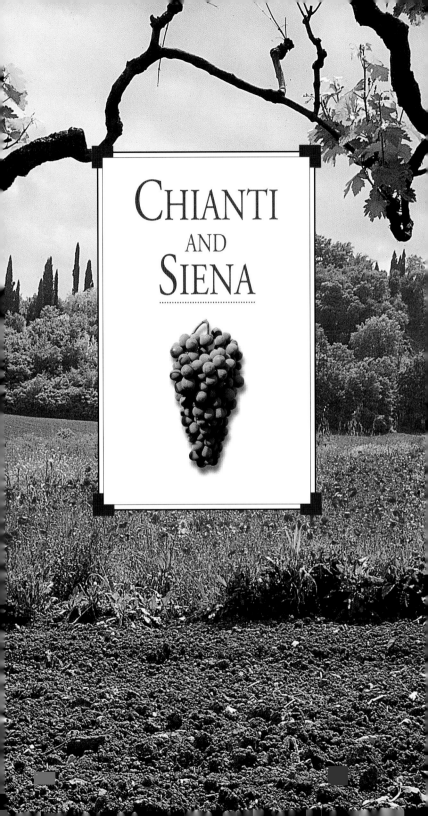

CHIANTI
AND
SIENA

Chianti and Siena

ITALY'S BEST-KNOWN WINE comes from this region. The geographical region of Chianti, which had the name long before the wine, is only one part of the winegrowing area of the same name. Chianti wine is produced over a huge area of central Tuscany. The area that gave birth to Chianti wine now sports the Chianti Classico label on its bottles of wine, to indicate that it comes from the classic heartland of Chianti. This heartland, a hilly district stretching across the provinces of Florence and Siena, does not look like a wine-producing area. The woodlands are studded with ancient towns and villages, whose long history is visible at every gateway. On the hilltops, often screened from the main roads, stand country houses set in estates where the olive groves and vineyards are separated by extensive woodland. These villas and castles bear witness to the splendors of past nobility and prosperity, but also to bloody wars.

The old rivalry between Florence and Siena still smoulders, and, in fact, has helped to spur on the revival of wines that were produced in the past, and which have now regained much of their original character and vitality.

FLOR
FS

San Casciano
in Val di Pesa

Elsa

Montespertoli

Mercata
Val di Pe

Castelfiorentino
FS

Certaldo
FS

Tavernelle
Val di Pesa

Barberino
Val d' Elsa

San Gimignano   Poggibonsi   Castellin
in Chian

Colle di Val d'Elsa

Castel di San Gimignano
FS

Monteriggion

0 kilometers   10

0 miles   10

Cinta Senese pigs, which are easily distinguished by their dramatic markings, browse freely with herds of other pigs in the oak woods and meadows in Val di Pesa. In Tuscany the breed dates back to antiquity and you can spot them in celebrated Renaissance paintings, including those of Luca Signorelli.

STAR ATTRACTIONS

- MONTERIGGIONI (SI): Town wall, **(** 0577 280551
- SIENA: Palazzo Pubblico, **(** 0577 292263 Cathedral, **(** 0577 47321 Piazza del Campo
- SAN GIMIGNANO (SI): Cathedral, Palazzo del Podestà, **(** 0577 940340 Museo Civico, **(** 0577 940008

◁ **Spring landscape at Incisa Val d'Arno**

CHIANTI
The famous red wine was once identified by its distinctive straw-padded bottle. Nowadays, this bottle has fallen out of favor because of the high cost of production and difficulties of transportation and storage.

The vineyards in this area are often estates with large old country houses. The Cusona estate belongs to the noble Guicciardini Strozzi family and produces an excellent Vernaccia di San Gimignano.

Panforte, the rich fruitcake, is a symbol of Siena's gastronomic pleasures. Its origins lie in the honey breads of the Middle Ages *(see p106).*

Incisa in Val d'Arno

Figline Valdarno

Greve in Chianti

San Giovanni Valdarno

nzano Chianti

Radda in Chianti

Montevarchi

Gaiole in Chianti

Bucine

Pergine Valdarno

Chianti

Castelnuovo Berardenga

ENA

Monte San Savino

TOURIST OFFICES

• SIENA Via Carlo Cammeo, 2 w www. siena.turismo.toscana.it

• COLLE DI VAL D'ELSA Via Campana, 43 0577 922791.

• SAN GIMIGNANO Piazza Duomo, 1 0577 940008. w www. sangimignano.com

• CASTELFIORENTINO Via Ridolci 0571 629049.

Chianti extra-virgin olive oil is the most famous and celebrated of Tuscany's oils in other parts of the world. The quality is excellent, but it is not produced in the same quantities as the oil from other regions, and it is expensive.

Places of Interest pp112–123
Restaurants pp185–187

Wines

The chianti area is very extensive, covering six of the region's provinces, all with very different terrains and microclimates. Its beauty is reminiscent of a magical Renaissance atmosphere, and the area has attracted many foreign investors and businessmen from northern Italy who have settled here, invested in vineyards, and made an essential contribution to reviving the region's wine. This is the realm of the Sangiovese vine, which seems to have originated here. It is used for making numerous wines, often in large quantities, especially the Chianti DOCG.

Other important red grapes are Canaiolo Nero and Colorino. The main whites are Trebbiano Toscano and Malvasia del Chianti or Malvasia Bianca, used in small amounts in Chianti but more important for wines such as Vin Santo. Vernaccia di San Gimignano, a very compact thin-skinned white grape is an important grape which gives its name to the wine it is used for.

The properties of the soil and climate in this area make it possible to get good results from Cabernet Franc, Chardonnay, Merlot, Syrah, and Pinot Nero red grapes, and Chardonnay and Sauvignon white grapes. Formerly, grapes were dried on racks and then added to the must while it was still young to make Chianti mellow (a practice known as *"governo"*), but this technique is very rare nowadays.

Sangiovese, also called Sangioveto, is the most important red grape vine not only of the Chianti area but of all of Tuscany.

CHIANTI

The label on a bottle of this wine may say Chianti or it may have the name of one of seven subdenominations: Colli Aretini, Colli Fiorentini, Montalbano and Rùfina *(see pp24-6)*, Colline Pisane *(see p81)*, Colli Senesi, and Montespertoli. This last one goes back only to 1997 and has just reached the market. Chiantis from the various subzones differ in body, bouquet, and the length of the aging time.

With Chianti Superiore there is a lower yield per acre; Chianti Superiore Riserva is aged for at least two years and is stored in the bottle for three months.

CHIANTI COLLI SENESI
This wine has many of the qualities of Chianti Classico but is not as full-bodied and mellow. It can be served with the same dishes as a young Chianti Classico.

CHIANTI CLASSICO
The Chianti Classico area was defined in 1932 as the "most ancient area of origin" whose boundaries were laid down by the Grand Duke Cosimo II in 1716. The label Chianti Classico distinguishes the Chianti made in this historical area from the Chianti produced elsewhere in Tuscany. The wines made here are full-bodied and suited to lengthy aging.

The Riserva complements red meat dishes such as bistecca alla fiorentina and the strong flavor of mature pecorino cheese.

Young Chianti Classico goes well with the traditional local antipasti, and with pollo alla diavola (spicy chicken) and spit-roasted pork.

THE GALLO NERO COMMUNES
The Chianti Classico area stretches between Florence and Siena and comprises the communes of Castellina, Gaiole, Greve, and Radda, and part of Castelnuovo Berardenga, Barberino Val d'Elsa, Poggibonsi, San Casciano, and Tavernelle Val di Pesa. Only 10 percent of this area (173,000 acres/70,000 hectares) is earmarked for Chianti Classico DOCG. In 1924, the producers of Chianti Classico founded a consortium and chose as its emblem a black rooster (gallo nero), the historic badge of the Chianti military league. In 1966, Chianti Classico received independent DOCG status.

San Casciano Val di Pesa

Greve in Chianti

Tavernelle Val di Pesa

Barberino Val d'Elsa

Radda in Chianti

Poggibonsi

Castellina in Chianti

Gaiole in Chianti

Castelnuovo Berardenga

GALESTRO
This is a fairly recent white wine, born from the marriage of Tuscan vines such as Trebbiano and Malvasia and foreign varieties that may include Chardonnay and Pinot Blanc.

VERNACCIA RISERVA
This wine has to age for at least a year, with four months' storage in the bottle. Some producers age the wine in wood, others do not. This results in a wide variety of different and very interesting styles. It is good served with baked fish and white meats.

VERNACCIA DI SAN GIMIGNANO
One of Tuscany's most famous wines, this white DOCG is produced on the hills of San Gimignano. It has a dry, harmonious flavor which has been greatly enhanced by modern techniques of processing at low temperatures. The young wine is ideal with first courses and shellfish dishes.

Grapes for Vernaccia di San Gimignano wine

CINGHIALE AL VINO BIANCO

2¼ lb (1 kg) leg of wild boar • 1 glass red wine vinegar • 1 glass white wine • 3 cloves garlic • 1 lemon • chilli pepper • extra-virgin olive oil • salt • pepper

Crush one of the garlic cloves and mix it with the vinegar. Season with pepper. Marinate the meat in this mixture overnight. The next day, heat the oven to 325°F (160°C). Dry the meat and sprinkle with the remaining garlic, chopped, and the chilli pepper and salt. Place the meat in an earthenware dish greased with olive oil and baste with the white wine. Cook in the oven until it begins to sizzle, then add the lemon cut in slices. Roast for 3 hours, adding a little more white wine if necessary. Serve the leg cut in slices. Skim the fat off the cooking juices and serve the juices as gravy.

SAN GIMIGNANO ROSATO
This is one of the seven new varieties of DOC San Gimignano, comprising three reds (Riserva and Novello), two rosés (one from Sangiovese alone), and two types of Vin Santo (white and rosé).

Grapes hung to dry for making Vin Santo

VIN SANTO
Vin Santo almost certainly originated in Tuscany and possibly in Chianti, although it is produced in other regions as well – there are about 20 different types. It owes its distinctive flavor to grapes that are hung up or set on racks to dry. Vin Santo is sold either as a dry wine (though it is never perfectly dry) or as a dessert wine, for which demand is falling. It is particularly well suited to the dry confections of the Siena area, such as *biscotti* or *cantuccini (see p34).*

VIN SANTO DEL CHIANTI
The Vin Santo of Chianti Classico has earned its own DOC label, and from the 1997 vintage also that of Chianti. However, the leading estates avoid using the DOC appellation and continue to label their products as "Vino da tavola" (table wine).

WINE TYPE	GOOD VINTAGES	GOOD PRODUCERS
Red Wine		
Chianti Classico	98, 97, 95, 93, 90	**Fonterutoli di Castellina in Chianti, La Massa di Panzano in Chianti**
Super Tuscans *(see p130)*	98, 97, 95, 90	**Felsina di Castelnuovo Berardenga, S. Giusto & Rentennano di Gaiole in Chianti, Fattoria di Nozzole di Greve in Chianti, Vicchiomaggio di Greve in Chianti**
White Wine		
Vernaccia di San Gimignano	99, 97, 95	**Montenidoli di San Gimignano, Panizzi di San Gimignano**

OTHER WINES WORTH TRYING
Combining the traditional local vines with foreign varieties has produced a profusion of original wines. They include the so-called Super Tuscans *(see p130),* many of which are very expensive. The DOC **Colli dell'Etruria Centrale** is a range of wines, labeled Bianco, Rosato, Rosso, Novello, Vin Santo. A less successful initiative is the creation of four new-style Tuscan wines identified by the term **Capitolato**: **Muschio** (Chardonnay and Pinot Bianco) and **Selvante** (Sauvignon) for the white wines, **Biturica** (Cabernet and Sangiovese) and **Cardisco** (Sangiovese) for the reds.

Cinta Senese Pork

CINTA SENESE PIGS are a very old local breed with a long history in the area's art as well as its cuisine. They appear in paintings dating back to the 14th century, including Ambrogio Lorenzetti's celebrated fresco of the *Effetti del Buongoverno* (Results of Good Government) in Siena. Cinta Senese pigs have a dark coat with a white belt round their forequarters. They are not, as most people will tell you, a cross between a wild boar and a pig. Some years ago the breed was almost extinct because the pigs can only be reared semiwild in lightly wooded areas; today local breeders are working hard to save the breed. The pigs graze freely on tubers, roots, truffles, and acorns. Although they look leaner than other breeds, they have a thick layer of fat, and their flesh is very firm with a delicate flavor. Inevitably, the quality of the meat, both fresh and cured, combined with the high cost of breeding the pigs, makes Cinta pork products much more expensive than those from other types of pig.

BURISTO DI CINTA

This pork specialty is made from the flesh of the pig's head, including the tongue and some of the skin. The meat is boiled and ground, then spices, pig's blood, and boiled fat are added. The mixture is stuffed into a natural casing made from the pig's small intestine and slowly boiled.

Two Cinta pigs grazing in an oak wood

The hoof of the Cinta hindquarter is black.

CINTA PROSCIUTTO

Prosciutto crudo from Cinta pigs is seasoned with plenty of pepper in the traditional Tuscan way. It is then left to mature for at least 18 months, resulting in a very tasty ham. Unlike other hams, the foot and hoof are always left on this one.

GRIFI

2¼ lb (1 kg) meat from the muzzle of a Cinta pig, cubed • 2 cloves • 1 onion, chopped • 1 clove garlic, chopped • 1 sprig of thyme, chopped • 1 sprig of rosemary, chopped • 2 glasses Chianti • 1 dessertspoon tomato purée • 1 sprig of tarragon, chopped • salt • pepper

Put the meat in a flameproof earthenware casserole, add the cloves, and cover with water. Bring to the boil, then simmer until the water has evaporated. Add the onion, garlic, thyme, and rosemary. Stir in the wine mixed with the tomato purée and season with salt and pepper. Cover and simmer gently, adding a little hot water if it starts to dry out. When the meat is almost tender, add the tarragon and cook for a further 5 minutes.

The hoof of the forequarter is usually a light color.

SPALLA (SHOULDER)
Cured shoulder is drier and saltier than the ham made from a leg of pork and tastes more peppery. It costs much less than *prosciutto crudo*.

ARISTA (CHINE OF PORK)
Salted *arista* has a thick layer of fat, which makes it look almost like pig's cheek.

RIGATINO
This is a very peppery *pancetta* (bacon) used a great deal in Tuscan cooking. It is also excellent in *antipasti* and Tuscan unsalted bread.

SOPPRESSATA DI CINTA
This salami is much the same as ordinary *soppressata* except that the meat used to make it is high-quality Cinta.

CINTA SALAME
Drier and firmer than normal Tuscan *salame*, but seasoned in the same generous way, this type is generally a medium–to-small in size.

Coarsely ground meat is mixed with fat chopped with a knife.

OTHER CINTA PORK PRODUCTS WORTH TRYING
The **fresh meat**, sold in the usual pork cuts, can be found only at specialized butchers. The tasty meat is very fashionable in Tuscany and much in demand among restaurateurs. Apart from the *salumi* illustrated above, the meat is used to make **guanciale** (pig's cheek), **capocollo** (dry-cured sausage), **lardo,** and **fresh and cured sausages**.

Sienese Fruit Cakes

SIENESE CAKES ARE MADE with dried and candied fruits – candied pumpkin is especially popular – and sometimes contain nuts. They are bound together with egg whites and sweetened, at least originally, with honey. Nuts and dried figs were once high-energy foods for the poor, and these cakes were nourishing as well as being a good way of using up egg whites when the yolks had been used in other dishes. The cakes have the added advantage of keeping well, so they can be made in advance. Recipes date back to the Middle Ages: *panforte* dates from the 13th century, when it was originally a variant of *pan pepato* (pepper cake), and *dolceforte,* made with spices and honey, was a medieval staple. Arab influences are also evident in some of the spices and other flavorings. These cakes are worth sampling freshly made, if possible: fresh *panforte,* in particular, tastes very different from the commercial product.

PANFORTE DI SIENA
This is Siena's most famous cake, made from flour, almonds, egg whites, sugar, and honey. It is flavored with dried and candied fruits – especially pumpkin and citrus fruits – and scented with vanilla, cloves, cinnamon, nutmeg and, occasionally, a little cocoa powder.

The flat cake is dusted with confectioner's sugar, sometimes mixed with a little ground cinnamon.

PAN PEPATO
This cake is older than *panforte,* and there are many different recipes in existence from various parts of Italy. In the Siena area it is often called *panforte scuro.* It contains larger quantities of cocoa powder and more spices, including pepper, than *panforte.*

CAVALLUCCI
These pale cookies are made with almonds, dried fruit, flour and egg whites, and are sweetened with sugar and honey.

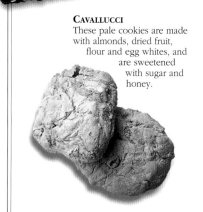

TORTA NATALIZIA RUSTICA

6 eggs, separated • 8 oz (200 g) flour • 1¼ lb (500 g) dried figs, finely chopped • 1¼ lb (500 g) walnuts, crushed • 8 oz (200 g) caster sugar • 4 oz (100 g) lard, melted

Preheat the oven to 325°F (160°C). Whisk the egg whites until stiff. Sift the flour and gradually add to the egg whites. Beat the yolks, sugar, and lard and fold into the whites. Stir in the figs and nuts. Spoon into a greased cake pan and bake the cake for 30 minutes.

CANTUCCI OR TOZZETTI
These crisp cookies are almost identical to the *biscottini* or *cantuccini di Prato (see p34)*, except these cookies sometimes contain aniseed, in which case they are called *anicini*. They are made with flour, eggs, almonds, sugar, and pine nuts. The dough is shaped into a long loaf, baked and cut into slices. The slices are returned to the oven to dry. They are eaten dipped in Vin Santo.

PANE CON I SANTI
This large, shallow loaf is made from sweetened bread dough flavored with raisins, nuts, and pepper.

The cookies are sprinkled with confectioner's sugar.

RICCIARELLI
These cookies are made from a simple almond paste mixed with sugar and egg whites to soften them. They are flavored with vanilla, lemon zest, and honey, then baked on a wafer base made from rice flour.

The dough is cut into lozenge shapes.

SCHIACCIATA CON L'UVA OR CIACCINO CON L'UVA
This sweet *focaccia* covered with raisins probably came originally from Gaiole in Chianti.

OTHER FRUIT CAKES WORTH TRYING
Schiacciata di Pasqua is a raised sweetened loaf flavored with aniseed that is made for Easter. **Torta di Cecco** or **torta al cioccolato** is taller than *pan pepato*, has more candied than dried fruit, and is covered with chocolate icing. A popular recent innovation is **ricciarelli**, covered with chocolate. Also typical of Siena is **torrone** (nougat) in jaw-breaking or softer versions, covered in chocolate or plain. The **torta natalizia rustica** (rustic Christmas cake) made by peasant families from nuts and dried figs is probably the origin of most modern-day Sienese fruit cakes.

Traditional Produce

IN FLORENCE EVER SINCE the Middle Ages there has been the saying: "You're as rich as if you had a farm in Chianti" because this was the wealthiest area of the countryside around Florence. Here, the old, established families of Florence and Siena still have their farms and estates, together with people from all over the world. In the shops, restaurants, and the *agriturismi* of Chianti you hear dozens of languages spoken, not just because of the visiting tourists but because many foreigners live and work here, most of them from other parts of Europe and the United States. They share a great love of Tuscan history and traditions. And, paradoxically, it is these newcomers, together with some of the younger members of the old families, who struggle to preserve the area's traditional products. As long as farms avoid specializing and continue to produce a wide range of foodstuffs, they will enable small local firms to obtain genuine local produce, from pork and vegetables to cheese, oil, and vinegar.

BLACK CABBAGE
Cavolo nero is the prince of Tuscan vegetables, cultivated throughout Tuscany. With its long, dark, crinkly leaves and delicate, sweetish flavor, it is essential for *ribollita* (vegetable soup) and many of the more celebrated regional soups.

PICI
The typical Sienese pasta is a kind of thick *spaghetti* made of ordinary wheat flour (not the hard durum wheat) and water. The dough is cut into long strips which are then rolled with the flat of the hand to make them thinner and rounded. *Pici* are sold both fresh and dried in the shops.

MARZOLINO
At one time this cheese was made only in the spring from the milk of ewes that had been grazing on the first fresh grass of the year.

This cheese is oval.

PESTO TOSCANO

1¼ lb (500 g) black cabbage • young extra-virgin olive oil (produced in November and December) • 3 cloves garlic • 2 dessertspoons mature grated pecorino • 1 dessertspoon pine nuts • salt • pepper
Plunge the cabbage into a pan of boiling water and leave until the water boils again. Drain, cool, then process in a blender with the garlic and pine nuts until finely chopped. Stir in the *pecorino* and add salt and pepper. Stir in enough oil to give a creamy consistency. Spread on bread croutons.

VINEGAR
Many celebrated wine-making estates offer excellent single-grape or Chianti vinegars, often aromatized with herbs.

CHIANTI OLIVE OIL
The oil from the Chianti DOP (Denomination of Protected Origin) comes from the same areas that produce the famous wine. Other areas produce a Terre di Siena DOP. Fruity with a fresh scent, full-bodied, and astringent, they have medium fluidity, with a slightly bitter and intensely pungent aftertaste, some herbal notes and a faint tinge of sour tomato.

BREAD FROM WOOD-FIRED OVENS
In Chianti you still find Tuscan bread baked the traditional way in wood-fired ovens.

GRAPPA
The skins and seeds of grapes left from making Chianti wine are used to produce very fashionable, modern grappas.

TONNO DEL CHIANTI
Despite its fancy name of "Chianti tuna," this is steam-cooked, brine-cured pork, produced by Cecchini, an unusual butcher's shop in Panzano in Chianti *(see p119)*.

WHAT TO SAMPLE
Though rare, you can still find **pecorino** made the local way from a fresh paste curdled with the flower tufts of the wild artichoke. It is rich in milk fat and usually matured before eating. This area also has the most authentic producers of Tuscan *salumi*: they make excellent traditional **guanciale**, **finocchione**, **prosciutto crudo**, **salame,** and **sausage**, as well as some innovative variations. The meat is excellent, especially **pork** from **Grigio** pigs, **lamb**, and **Chianina beef** (more likely to be found in shops here than the rest of Tuscany, but nearly all imported from the Arezzo area). San Gimignano has **white truffles**. Val di Pesa has fine fruits, especially **peaches**.

Wild Produce

GRISETTE
(Amanita vaginata)
Grisette *(fungo gentile)* is one of the most common amanita mushrooms found in woods from May to November. The colors vary, but it can be identified by the furrowed edge of the cap and the absence of a ring on the stalk; however, it should always be shown to an expert before eating. It is a very delicate mushroom and is excellent cooked with garlic and parsley.

MAN-ON-HORSEBACK MUSHROOM
(Tricholoma equestre)
Common in mixed pine woods in the fall, this yellow mushroom *(equestre)* adds a delicious flavor to sauces or savory pies and goes well with garlic and parsley. It can also be preserved in oil. There is a poisonous mushroom that looks very similar, so this one must be checked by an expert before it is eaten.

GRAY WAX-CAP MUSHROOM
(Hygrophorus limacinus)
This handsome mushroom *(limaccioso)* has a gray cap with thick, fleshy white gills and a white stalk covered in gray viscous gluten. It is common in pine woods in the fall. The white flesh, with its rich aroma, is excellent in pies and stuffings, or preserved in oil.

DOVE-COLORED TRICHOLOMA
(Tricholoma columbetta)
It takes experience to recognize these fleshy white mushrooms *(columbetta)*, which sometimes have green patches at the foot of the stalk. They are common in chestnut and oak woods in the fall. They are excellent with meat or bottled in oil, and go well with man-on-horseback mushrooms and the related gray tricholoma mushroom *(see opposite)*.

TAGLIATELLE AI FUNGHI

extra-virgin olive oil • a bunch of parsley • 3 cloves garlic • small piece of chile, chopped • 1¼ lb (600 g) mixed mushrooms, sliced • 4 oz (100 g) fresh sausages, chopped • 18 oz (500 g) peeled, plum tomatoes • 18 oz (500 g) egg tagliatelle • *salt*

Heat some oil in a pan and add the mushrooms, parsley, garlic, chile, and sausage. Season. Cook over a high heat until the mushrooms have shed their water. Lower the heat and cook until the liquid has evaporated. Add the tomatoes and simmer until cooked. Meanwhile, cook the *tagliatelle*. Serve the sauce with the pasta.

MARMELLATA DI ROSA CANINA (ROSE HIP JAM)

• *dog rose hips* • *sugar*

Cut open the hips and remove the seeds and bristles inside. Wash the hips well in running water. Pour enough water into a preserving pan to come 1–2 inches (2.5–5 cm) up the side. Weigh the rose hips and put them in the pan with half their weight in sugar. Cook until all the water has evaporated and the fruit is soft. Sieve the fruit, return it to the pan, and continue cooking until it reaches the desired density. Bottle at once.

DOG ROSE
(Rosa canina)
Dog rose *(rosa di macchia)* hips, picked after the first frosts, are excellent in jams, sweet sauces, fortified wines, and liqueurs. The bristles around the seeds need to be removed before cooking.

BLACKTHORN
(Prunus spinosa)
The blackthorn *(marruche)* is a common tree on the edges of woods and fields. Its very astringent fruit, sloes, can be eaten after the first frosts. They are very good in liqueurs and syrups.

GRAY TRICHOLOMA MUSHROOM
(Tricholoma terreum)
Little gray tricholoma mushrooms *(moretta)* spread through pine woods in their thousands in the fall. The mushroom cap is covered in what looks like mouse fur, and the gills and stalks are a grayish white. Always have them checked by an expert before eating since they are similar to poisonous tricholomas. They are exquisite in sauces, savory pies, and with fish. They can also be preserved in oil.

BUTCHER'S BROOM
(Ruscus aculeatus)
In springtime the young shoots of this attractive bush *(pungitopo)* are delicious, though slightly bitter. They can be preserved in oil, or simmered and served with egg sauces. Here, they are shown growing with the true wild asparagus *(Asparagus acutifolius)* – both are picked and eaten.

Places of Interest

THE RUSTIC ORIGINS of many of the gastronomic suppliers listed here are preserved intact. The farmhouses, for instance, are nearly all historic mansions crammed with colorful works of art. When shopping you can hear a mixture of many languages from all the French, American, German, and Japanese visitors mingling with the local Italian population. Despite the high numbers of tourists, the quality of the regional food produce has hardly suffered at all – unlike the situation in some of the big cities. Often, in fact, the foreigners shopping in Chianti are even more discerning than the local customers.

BARBERINO VAL D'ELSA (FI)

🍇 Casa Emma

località San Donato in Poggio
☎ 055 8072859

The Merlot Soloìo produced here is very fine, with unusual body and bouquet. There is also a mellow Chianti Classico Riserva, which is very good.

🍇 Fattoria Isole & Olena

località Isole, 1
☎ 055 8072763 ⬛ Sat

From a truly skilled professional comes a series of wines of the greatest interest: Chianti Classico, Cepparello (based on Sangiovese), Eremo (on Syrah), and Cabernet Sauvignon Collezione De Marchi. The extra-virgin olive oil is very fine.

🍇 Castello di Monsanto

via Monsanto, 8
☎ 055 8059000 ⬛ Sat

This estate can justly claim to have played an important role in the region's wine-making revival by its foresight and enterprise. Its wines are excellent: the Chianti Classico, elegant and full-bodied, plus the reds Fabrizio Bianchi (Sangiovese) and Nemo, based on Cabernet.

🫒 Fattoria Pasolini Dall'Onda

piazza Mazzini, 10
☎ 055 8075019

Extra-virgin olive oil with an intense fruity flavor is produced from olives grown and pressed on the estate. Olive oil production goes back a long way here – it has been made on the estate since 1573.

Wine aging in barrels in Chianti

PAPPA COL POMODORO

⅔ lb (300 g) stale bread
• 4 cloves garlic, chopped
• 2 lb (850 g) small ripe tomatoes, peeled
• a few basil leaves, torn
• extra-virgin olive oil
• vegetable stock • salt
• pepper

Soak the bread in cold water for a few hours, then lightly squeeze out the water with your hands. Put the bread in a pan with the garlic, tomatoes, basil, and plenty of olive oil. Bring up to simmering point, then simmer gently for at least 30 minutes until the bread is well mixed with the other ingredients. Remove from the heat and season to taste with salt and pepper. Serve with extra-virgin olive oil to drizzle over the top.

CASTELLINA IN CHIANTI (SI)

🍇 Casina di Cornia

località Casina di Cornia
☎ 0577 743052

This family-run winery is located in a traditional farmhouse with an underground cellar. Apartments are available if you wish to stay the night. Among the wines on offer are Chianti Classico, as well as Riserva Vigna La Casina and L'Amaranto (Cabernet Sauvignon). Oil can also be purchased.

🍇 Gagliole

località Gagliole, 42
☎ 0577 740369

The favorable position of these vineyards and their organic cultivation have produced excellent results in both the Gagliole Rosso (Sangiovese with

Cabernet Sauvignon)
and Gagliole Bianco
(Trebbiano with a little
Chardonnay).

🍇 Castello La Leccia

località La Leccia
☎ 0577 743148

Azienda Agricola Villa Cerna at Castellina in Chianti

This winery in an 11th-century castle on a hill offers views over Siena and San Gimignano. Products for sale include Chianti Classico and Riserva, Bruciagna (Sangiovese), grappa, and oil. Rooms with bathrooms can be rented, as can a larger dwelling with 12 beds and a swimming pool. There are no guided tours of the cellars, and there is a charge for tastings.

🏛 Apicoltura Lecchini

Fattoria San Giorgio alla
Piazza, località La Piazza
☎ 0577 733560

Local honey, especially from chestnut, acacia, and wild flowers, as well as honey-based energy-boosters and beauty products are sold here.

🍇 Castello di Lilliano

località Lilliano
☎ 0577 743070

The Chianti Classico and Riserva, both wines of distinctive, forceful character, are backed up by Anagallis, a red wine from Sangiovese and Colorino grapes matured in oak barriques.

🍇 Rocca delle Macìe

località Le Macìe
☎ 0577 7321
⏺ Sat

An attractive, dynamic estate with a carefully gauged production centered on the red wines of the region. The Chianti Classico is vinified from various crus, including La Tenuta Sant'Alfonso. Also interesting is the

Roccato (Sangiovese and Cabernet) and Ser Gioveto (Sangiovese). It also has a mellow grappa and extra-virgin olive oil.

🐂 Macelleria Stiaccini

via Ferruccio, 33
☎ 0577 740558
⏺ Wed pm

This butcher's shop sells its own fresh sausages, as well as a good selection of Tuscan salumi with some Sienese specialties as well. It has Chianina beef plus various other cuts of meat, all from animals that have been carefully selected by the owners from herds in the province. It also offers ready-to-eat spiedini (kebabs), fegatelli, and other seasoned meats.

🍇 Azienda Agricola Villa Cerna

località Cerna
☎ 0577 743024
⏺ Sat

This estate is owned by the Cecchi family. It offers a Chianti Classico with a good structure and a Riserva matured in wood, both in large barrels and oak barriques. The estate also makes a Vin Santo that is allowed to ferment in casks.

PANFORTE

6 oz (150 g) caster sugar • 6 oz (150 g) honey • 1 dessertspoon cocoa powder • 6 oz (150 g) each of peeled almonds and hazelnuts, roasted and halved • 2 oz (50 g) chopped walnuts • pinch each of ground cinnamon, cloves, and nutmeg • vanilla essence • 3 oz (70 g) flour • ½ lb (250 g) diced candied fruit • confectioner's sugar • rice flour wafer or rice paper

Preheat the oven to 325°F (160°C). In a pan (preferably copper), heat the sugar and honey over a gentle heat until a drop of the mixture forms a soft ball when dropped into cold water. Remove from the heat and add the cocoa, nuts, fruit, spices, few drops of essence and 2 oz (60 g) of the flour; stir carefully. Pour into a shallow cake pan lined with the wafer or rice paper. Mix the remaining flour with 2 dessertspoons confectioner's sugar and a little cinnamon. Sprinkle it over the mixture, then bake in the oven for 30 minutes. Cool, turn out, and sprinkle with confectioner's sugar mixed with cinnamon.

CASTELNUOVO BERARDENGA (SI)

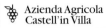

🍇 Azienda Agricola Castell'in Villa

località Castell'in Villa
📞 0577 359074
⚫ Sat

The wine here is of a consistently high quality, thanks to the skilled hand of a wine-maker on this estate who excels at the production of Chianti Classico as a young wine and a Riserva. Also worth noting are the Poggio delle Rose, made from Sangiovese alone, and the Vin Santo.

🍇 Fattoria di Felsina

strada Statale Chiantigiana, 484
📞 0577 355117

This is one of the most interesting cellars in Tuscany, containing a wide range of fine wines, from Chianti Classico to the Berardenga and Rancia selections (at their best in the Riserva version). The Fontalloro (from pure Sangiovese) and Maestro Raro (Cabernet) are also excellent. In addition, the estate produces a very good Vin Santo and two whites: I Sistri (Chardonnay) and Pepestrino (made from Trebbiano, Sauvignon, and Chardonnay grapes).

FAGIOLI ALL'UCCELLETTO

2 cloves garlic, chopped • sprigs of sage, chopped • extra-virgin olive oil • 3¼ lb (1.5 kg) fresh beans or 1 lb (450 g) dried beans, soaked overnight • 1¼ lb (600 g) tomatoes, sliced • salt • pepper

Lightly fry the garlic and sage in the oil. Add the beans, tomatoes, and about 14 fl oz (400 ml) water. Season to taste with salt and pepper and simmer for about 30 minutes.

⊛ Pasticceria Lodi Pasini

via Fiorita, 6
📞 0577 355638
⚫ Mon, Sun pm

Traditional Sienese cakes and fresh stuffed pasta are the two specialties here – try their lemon-scented ravioli filled with a mixture of ricotta and other cheeses.

🍇 Fattoria di Petroio

località Quercegrossa, via Mocenni, 7 📞 0667 98883; 347 7713252

The two classic wines of this part of Tuscany are produced on the richly endowed land of this small estate – Chianti Classico and Chianti Classico Riserva.

🍇 Agricola San Felice

località San Felice
📞 0577 359087

This estate has produced good results with some of its wines, such as the Riserve di Chianti Classico Poggio Rosso, Il Grigio, and the Vigorello red, which is made from Sangiovese plus small amounts of Cabernet Sauvignon grapes. The olive oil is very good.

COLLE VAL D'ELSA (SI)

🍷 Frantoio Roncucci

località Menzanello
📞 0577 971080

The oil comes exclusively from the estate's own groves (70 percent Correggiolo olives) and is sold by measure straight from the press while it is operating. As the oil is not

The Castello di Brolio of the Tenuta Ricasoli

*bottled, you need to take
a suitable container with
you to carry your oil home.*

GAIOLE IN CHIANTI (SI)

Agricoltori del Chianti Geografico

via Mulinaccio, 10
☎ 0577 749489

*This cooperative winery,
run by a great wine-
maker, is based on two
estates. The Gaiole estate
produces the red wines,
especially Chianti Classico
with the Contessa di Radda
selection, the Riserva Monte
Giachi, and the Capitolare
di Biturica (based on
Cabernet Sauvignon and
Sangiovese). The San
Gimignano estate mainly
produces whites and
Chianti Colli Senesi.*

Le Antiche Delizie del Bianchi

via Ricasoli, 44/46
☎ 0577 749501 ● Tue

*This bakery's philosophy
is to keep a close rapport
with the surrounding
district and use natural
ingredients. It has bread
made with fresh yeast and
kneaded by hand, like the
classic Tuscan loaf and
what is called "Etruscan
bread," made with spelt
and a mixture of flours.
It also sells traditional
cakes and the firm's own
creations, like the Torta
Chiantigiana, made with
extra-virgin olive oil.
Their ice cream is made
with good-quality natural
ingredients. The
delicatessen has a select
range of local specialties,
and the small restaurant,
Lo Sfizio del Bianchi,
offers real local cuisine.*

Apiari Floridea

località Badia a Coltibuono
L'Osteria, 27
☎ 0577 749479

Badia a Coltibuono

*This apiarist is rigorous
about the production of
honey by natural methods.
Honeys include ones
made from pollen from
chestnut trees, woodland
flowers, broad-leaved
trees, acacia, and heather.*

Badia a Coltibuono

località Badia a Coltibuono
☎ 0577 74481
● Sat; Aug

*This estate, with its old
monastery buildings dating
from the 11th century,
favors a traditional
approach to production
with particular emphasis
on Sangiovese vines. Its
star product is Sangioveto,
made from Sangiovese
alone. Also noteworthy is
the Chianti Classico Riserva.*

Barone Ricasoli – Castello di Brolio

località Brolio
☎ 0577 7301
● Sat, Sun (winter)

*This is one of the oldest
and most renowned of the
Chianti Classico wineries.
Much of the production is
Chianti Classico Brolio
(also Riserva). This is
followed in volume by
Casalferro, a Sangiovese
from a particular clone
with the Merlot grape. In
recent years the Sangiovese
vine used for producing
the Casalferro has been
used to make Formulae, a
young wine that offers very
good value for money.*

Castello di Cacchiano

località Cacchiano,
frazione Monti in Chianti
☎ 0577 747018

*The Ricasoli Firidolfi
family has drawn on
expert help to enhance the
Sangiovese grapes in the
Chianti Classico, the
Riserva, and the Rosso R.F.
from Merlot, Sangiovese,
and Canaiolo, matured in
small casks. The Vin Santo
is very good.*

Macelleria Chini

via Roma, 2
☎ 0577 749457
● Mon and Wed pm

*The Chini family has
worked in the meat trade
since the 17th century.
Their products are of the
highest quality – there is
salumi made from pure-
bred Cinta Senese pigs ,
plus meat from other
local animals.*

POLLO ALLA DIAVOLA

*1 free-range chicken •
marinade of sliced garlic,
rosemary leaves, extra-
virgin olive oil, and salt*

Cut the chicken down
the backbone, open it
out, and flatten with a
meat mallet. Pour over
the marinade and leave
for 1 hour. Grill over hot
embers, turning it every
6–7 minutes until tender.

🍇 Castello di Meleto

località Meleto
☎ 0577 749217;
0577 749129

The castle of Meleto, built in the 11th century and partially restored in the 1700s, dominates the hills of Chianti. The cellar, dug out of the rock beneath the castle, has a secret passage leading outside. There is a fee for tastings; it is possible to match wine to food and there is even a special menu for the wines on offer. Among the products for sale: Chianti Classico and Riserva, Fiore (Sangiovese, Merlot), oil, grappa, and honey. It is possible to rent B&B-style rooms and apartments.

🍇 Azienda Agricola Riecine

località Riecine
☎ 0577 749098

This property has changed hands and at present it seems that the previous style is continuing with just

POLLO CON LE OLIVE

3 spring chickens, each cut into 8 pieces • 10 oz (300 g) pitted green olives • 3 bay leaves • flour • 3 cloves garlic • extra-virgin olive oil • about 14 fl oz (400 ml) dry white wine • chicken stock • salt • pepper

Coat the chicken pieces in flour. Heat some oil in a frying pan, add the chicken and fry over a brisk heat to seal on all sides. Add the bay leaves, garlic, and wine and cook until the wine has evaporated. Add the olives and a little stock. Cover and continue cooking until the chicken is tender, adding more stock if required. Adjust the seasoning and serve.

Vineyards of a Vistarenni estate

a few great wines: Chianti Classico, Chianti Classico Riserva, and La Gioia di Riecine (Sangiovese).

🍇 Rocca di Castagnoli

località Castagnoli
☎ 0577 731004 ◑ Sat

Two vineyards belong to this estate – one in Gaiole, the other in Castellina. The wine most representative of the "Super Tuscan" style is Stielle, made from Sangiovese and Cabernet grapes, followed by Buriano (Cabernet Sauvignon). Chianti Classico Riserva, Poggio a' Frati, and Capraia are all produced in the traditional style. The estate also has a shop in Gaiole (via Ricasoli, 45).

🍇 Fattoria di San Giusto a Rentennano

frazione Monti in Chianti, località San Giusto a Rentennano
☎ 0577 747121

This estate limits its wines to three different types, all of them of high quality. The Chianti Classico, especially the Riserva, is a powerful wine with complex perfumes. Percarlo (Sangiovese) has good character, and the estate's Vin Santo is held to be one of the best in Tuscany.

GAIOLE IN CHIANTI – MONTI IN CHIANTI (FI)

🍇 Rocca di Montegrossi

località Monti
☎ 0577 747977

This winery is situated in a village with a 12th-century Romanesque church. The cellar has arches and a specific structure for the drying of Vin Santo grapes. The wines produced here include Chianti Classico and Riserva Vigneta San Marcellino, Geremia (Sangiovese), and Vin Santo del Chianti Classico (Malvasia). Oil is also available. Guided tours and tastings can be arranged for a fee, and there are apartments with swimming pool to rent.

GREVE IN CHIANTI (FI)

❋ Gelateria Cabana

località Strada in Chianti, via Mazzini, 32
☎ 055 8588659
◑ Mon (spring), Mon–Fri (winter)

Very fine cream and fruit ice creams in a variety of flavors, all from natural ingredients, are sold in this ice-cream parlor. It also has ice-cream cakes and pastries – the zuccotto *and the* millefoglie *both merit a special mention.*

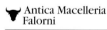

Le Cantine

Galleria delle Cantine, 2
055 8546404

This wine shop, owned by the famous Falorni butcher's shop, is located under a new shopping center. It offers about 1,000 labels, all of them Tuscan. Of these, more than 100 are rotated weekly for sale by the glass in an unusual, automated self-service system. As well as the wines, salumi, *20 or so Tuscan oils, and a few cheeses are on offer.*

Casa Vinicola Carpineto

località Dudda
055 8549062;
055 8549086 Sat

A good Chianti Classico, also in a Riserva version, is produced here as well as Cabernet Sauvignon Farnito and Vino Nobile di Montepulciano.

Antica Macelleria Falorni

piazza Matteotti, 69
055 853029
daily, including Sun

This large store with a wine cellar sells a wide range of salumi *that can be sampled with the wine. The family firm has long been linked to traditional Tuscan products, including Chianina beef, Cinta pork, wild boar, and local* salumi. *It also has a modern outlook, producing best-selling items like* zampone *(stuffed pig's feet) and packaging its own sliced hams and other meats*

in sealed containers. However, the traditional spirit and methods remain, evident in the excellent fresh meat and local game, and salumi *from both Cinta and ordinary pigs and wild boar.*

Castello di Querceto

Lucolena, frazione Dudda
055 85921

This family firm produces Chianti – the younger version and the Riserva il Picchio are noteworthy – and draws on Sangiovese vines for its La Corte red.

Castello Vicchiomaggio

via Vicchiomaggio, 4
055 854079

This farm is located in a fortress that later became a Renaissance villa. The underground cellars date back to the 10th century. There are apartments to

rent and a restaurant that offers typical Tuscan fare. A fee is payable for tastings. An intensely fruity extra-virgin olive oil, one of the best in the region, is made here. Also in production are Chianti Classico (with various reserves), Ripa delle Mandorle (Sangiovese, Cabernet Sauvignon), the splendid Ripa delle More (Sangiovese), and grappa.

MERCATALE VALDARNO (AR)

Fattoria Petrolo

via Petrolo, 30
055 9911322

The line of extra-virgin olive oil is excellent and can be purchased directly at the estate together with its Vin Santo. The wines (Torrione from Sangiovese alone, Galatrona from Merlot, Terre di Galatrona from Sangiovese with a little Merlot) are found only in wine shops, and they are expensive.

RIBOLLITA (VEGETABLE SOUP)

10 oz (300 g) dried cannellini beans • 3 zucchini • 3 carrots • 1 stalk celery • 10 oz (300 g) potatoes • 3 tomatoes • 12 oz (350 g) onions • 4 oz (100 g) guanciale (pig's cheek) • extra-virgin olive oil • 8 oz (200 g) peas • ½ black cabbage, cut into strips • a few sprigs of parsley • meat stock • stale Tuscan bread, sliced • salt • pepper

Rinse the beans, soak overnight, and then cook them in the same water over a very low heat. Meanwhile, chop the zucchini, carrots, celery, potatoes, tomatoes, half the onions, and the *guanciale* and fry them in oil in a large pan until softened. Add the peas, cabbage, and parsley, moisten with the bean cooking water and some stock. Add salt and pepper. Simmer for 1 hour. Purée some of the beans in a vegetable mill and add to the soup with the whole beans. Arrange the bread slices in an ovenproof dish. Pour the soup over the bread and leave to cool. Preheat the oven to 350°F (180°C). Finely slice the remaining onions and add them to the soup with more oil. Bake in the oven until the oil simmers and the onion forms a golden crust.

MERCATALE VAL DI PESA (FI)

Castelli del Grevepesa

località Ponte di Gabbiano,
via Grevigiana, 34
055 821911

*This large cooperative
winery has a wide variety
of good wines. Notable
among them is the Chianti
Classico Clemente VII
(which also comes in a
Riserva version).*

Fattoria Castello Il Palagio

via Campoli, 140
055 8218157

*This estate is situated
near the Romanesque
parish of Santo Stefano
a Campoli and the castle
of Il Palagio. It is possible
to organize gala dinners
in the castle. Among
the numerous wines
produced, the best are
Chianti Classico and
Riserva, Vin Santo, Rosso
Colli della Toscana
Centrale (Sangiovese,
Canaiolo, Merlot,
Lambrusco Maestri),
and Montefolchi (Merlot).
Oil and grappa are also
produced and there is
a farmhouse available
to rent.*

Tenuta Montecalvi

via Citille, 85
055 8544665

*The old farmhouse within
which this winery is located
was once part of the castle
of Uzzano. It still features
the architectural structure
typical of a Chianti pigeon
loft. The cellar is small,
but furnished with
innovative equipment,
including a high-density
plant. Among the wines
made here are Montecalvi
Rosso Alta Valle delle Greve
(made from a blend of
Sangiovese, Merlot, Syrah,
and Cabernet Sauvignon
grapes), and oil. There is
a fee for tastings.*

Solatione

via Valigondoli, 53a
055 821623

*This winery near Badia
a Passignano is superbly
located on a high hill over
the valley of the Chianti. It
offers splendid panoramic
views over Florence. From
October to March it is
possible to take a guided
tour of the cellar and
witness the drying process
of the grapes for Vin
Santo. The grapes are
hung all the way from
the ceiling to the floor in
specially designed rooms.
It is possible to taste wines*
*such as Chianti Classico
Solatione and Riserva,
and Vin Santo (also
Riserva Re Nato).*

MONTESPERTOLI (FI)

Fattoria Le Calvane

via Castiglioni, 1/5
0571 671073;
338 3138969

*A Chianti Colli Fiorentini
Il Quercione, a Riserva Il
Trecione, and Vin Santo
Zipolo d'Oro are all
offered here. There are
also wines made from
vines not traditional to
the area, including
Borro del Boscone, from
Cabernet Sauvignon
matured in new oak
barriques, Sorbino from
Chardonnay grapes, and
Collecimoli made from
Chardonnay, Sauvignon
Blanc, and Traminer.*

MONTEVARCHI (AR)

Fattoria La Rendola

località Rendola, 85
055 9707594

*Mentioned in documents
from the 13th century,
this winery has been
owned over the centuries
by many noble families,
including the Ricasoli,*

The splendid hill panorama of Montespertoli

the Canevaro, and the Firidolfi. The 18th-century cellar has been restored and now holds barriques and a bottling plant. The wines produced include La Pineta (Sangiovese), L'Incanto (Sangiovese, Merlot, Cabernet), Merlot di Toscana, Chardonnay di Toscana, and Bianco Toscano (Chardonnay, Pinot Bianco). Oil is also available. Upon request and on payment of a fee, food can be arranged.

PANZANO IN CHIANTI (FI)

🍇 Enoteca Baldi

piazza Bucciarelli, 25
📞 055 852843
⭕ daily, including Sun

This is a first-rate wine bar, offering an excellent selection of Italian and international wines and, a wide range of the delicacies of central

---

CARNE IN GALERA

2¾ lb (1.2 kg) sirloin or fillet of beef • 1 sprig of sage, finely chopped • 2 or 3 sprigs of rosemary, finely chopped • 1 clove garlic • 4 fl oz (100 ml) white wine vinegar • 8 fl oz (200 ml) hot beef stock, plus extra, if necessary • extra-virgin olive oil • salt

Heat some oil in a pan, add the beef, and fry until well browned and sealed on both sides. Add the garlic and herbs and fry for 1–2 minutes. Lower the heat, add the vinegar and stock. Cover and cook over a low heat until the liquid has evaporated. Add salt when the meat is half cooked. Add more stock if it evaporates before the meat is tender.

The Antica Macelleria Cecchini

Tuscany. There are good gourmet savories to sample with the wines.

 Antica Macelleria Cecchini

via XX Luglio, 11
📞 055 852020
⭕ Wed, Sun pm

At first glance you seem to have entered an ordinary butcher's shop when you go in. Then you notice the classical music playing softly in the background, and behind the counter a second room opens out with a fine table for sampling wine and hams, with other local and traditional specialties hanging from the ceiling. Then you start to browse through the large, elegant 16-page menu (at present reduced for renovation), which looks more like a restaurant menu than a butcher's price list. It offers 22 cuts of Tuscan lamb ready to cook (seasoned, dressed, and packaged); nine types of meat for roasting (from Chianina beef to pigeons); 12 stuffed-meat dishes; 13 different meats for grilling; 12 kinds of sausage, 12 meat preparations for cooking in a saucepan; 10 for cooking in a frying pan; 18 unusual sauces and delicacies, all of them made by the firm; nine pork products; 12 terrines and pâtés; and eight different cuts of cold meats (tongue, boned calf's head, galantines). In addition, there are

chestnuts, pulses, extra-virgin olive oil, Vin Santo, herbs, and fresh produce from the firm's farm. These products are presented with faithful devotion to tradition, a careful search for the oldest recipes (some are reprinted on the menu), and a careful choice of authentic ingredients. All these factors add a cultural dimension to the gourmet extravaganza, making it an unmissable experience for meat lovers.

🍇 Azienda Agricola Cennatoio

via San Leolino, 35
📞 055 852134 ⬤ Sat

The star product from this estate is its Vino Etrusco from Sangiovese grapes. The Chianti Classico Riserva, Etrusco Toscana, and Vin Santo Occhio di Pernice are also good.

🍇 Tenuta Fontodi

via San Leolino, 89
📞 055 852005 ⬤ Sat

This carefully managed estate produces high-quality wines, starting with its Chianti Classico Riserva Vigna del Sorbo, which is among the finest in its class. Outstanding among the varietals are the Colli della Toscana Centrale Flaccianello della Pieve, from Sangiovese, Meriggio, and Syrah. The estate also makes a good extra-virgin olive oil.

RICCIARELLI (ALMOND COOKIES)

9 oz (250 g) peeled almonds • **10 oz (300 g)** caster sugar • **1** egg white • **1** dessertspoon honey • pinch of ground cinnamon • grated zest of **1** lemon • confectioner's sugar • **1** rice flour wafer or rice paper

Preheat the oven to 275°F (140°C). Crush the almonds in a blender and mix them with the sugar. Beat the egg white and mix it into the almonds with the honey, cinnamon, and lemon zest. Mix well. Roll out the dough on a work surface sprinkled with confectioner's sugar until it is ¾ inch (2 cm) thick. Cut out lozenge shapes 3 inches (7.5 cm) in length. Place each on a slightly larger piece of wafer or on rice paper. Bake in the oven for about 15 minutes, taking care not to let the cookies brown.

All kinds of good things can be found in this food store-cum-butcher's-cum wine shop. Apart from the fine wares on display, the staff will procure all kinds of specialties on request. It has real Chianina beef, Sienese cakes bearing the shop's own hallmark, local marzolino cheese matured in the store's cellars, and its own salumi, including its own creation "tonno di Radda" (dried lean pork) and sausage flavored with black truffles (not the synthetic aroma). It also has a rich selection of the region's olive oils, wines, and local honey. Another shop selling only wine is at via dei Portici, 3.

POGGIBONSI (SI)

🍇 San Fabiano Calcinaia

località San Fabiano
☎ 0577 979232

This estate dating back to the 11th century offers a superb view over the valley of the Elsa. It also has apartments to rent. The wines have an excellent reputation. They include Chianti Classico San Fabiano Calcinaia and Riserva Cellole, Cerviolo Bianco (Chardonnay and Sauvignon), and the unmissable Cerviolo Rosso (Sangiovese, Cabernet Sauvignon, and Merlot). Olive oil is also produced.

RADDA IN CHIANTI (SI)

🍇 Castello d'Albola

via Pian d'Albola, 31
☎ 0577 738019

Belonging to the Zonin family, this estate is known for two innovative classics – Acciaiolo from Sangiovese and Cabernet Sauvignon grapes, and Le Fagge from Chardonnay. The Chianti

Classico Riserva and the Novello Sant'Ilario are both very good.

🍇 Enoteca Arte Vino

viale XI Febbraio, 21
☎ 0577 738605
⏺ Tue

This wine bar specializes in local wines and serves hot and cold dishes with them, including crostini, local salumi, and pecorino.

🍇 La Brancaia

località Poppi, 42b
☎ 0577 742007 ⏺ Sat

This recently built winery belongs to a Swiss family that now lives in Tuscany. Brancaia (Sangiovese, Merlot, Cabernet Sauvignon) and Chianti Classico Brancaia deserve a special mention. There are guided tours on Wednesdays; a fee is payable for tastings.

🏛 Casa Porciatti

piazza IV Novembre, 1
☎ 0577 738055
⏺ Wed pm, Sun pm (May–Oct); Sun (Nov–Apr)

🍇 Azienda Agricola Terrabianca

località San Fedele a Paterno
☎ 0577 738544

The star wine here is definitely Campaccio, which also comes in a Riserva version, from Sangiovese and Cabernet Sauvignon. It is backed up by one of the finest Tuscan whites, Piano della Cappella. Try the Chianti Classico Vigna della Croce and the estate's other white, Fior di Fino, from Malvasia and Trebbiano.

🍇 Castello di Volpaia

località Volpaia
☎ 0577 738066

One of the finest estates in Tuscany, this has excellent agriturismo (farm vacation) facilities and quality products. The Chianti Classico Riserva, the Coltassala (Sangiovese), and the Balifico (Sangiovese and Cabernet) are all noteworthy. The estate has excellent extra-virgin olive oil and a whole line of vinegars.

The village of Castello di Volpaia

SAN CASCIANO IN VAL DI PESA (FI)

🍷 Tenuta Castello il Corno

via Malafrasca, 64
📞 055 8248009

This ancient farm in the Val di Piesa is located in a villa, the oldest part of which dates back to the 1200s. It has a high, battlemented tower. The villa stands at the heart of 510 acres (210 hectares) of vineyards that produce Chianti Classico, Colorino, Corno Rosso da Sangiovese, and Cabernet. There are also 11,000 olive trees that yield an excellent oil. Upon request, a typical Tuscan lunch can be organized, and there are 19 apartments available to rent. Tastings are upon payment of a fee; salumi and cheeses are supplied.

🍇 Fattoria Corzano e Paterno

località San Pancrazio, via Paterno, 10
📞 055 8249114;
055 8248179

This firm is made up of two farms lying over two hills: Paterno, where cheese is made, and Corzano, where the winery, the farmhouse, and the cellars are located. The buildings date back a long time and have been subjected to many restorations over the centuries. Among the

wines that offer the best quality–price ratio are: Chianti Terre di Corzano, Chianti Riserva I Tre Borri, Aglaia (Chardonnay), Vin Santo, and the unmissable Corzano (Sangiovese, Cabernet Sauvignon, Merlot). There is a fee for tastings. The agriturismo facilities operate between April and October. An excellent oil is also made.

🫒 Oleificio Giachi

località Mercatale in Val di Pesa, via Campoli, 31
📞 055 821082

This firm bottles excellent extra-virgin olive oil, mostly from local olive presses, including its own blend, Colle dei Giachi.

🐓 Azienda Agricola Massanera

via di Faltignano, 76
📞 055 8242360

Free-range Cinta Senese pigs are raised here and turned into fine salumi, but prices are high. The estate also makes very good, but expensive, oil and wine.

SAN GIMIGNANO (SI)

🍇 Azienda Agricola Il Casale-Falchini

via di Casale, 40
📞 0577 941305 ◑ Sat

This estate was one of the first to revive production of Vernaccia, a policy that has produced the excellent wines Vigna al Solatio, enriched with a little Chardonnay, and Ab Vinea Doni. Among its other wines, Càmpora, a red from pure Cabernet Sauvignon, is very good.

🍇 Fattoria Cusona

località Cusona, 5
📞 0577 950028 ◑ Sat

The Guicciardini Strozzi firm owns this centuries-old property. It makes a good Vernaccia, which also comes in a Riserva version, made from grapes gathered late in the harvest and then fermented in barriques. There is also a spumante version. Among the red wines is Sodole, which is produced from Sangiovese grapes. Accommodation is also available (0577 907185).

The towers of San Gimignano

PAPPARDELLE SULLA LEPRE (PASTA WITH HARE)

4 dessertspoons olive oil • 1 onion, chopped • 1 carrot, chopped • 1 stalk celery, chopped • a few sage leaves • a handful of parsley, chopped • 6 oz (150 g) guanciale *(pig's cheek), chopped • shoulder, neck, and breast of a hare, cut into pieces • hare giblets (lights, heart, liver) and blood • 2 glasses Chianti • vinegar • beef stock • 4 fl oz (100 ml) milk • 1¼ lb (600 g) fresh* pappardelle *• grated Parmesan cheese • salt • pepper*

Heat the oil in a pan (preferably earthenware) and fry the onion, carrot, celery, sage, parsley, and *guanciale* lightly. Gradually add pieces of hare and the lights and stir-fry until browned. Add the red wine and allow it to evaporate. Moisten with the blood and a little vinegar. Simmer gently for 10 minutes. Add salt and pepper. Warm the milk and add to the pan, cover and simmer for 1 hour, adding a little stock if it starts to dry out. Bone the pieces of hare and return them to the pan with the chopped heart and liver. Simmer for another 5 minutes. Meanwhile, cook the *pappardelle*. Drain the pasta and serve it with the sauce and Parmesan cheese.

🍇 Azienda Agricola Fontaleoni

località Santa Maria, 39
☎ 0577 950193

With its 37 acres (15 hectares) of vines, this estate focuses on the area's classic wines. There are two styles of Vernaccia, the normal and the Vigna Casanuova.

🍇 Montenidoli

località Montenidoli
☎ 0577 941565

A small estate with a very good Vernaccia. The traditional version is good value for money, and there are two choices, Carato and Fiore.

🍇 Azienda Agricola Panizzi

località Racciano, 34, Santa Margherita
☎ 0577 941576 ⬛ Sat

The estate's care for its vines and the quality of its wines is apparent in the Vernaccia with a Riserva version partly fined in barriques. The Chianti Colli Senesi is full-bodied and structured.

🍇 Fattoria di Pietrafitta

località Cortennano
☎ 0577 943200
⬛ Sat, Sun; Nov–Mar

Agriturismo facilities include two- to ten-bed apartments and B&B-style accommodation. Organic wines are produced in a cellar that dates back to the 1400s. There is a fee for tastings; four wines (Vernaccia di San Gimignano, Chianti Colli Senesi, San Gimignano

Rosato and Rosso) are made available, as well as bruschetta *and cheeses. Other products are oil, grappa, and Vin Santo.*

🐦 Fattoria San Quirico

località Pancole, 39
☎ 0577 955007

Surrounded by vineyards and olive groves, this certified organic farm produces saffron, oil, and wines bearing a DOC label.

🍇 Teruzzi & Puthod – Ponte a Rondolino

località Casale, 19
☎ 0577 940143 ⬛ Sat

This certified organic estate boasts the latest technology. No tastings are held in the cellar, but it is possible to taste the wines at the sales center located in località Montegonfoli (0577 941 722; open from March to October). The wines include Terre dei Tufi (Vernaccia, Malvasia, Vermentino, Chardonnay), Vernaccia di San Gimignano Vigna Rondolino, Carmen Puthod (Sangiovese), and Peperino (Sangiovese).

SIENA

✴ Pasticceria Buti

via Vittorio Emanuele II, 53
☎ 0577 40464
⬛ Mon, Sun pm

The Teruzzi & Puthod estate at Ponte a Rondolino

Sienese cakes, including an authentic spicy pan pepato, *are sold here.*

Enoteca Italiana

Fortezza Medicea, 1
0577 288497

This interesting wine shop has an enormous range of Italian wines – there are over 1,000 names from all regions plus 500 Tuscans, chosen by experts. A dozen wines are opened in turn daily for tasting with assorted snacks.

Forno dei Galli

via dei Termini, 45
0577 289073

Bread, fresh pasta, and traditional Sienese cakes are sold here.

Bar Impero

via Vittorio Emanuele, 10/12
0577 47424
Mon

Excellent ice cream is made and sold here all year round.

Drogheria Manganelli

via di Città, 71/73
0577 280002

The original furnishings date back 120 years in this real old-fashioned grocer's shop. It makes its own traditional Sienese cakes and has a choice selection of products from all over Italy, as well as some imported delicacies, all from high-quality producers. There is a good range of wines.

Gastronomia Morbidi

via Banchi di Sopra, 75
0577 280268
Sat pm

This is a delicatessen for gourmets, selling a small, select range of wines with choice grappas, plus the firm's own traditional salumi *and an array of hams and sausages from other regions. It also has an assortment of cheeses from its own dairy and other parts of Italy, and a range of international dishes, both fresh and ready-cooked. Another branch is at via Banchi di Sotto, 27.*

Bar Nannini

via Banchi di Sopra, 24
0577 236009

At this long-established café, it is possible to sample traditional Sienese cakes.

La Nuova Pasticceria di Iasevoli

via Dupré, 37
0577 41319
Mon, Sun pm

Fine traditional Sienese confections, including cantucci *(cookies) and* pane con i santi *(sweet bread containing fruit), can be found here.*

Pasticceria Parini

via Mencatelli, 2
0577 283159
Mon, Sun pm

This confectionery shop makes excellent Sienese cakes. They are also sold at a shop at via Quinto Settano, 5 (0577 50593).

Enoteca San Domenico

via del Paradiso, 56
0577 271181
daily, including Sunday

A selection of Italian wines is sold here – not just the big names but also fine wine from smaller producers – plus a choice of liquors, champagne, Tuscan olive oil, and the firm's own traditional cakes.

TAVARNELLE VAL DI PESA (SI)

Azienda Agricola Poggio al Sole

frazione Sambuca, località Badia e Passignano
055 8071504

The area's classic red grapes can be found in the juicy Seraselva, produced from Merlot and Cabernet, and the full-bodied Chianti Classico Casasilia (Sangiovese and Syrah).

AGNELLO IN FRICASSEA (LAMB FRICASSÉE)

1 leg and 1 shoulder of lamb • 2 onions • 1 carrot, chopped • 1 stalk celery, sliced • 2 dessertspoons flour • 4 egg yolks • juice of 1 lemon • a few calamint (or mint) leaves • extra-virgin olive oil • salt • pepper

Bone the lamb. Slice 1 onion. Put the bones, sliced onion, carrot, and celery in a pan of water and cook for 2 hours to make stock. Cut the meat into pieces 2–2½ inches (5–6 cm) long. Finely chop the remaining onion. Flour the pieces of meat and brown them in the oil with the onion. Add salt and pepper and moisten with the stock. Cover and simmer until the meat is cooked. Add enough stock to make a sauce. Beat the egg with the lemon juice, pepper, and calamint. Remove the pan from the heat, add the egg and stir briskly. The sauce should have the consistency of mayonnaise. Serve hot or cold, but do not reheat.

MONTALCINO
AND THE
SIENESE CRETE

Montalcino and the Sienese Crete

IN THIS GOURMET GUIDE, the southern part of the province of Siena has been separated from the north because the zone of Chianti Classico wine and the zone of Brunello and Vino Nobile deserve separate treatment. A corner of the province of Arezzo has been added to this section because Lucignano and Monte San Savino are influenced more by Sienese gastronomic habits than by their own.

The clay hills known as the Crete have fine truffles, rounded and regular, without knobby bits or cracks, especially San Giovanni d'Asso, Trequanda, Buonconvento, and Asciano. In fact, the commune of San Giovanni d'Asso has the highest production of truffles in Italy. There is nothing smooth and regular about the eroded hillocks that give the Crete its name. The sunny rolling hills have tremendous, jagged gashes in them, spectacular gulleys denuded of topsoil by heavy rain so they are bare of vegetation. Great slashes suddenly open in wheat fields, vineyards, olive groves, and young oak scrub. The Crete, like the wooded areas of Montalcino, the valley of the Merse and the Val d'Orcia, is studded with ancient farms set in woods rich with mushrooms, herbs, and fruits. The farms often have a complete food production cycle (cereals, cattle, sheep, and pigs, cheese-making, olive groves, and presses).

Colle di Val d'Elsa

Monterig...

Casole d'Elsa

Sovi...

Colline Metallifere

Chiusdino

Monticiano

STAR ATTRACTIONS

- CHIUSI (SI): National Etruscan Museum, ☎ 0578 227667
- MONTE OLIVETO MAGGIORE (SI): Abbey, ☎ 0577 707017
- MONTEPULCIANO (SI): Cathedral, Madonna di San Biagio, ☎ 0578 75887
- MONTE S. SAVINO (AR): Loggia dei Mercanti, ☎ 0575 843098
- PIENZA (SI): Cathedral, ☎ 0578 749071
- SANT'ANTIMO (SI): Abbey, ☎ 0577 835659

Pecorino cheese made in the Crete – especially the mature *pecorino* of Pienza – is world-famous *(see pp132–3)*.

Beekeeping at Montalcino has reached very high quality levels with a whole range of unusual honey-based products *(see pp134–5)*.

WHITE TRUFFLES

The Sienese Crete area is blessed as far as truffle lovers are concerned because it has a rich supply of the white truffle *(Tuber magnatum)*. San Giovanni d'Asso is the truffle center and holds a truffle fair every November.

◁ **The Tuscan hills dominated with cypresses**

Large old estates in this area often produce the celebrated Brunello di Montalcino DOCG, one of the great internationally famous wines. These farms were once bustling villages: around the main landowner's house were a wine cellar, an olive press, shops and workshops, a herbalist, dairy, butcher, and church. In many cases, such as Fattoria dei Barbi at Montalcino, the estate pictured here, these activities still continue.

Cakes and cookies are another well-known Montalcino product.

TOURIST OFFICES

• CHIANCIANO TERME
Via Sabatini, 7
☎ 0578 63648.
w www.chianciano.
turismo.toscana.it

• MONTEPULCIANO
Via di Gracciano, 59a
☎ 0578 757341. w www.
prolocomontepulciano.it

• PIENZA Corso
Roffellimo, 59 ☎ 0578
749071. w www.infinito.it/
utenti/ufficio.turistico

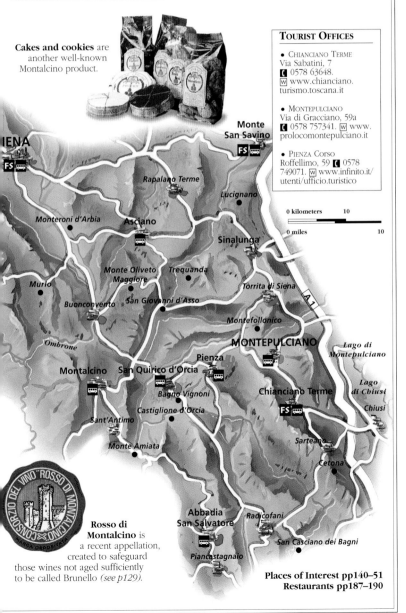

Rosso di Montalcino is a recent appellation, created to safeguard those wines not aged sufficiently to be called Brunello *(see p129)*.

Places of Interest pp140–51
Restaurants pp187–190

Wines of Montalcino

THE MAJESTIC RED WINE grown around Montalcino, south of Siena, is one of Italy's greatest wines. Brunello di Montalcino DOCG dates from the late 19th century, which is relatively recent compared with other noble wines. Its fortune and that of all Sienese wine-making lies with the Sangiovese Grosso vine, the only grapes used to make this wine. The same is true of the Rosso di Montalcino. The great Sienese reds were born out of patient effort and a careful eye on the market, and the work of Tuscan and foreign vine-growers who have preserved the link with the local tradition.

There are subtle variations in the bouquet and flavor of Montalcino wines, depending on where they come from. The area around the city is like a large pyramid with four sides sloping to the valleys. On the north side, the wines are elegant and have good body; to the east, the cooler climate confers a more austere structure and great potential for aging; to the south, the body is sustained but the perfume is less elegant; to the west, the wines are especially well balanced and pleasant to drink.

MOSCADELLO DI MONTALCINO

Few estates produce this wine, so it is not easy to find on the market. In the most common versions it is liqueurlike, but it can also be sweet and sparkling. It is a pale yellow or golden color and has the typical muscatel scent. It is perfect with the sweet dry cookies of Siena and with fruit. It should be made from the ancient Moscadello vine, which has largely disappeared; attempts are being made to nurture some of the original vines. Moscato Bianco is widely used in its place.

The Sangiovese grape grown in Montalcino is called Brunello.

The oldest wines are sometimes called "wines for meditation."

BRUNELLO DI MONTALCINO

Described in Tuscany as the king of wines, this wine has found worldwide fame. It is aged for at least four years before it is sold; five years if it bears the Riserva label. The high price is justified by this lengthy aging process. The wine's ruby-red color takes on a garnet red hue as it ages. The elegant bouquet is intense and the taste very well balanced. It is a great wine to drink with roasted or braised meats and strong, mature cheeses.

WINE TYPE	GOOD VINTAGES	GOOD PRODUCERS
Red Wine		
Brunello di Montalcino	97, 95, 94, 90	Siro Pacenti, Capanna, Salvioni La Cerbaiola, Lisini, Fattoria del Casato, Caparzo di Montalcino
Rosso di Montalcino	97, 95, 90	Altesino di Montalcino, Argiano di Montalcino
Super Tuscans (see p130)		Argiano di Montalcino

PICI CON L'ANATRA MUTA

1 muscovy duck • 1 carrot • 1 red onion • 1 bunch of parsley • extra-virgin olive oil • 1 glass red wine • 2¼ lb (1 kg) peeled, plum tomatoes, chopped • 2 tablespoons tomato purée • salt • pepper

Bone the duck, leaving the neck, legs, and wings complete. Use the bones and the neck to make stock. Grind up the rest of the duck meat, giblets, carrot, onion, and parsley. Fry this mixture slowly in the olive oil with the whole parts of the duck. Season to taste. Continue cooking slowly, moistening with the red wine. When the wine has all evaporated, add the fresh tomatoes and the tomato purée, then simmer gently for 3 hours. Check from time to time and add some of the duck stock if it looks as if it is becoming dry. Serve the duck sauce on the local *pici* pasta. (At Trequanda this pasta is also known as *pinci* or *lunghetti*).

ROSSO DI MONTALCINO

Brunello grapes are used to make this younger, less austere wine. Very dry with an intense ruby-red color, it is a versatile table wine which goes with Sienese cuisine's many savory dishes, such as first courses with meat sauces and second courses of pork, stewed meats, and meat with sauces.

NOVELLO

Many estates are successfully making this young wine, which has earned a place for itself in the market. Produced by the *macération carbonique* method, where grapes are fermented whole in a closed vat, it is richly perfumed and suited to drinking with all courses. However, it can be expensive for the quality and does not age well.

The Azienda Col d'Orcia at Montalcino

Other Wines from South of Siena

The province of Siena boasts the richest and most diverse wine production in the whole of Tuscany. The area south of Siena produces not only Brunello but also two great DOCG wines, Vino Nobile di Montepulciano and Chianti Colli Senesi made from Sangiovese Grosso grapes. In the Montepulciano area the Sangiovese Grosso vine is called Prugnolo Gentile, because of the elongated shape of its grapes and their plummy blue color and scent. This vine attains its full potential in the Colli Senesi, either with the grapes used alone or in combination with other reds such as Cabernet Sauvignon, Cabernet Franc, Pinot Nero, and Merlot. Sangiovese Grosso forms up to 80 percent of Chianti while it varies from 60 percent to 80 percent in Vino Nobile and Rosso di Montepulciano. Other red grapes are also added to these wines, including Canaiolo for mellowness and Mammolo for its bouquet.

The Sienese region also has a long tradition of white grape vines. The most common is Trebbiano Toscano, but the present trend is to reduce the quantity of this grape and gradually replace it with other grapes such as Chardonnay, Pinot Bianco, Sauvignon, Traminer Aromatico, Rhineland Riesling, Pinot Grigio, and Muller Thurgau, which have long been grown here. The second traditional white grape is Malvasia Toscana, then there are other lesser varieties like Grechetto Bianco, also called Pulcinculo because of the dark spot found on the tip of the grape.

Vin Santo di Montepulciano

This highly prized traditional Vin Santo is made with Pulcinculo in addition to the other traditional grapes. It can be labeled Riserva after it has aged for at least five years in wood. Served as a dessert wine, it goes well with sweet dry cookies. The price varies, but it can be very expensive. Some estates produce it in a *"Vendemmia Tardiva"* version, from grapes left to dry on the vines instead of picking them and drying them on racks.

The white version from white grapes.

This attractive amber-colored Vin Santo, called Occhio di Pernice, is made from at least 50 percent Sangiovese grapes.

The Super Tuscans

Many Tuscan estates have long been engaged in producing wines outside the rules of the DOC or DOCG wines. The choice of vines and methods of production aim at the very highest quality. The techniques vary from one estate to another – they may be based on traditional Tuscan vines alone or combined with noble vines like Cabernet Sauvignon and Merlot. Some excellent wines have been produced and they are much in demand internationally. These wines are called Super Tuscans, an appellation which indicates prized wines much sought-after abroad.

CHIANTI E CHIANTI DEI COLLI SENESI

Chianti is made from Tuscan grapes vinified in the Siena area; Chianti dei Colli Senesi is made from grapes that have been grown and vinified locally.

VINO NOBILE DI MONTEPULCIANO

This DOCG wine can be one of Italy's most impressive reds. The area of production for the wine stretches west from Valdichiana and east into another small area. Specific areas that produce superior wine include Argiano, Caggiole, Canneto, Casalte, and Valiano. The wine is aged for two years in casks, or three years in the case of the Riserva. It is a deep red color, with an intense, balanced bouquet, excellent with *bistecca alla fiorentina*, grilled meats, and mature cheeses.

ROSSO DI MONTEPULCIANO

This red wine, which has practically no aging, was created to bring Montepulciano wine closer to the general public. It is a bright ruby red with an intense bouquet and a pleasant dry flavor. It is ideal as a general table wine with full-bodied dishes, such as grilled meats.

VAL D'ARBIA

Made mainly from Trebbiano Toscano and Malvasia grapes, this dry white wine is a pale yellowish color with a hint of green. Fruity and fresh-tasting, it makes a good aperitif or it can be served with fish. Also available in a Vin Santo version.

WINE TYPE	GOOD VINTAGES	GOOD PRODUCERS	WINE TYPE	GOOD VINTAGES	GOOD PRODUCERS
Red Wine			**Super Tuscans** *(see p130)*	98, 97, 95, 90	Avignonesi di Montepulciano
Rosso di Montepulciano	97, 90	Avignonesi, Poliziano, Dei di Montepulciano	**White Wine**		
Chianti *and* Chianti dei Colli Senesi	98, 97, 95, 93, 90	Farnetella di Sinalunga, Fattoria del Colle di Trequanda	Vino Nobile di Montepulciano	97, 95, 90	Avignonesi, Fattoria del Cerro, Poliziano di Montepulciano

Pecorino from the Sienese Crete

S OUTH OF SIENA, in the primeval landscape of the Crete, shepherds tend sheep whose milk is used to make *pecorino* cheese. The ancient craft of cheese making is now largely practiced by Sardinian shepherds who have settled here in recent decades, but this has not altered the traditional quality of the cheese – the Sardinians have preserved their own sheep-tending skills, while absorbing the habits and tastes of the Sienese people. The Crete and the southern part of the province of Siena produce the most prized *pecorino* in Tuscany.

MATURE PECORINO DI PIENZA

This is the most prized and famous of Tuscan *pecorini*, prepared with milk solely from the Crete and Montalcino areas. The secret of its quality lies in the use of fresh, unpasteurized milk and a covering of olive oil lees (skins after the olives have been pressed) to keep the inside soft and slightly mellow. (Avoid cheeses covered with plastic film, which ruins the cheese.) These cheeses are matured for anything from 5 to 18 months.

The whitish color of the crust is due to the olive oil lees.

MATURE PECORINO

The area of production for this cheese is the same as for the traditional Pienza cheese and the two are quite similar, except that this cheese does not have the olive oil crust, so the inside has a drier texture and a stronger flavor.

This cheese has a hard, deep yellow crust.

SEMIMATURE PECORINO

After 90–120 days of maturing, *pecorino* is still beautifully mellow, ideal for eating with *salumi*, with pears, or in thin slices on meat, *crostini*, or baked vegetables. Sometimes chiles, black pepper, or black truffles are incorporated into the cheese. It is rare, however, to find a cheese-maker who uses pieces of fresh truffle; most use semiprocessed truffles or the synthetic aroma, resulting in an inferior product.

A coating of extra-virgin olive oil on this white cheese keeps the inside soft.

This cheese is covered in tomato purée which keeps the inside soft and enhances its scent, giving it a red crust.

FRESH PECORINO

Sweet and creamy, with a markedly milky flavor, fresh *pecorino* is eaten within 90–120 days of being made. It is popular with all age groups and can be eaten at the end of the meal or as an *antipasto* dressed with extra-virgin olive oil from the Crete region and seasoned with salt and black pepper.

CIPOLLE IN FORNO

12 red onions • extra-virgin olive oil • white wine vinegar • 2 oz (50 g) pecorino, grated • 4 oz (100 g) breadcrumbs • salt • pepper

Preheat the oven to 400°F (200°C). Peel the onions, cut two slits to form a cross at the top of each and put them in a baking pan. Brush with oil and season with salt and pepper. Roast in the oven until well cooked. Moisten with the vinegar and return to the oven to evaporate the liquid. Mix the cheese and crumbs, sprinkle them over the onions and serve.

FRESH PECORINO WITH HERBS OR NUTS

Fresh *pecorino* may have herbs or nuts added to it. The cheese should be eaten within a week and is excellent as an *antipasto* or as a snack with a little extra-virgin olive oil from the Crete drizzled over it.

Chopped arugula in fresh pecorino is a recent innovation.

Adding small pieces of walnut to the cheese is an old tradition.

PECORINO SOTT'OLIO

In some families and farmhouses there is a tradition of preserving mature *pecorino* in olive oil mixed with herbs or spices.

OTHER EWE'S MILK PRODUCTS WORTH TRYING

Raviggiolo is a fresh curd cheese eaten within four days of making. Traditionally it is salted and eaten as an antipasto or sugared as a dessert. It is very delicate and should be kept in a sealed container in the refrigerator. The **ricotta** in this area is delectable, especially when made from raw milk: it is eaten on ribbon pasta or made into fillings for stuffed pasta such as ravioli. Another product of this area is **marzolino** *(see p108)*.

Honey

THROUGHOUT TUSCANY – from the mountains to the coast, where the Mediterranean landscape is dotted with wonderfully aromatic plants – honey *(miele)* is produced. Renowned for its therapeutic properties, honey is thought to help with disorders in all parts of the body, from liver to lungs to circulation. At Montalcino beekeeping (apiculture) has a long history, originating with the skill of the foresters who used to gather wild honey from hollow trees, and are still capable of hiving swarms of wild bees. Traditional honey production in Montalcino and the surrounding area is based on the flowering chestnut woods on the Apennine slopes. Many local firms take hives to other parts of Italy, so they can extend the honey-producing season.

Chestnut honey is a rich, dark brown color.

CHESTNUT HONEY
The aroma and slightly bitter taste of chestnut honey *(miele di castagno)* make it good for cooking and in confectioneries. It is believed to be useful for intestinal disorders and helpful in regulating the nervous system and in cases of anemia.

SUNFLOWER HONEY
This honey *(miele di girasole)* is thought to be mildly effective at soothing pain or fever and is a mild diuretic.

Sunflower honey is very dense with an opaque yellowish color.

WOODLAND HONEY
Rich in mineral salts and iron, woodland honey *(melata di bosco)* is very fortifying.

Woodland honey is a deep golden color.

CANTUCCI DI MONTALCINO

- 8 oz (200 g) unpeeled almonds
- 1¼ lb (500 g) plain flour
- 4 eggs • 1 teaspoon baking powder • ¾ lb (350 g) sugar
- 4 oz (100 g) chestnut honey • few drops of vanilla essence • butter • salt

Preheat the oven to 350°F (180°C). Roast the almonds for 4 minutes. Heap the flour on a work surface and make a well in the center. Beat the eggs and pour into the well with the baking powder, sugar, honey, vanilla essence, and a pinch of salt. Knead until the dough is smooth, then add the almonds. Roll out the dough and shape into long fingers. Transfer to a buttered and floured baking sheet and bake for about 20 minutes. Cut the fingers diagonally into ¾ inch (2 cm) slices and leave to dry.

SULLA CLOVER HONEY
Because it has a faint aroma, this honey *(miele di sulla)* can be used for sweetening foods without affecting their flavor. It is thought to help purify the liver and keep the intestines in good order.

This clear honey is a light golden color.

HEATHER HONEY
Delicately scented heather honey *(miele di erica)* is good for coughs and colds, as it helps to soothe sore respiratory organs.

Jellylike heather honey is brownish-orange.

ARBUTUS HONEY
Arbutus honey *(miele di corbezzolo)*, from the wild strawberry tree, is quite bitter. It is thought to be good for the circulation and blood.

Arbutus honey is a mustard color, or milky white if very pure. It is very thick and granular.

PRESERVES IN HONEY
The classics – hazelnuts, almonds, or walnuts in honey *(vasetti "sotto miele")* – are found in most parts of Tuscany. There is also the unusual delicacy of boiled chestnuts flavored with vanilla and conserved in acacia honey.

OTHER VARIETIES OF HONEY WORTH TRYING
Acacia honey, clear and very fluid, is probably the variety most commonly seen. It is not strong and suits a range of tastes. Rich in energy, it is fortifying and has mild laxative properties which are thought to help purify the liver. **Tiglio** (linden) honey, excellent for problems with the respiratory tract, is also useful for inducing sleep. **Millefiori** (wild flower) is versatile and very nourishing. **Eucalipto** (eucalyptus), helpful in disorders of the respiratory tract, is a decongestant and emollient for smokers. **Lavanda** (lavender) is richly scented and helps to calm the nervous system. **Rosmarino** (rosemary) has a strong flavor and is a mild diuretic. **Timo** (thyme), rich in fructose, is believed to be good for the circulation, as is **trifoglio** (clover) honey. At Montalcino, other honey specialities include grappa, candies, fruit cakes, and preserves.

Traditional Produce

THERE ARE PLENTY of genuine Tuscan specialities for the gourmet in this area, and they are nearly always produced with due respect for the environment. The *prosciutti* and *salumi*, cèpe mushrooms and truffles, extra-virgin olive oil, game birds and animals, Chianina beef, lamb, and fine vegetables produced in this part of Tuscany all have their own very distinctive character.

OSSI DI MORTO
These very hard cookies, made from egg whites and chopped almonds, are typical of Montalcino.

GRAPPA
In recent years a lot of work has gone into improving the grappa made by distilling the grape skins and seeds left over from the wine-making process. Leading wine-makers have staked their names on these grappas, some of interest to true connoisseurs.

COLLI SENESI OLIVE OIL
The olive oils produced in the Colli Senesi are of medium-to-high fruitiness, and generally full-bodied. They vary in taste, but all are peppery when young, usually with a slightly bitter aftertaste. Those produced in 26 towns on the hills around Siena (including Montalcino and Le Crete) boast the Terre di Siena DOP label.

POLLASTRELLA AL DRAGONCELLO

1 young free-range pullet • 1 apple • a large bunch of tarragon • 1 knob of butter • 1 dessertspoon plain flour

Preheat the oven to 350°F (180°C). Brown the pullet, then stuff it with the apple and tarragon. Sew up the bird with kitchen twine, wrap in wax paper, and roast in the oven for about 40 minutes. Remove the paper and pour off the cooking juices. Roast the bird for another 5 minutes until it is a golden color, then remove from the pan. Thicken the juices in the pan with the butter and flour; serve with the bird.

TARRAGON
One of the classic herbs of international cuisine, tarragon (*persia* in Tuscany, elsewhere *dragoncello* or *estragone*) is a common aromatic in the Siena area, where it is widely used in sauces and meat dishes.

AMIATA OLIVE OIL
This oil is produced at the foot of Mour Amiata, partly using a typical cultivar known as Olivastra Leggianese. It has a fresh scent of herbs and a rounded taste, rather astringent and pungent. The strong flavor has a markedly bitter, peppery aftertaste.

For this salami the meat is coarsely ground and the fat is chopped with a knife.

MORTADELLA
The local name for Tuscan salami encased in pig's large intestine is *mortadella* (while the smaller size is usually called *salame*). This salami is slightly less fatty than some types and its medium-to-high quality is due to the good local pork.

This meat is finely ground and rather fatty.

FINOCCHIONA
This salami, which is cured for eating raw, contains aromatic fennel seeds or flowers. It is similar to Florentine *sbriciolona*, but usually cured for longer.

Wrapped in straw paper, lombo can breathe.

LOMBO
Chine of pork is boned and salted and scented with fennel seed to add even more flavor to the good quality meat. If fresh, *lombo* is served dressed with olive oil and lemon.

BURISTO
Typical of the Siena area, *buristo* (blood pudding) is made from the flesh of the pig's head – including the tongue and some of the skin – finely ground and mixed with spices, pig's blood, and boiled fat. The meat is encased in the pig's stomach and slowly boiled. It is traditionally eaten strewn with chopped raw onion.

WHAT TO SAMPLE
Rigatino, salted belly of pork, is indispensable in local cooking. There are numerous traditional cakes, especially at Montalcino, where you can find Sienese classics such as **ricciarelli** and **panforte**. Specialities peculiar to Montalcino and the Crete are **pane coi santi**, bread dough with nuts, raisins, and aniseed mixed into it; **torta di Montalcino**, a soft cake containing raisins and covered with chocolate, hazelnuts, and almonds; **morselletti**, aniseed cookies (the original recipe also calls for olive oil); **pinolata**, made of pastry with cream and raisins, covered with pine nuts to look like a pine cone; **schiacciata di Pasqua**, a bread flavored with mint, rosewater, saffron, aniseed, and citrus peel. The local pasta, **pinci**, is like large spaghetti. **Saffron** grows wild in this area, and the medieval village of Murlo has grown **rice** for centuries.

Wild Produce

WHITE WAX CAP
(Hygrophorus penarius)
Late in the season this mushroom *(lardaiolo bianco)* is abundant in thick stands of evergreen and deciduous oaks. It remains white and fleshy after cooking and is good in sauces with white meats.

LESSER BOLETUS
(Boletus duriusculus)
The sturdiest and most prized of this group of *porcini*, the lesser boletus *(oppiarello)* grows under poplars along the coast. It is good cooked with garlic and parsley (it darkens when cooked). When young, these mushrooms are preserved in oil; mature ones are dried.

CHANTERELLE
(Cantharellus cibarius)
This mushroom *(giallarello)* has adapted to virtually all cuisines and is popular in many countries. Chanterelles grow in all kinds of woodland but in this area are found mainly under holm oaks. Less perfumed than the Alpine chanterelles that grow under beech and spruce, they are excellent fried with garlic and parsley, in cream, and in sauces.

PARASOL MUSHROOM
(Lepiota procera)
Common in both the coastal scrub and on grassy hillsides, this popular mushroom *(bubbola)* is very conspicuous because of its height – up to 20 inches (50 cm) – and the drumstick shape of its cap. It is excellent raw in salads or preserved in oil when young. When ripe, the cap is very good grilled, fried, or deviled. The woody stalk is dried and made into an aromatic powder.

FUNGHI CON LA NEPITELLA (MUSHROOMS WITH CALAMINT)

1¾ lb (800 g) mixed mushrooms, sliced • 3 cloves garlic, chopped • 1 sprig of calamint (or mint) • 1 dessertspoon tomato purée • extra-virgin olive oil • salt • pepper

Put the mushrooms in a pan with the garlic, sprig of calamint, plenty of oil, and salt and pepper. Cook over a high heat until the mushrooms shed their water, then lower and cook till the liquid evaporates (the oil should be clear again). Add the tomato purée and cook over a moderate heat for 10 minutes.

COMMON SOW THISTLE
(Sonchus oleraceus)
One of the best-known edible wild plants, sow thistle *(crespigno)* grows abundantly on the edges of vegetable patches and paths, on waste ground, and in orchards. Sweet and tasty when young, it is good raw. As it matures, it is eaten in mixed salads, stuffings, and omelettes.

WILD ASPARAGUS
(Asparagus acutifolius)
Plentiful early in spring growing by hedgerows, ditches, and on the edge of woods, picking wild asparagus *(asparago selvatico)* is a pleasant pastime. It is used in the same way as the cultivated variety.

WILD LETTUCE
(Lactuca serriola)
This salad vegetable *(lattuga di campo)* is well known to country people in Tuscany, who go looking for it. Check with an expert before you pick it: the rosettes at the base of many spring plants can look similar and not all are edible. Wild lettuce is very good raw or cooked and dressed with oil, lemon juice, or vinegar.

PENNE IN SALSA D'ERBETTE DI PRIMAVERA

1 young wild fennel plant • a few calamint (or mint) leaves • 1 rosette of common poppy leaves • 1 young borage plant • 1 small bunch of parsley • 20 basil leaves • 1 handful nettle tips • 1 handful of field eryngo • 1 head of wild chicory leaves • 2 heads of wild lettuce leaves • 3 young sow thistle plants • 1 sprig tarragon • 10 leaves lemon balm • 1 sprig marjoram • 6 walnuts • extra virgin olive oil • 1 chile • 2 cloves garlic • 1¼ lb (500 g) peeled, plum tomatoes • 1¼ lb (500 g) penne • salt

Make sure the herbs are dry. Chop them in a blender or food processor with the walnuts. Put them in a jar, cover with olive oil, and leave for at least 2 days. Heat a little oil in a pan, add the chile and garlic, and fry until softened slightly. Add the tomatoes and season with salt. Cook over a brisk heat. Add the herbs and walnuts and cook for a further 5 minutes. Meanwhile, cook the pasta. Drain well and serve with the tomato and herb sauce, mixing thoroughly.

STRAWBERRY TREE (ARBUTUS)
(Arbutus unedo)
The strawberry tree *(corbezzolo)* is common in Mediterranean thickets, where its colorful appearance – green leaves, white flowers, and red fruit – enlivens the scenery. When ripe, the fruit is creamy rather than juicy, and is very sweet. It can be eaten fresh (in moderation) or used in preserves.

Places of Interest

As with the Chianti region, the well-informed, polyglot clientele of this area want the genuine flavors of the past, thus helping to ensure the survival of these foods. There are fewer shops here, but there are many interesting farms, as well as some of the finest wine producers. The farms have such a wide range of products that they are almost self-sufficient: they offer not only olive oil and wine but also *salumi*, cheese, fresh vegetables, and local honey, all of them excellent.

A single wine, Poggio di Chiari from Sangiovese grapes alone, matured in French and Slavonian oak, is produced here. The owner, a supporter of local products, has reintroduced the cultivation of spelt and beans, and he also breeds Cinta Senese pigs.

ASCIANO (SI)

Tenuta Monte Sante Marie

località Monte Sante Marie
📞 0577 700020/43

This farm with agriturismo facilities makes a superb extra-virgin olive oil. In years when they have a bumper crop of fruit, they make and sell excellent cakes and jams as well.

BUONCONVENTO (SI)

La Bottega del Pane

via del Taia, 21
📞 0577 809016

This shop sells traditional Tuscan bread made with

fresh yeast, and a wide range of Sienese cakes. Its illustrious clientele includes Queen Elizabeth II and the Italian president Carlo Azeglio Ciampi.

Rabazzi Piante

strada per Monte Oliveto, 7
📞 0577 806302
🕐 Sat pm

This nursery offers an excellent selection of potted aromatic herbs.

CHIUSI (SI)

Azienda Agricola Colle di Santa Mustiola

via delle Torri, 86a
📞 0578 63462

LUCIGNANO (AR)

Apicoltura Nocciolini

località Selva, 50a
📞 0575 836097

All types of honey, from this and other areas, gathered by itinerant beekeepers is sold here.

Panificio Redi

località Croce
📞 0575 837037
🕐 Sat pm

At this bakery, Tuscan bread is made the old-fashioned way, kneading by hand before leaving it to rise.

CINGHIALE IN AGRODOLCE (BOAR IN SWEET AND SOUR SAUCE)

3¼ lb (1.5 kg) lean boar's meat • 3 pints (1.5 liters) red wine • 8 fl oz (250 ml) wine vinegar • juniper berries • 3 bay leaves • 1 dessertspoon plain flour seasoned with salt and pepper • extra-virgin olive oil • 2 carrots, finely chopped • 1 onion, finely chopped • 1 stalk of celery, finely chopped • meat stock • 4 oz (100 g) chopped panforte • 3 cavallucci (sweets) • 4 oz (100 g) dark chocolate • 1 oz (30 g) butter • 2 oz (50 g) raisins • 2 oz (50 g) pine nuts • 2 oz (50 g) chopped walnuts • salt • black peppercorns and ground pepper

Marinate the boar's flesh for 24 hours in the wine, half the vinegar, the juniper berries, bay leaves, and a few peppercorns. Remove the meat, reserving the marinade. Cut the meat into small cubes and coat with the seasoned flour. Heat some oil in a pan, add the meat, and brown on all sides. Add the vegetables and cook until they are tender, then moisten with a little stock. Simmer gently adding the marinade a little at a time. Meanwhile soak the *panforte* and *cavallucci* in the stock until they crumble, add the chocolate, butter, dried fruit, nuts, and the rest of the vinegar. When the boar is cooked, remove it from the pan and keep warm. Add the *panforte* mixture to the cooking juices and heat, stirring until it forms a thick, smooth sauce. Pour the sauce over the meat and serve.

An estate in Montalcino

🐂 Franco Scarpelli

via Matteotti, 121
📞 0575 836016
⏰ Mon, Wed, Thu pm

The owner of this butcher's is an expert on Chianina beef and is guided by an innate passion for the breed. He raises and butchers mostly Chianina beef following traditional methods. He also makes his own excellent hams and sausages from local pigs. The poultry comes from nearby farms.

MONTALCINO (SI)

🍷 Azienda Agricola Altesino

località Altesino
📞 0577 806208

This is one of the very few estates to produce brandy from Brunello. It takes courage to distil a wine destined to become Brunello. All the same, in less generous years, this is a good way to obtain something different. Production is limited and the brandy is aged in barrels for a minimum of 10 years. Outstanding among the wines is the Brunello di Montalcino Alte d'Altesi, based on Sangiovese grapes with a small amount of Cabernet Sauvignon, and Quarto d'Altesi, a pure Merlot.

🍇 Tenimenti Angelini Val di Suga

località Val di Cava
📞 0577 80411 ⏰ Sat

This estate by a small lake is surrounded by vineyards. The wines made include Brunello and Rosso di Montalcino, Brunello di Montalcino Vigna Spuntali, and grappa. A fee is charged for tastings.

🍇 Banfi

Castello di Poggio alle Mura
📞 0577 840111

Extending over 7,413 acres (3,000 hectares), this estate has vineyards, olive groves, and plum trees. The 13th-century Castello di Poggio alle Mura houses the Museum of Glass and Bottles (a fee is charged). A wine shop on the estate organizes tastings for a fee. The wines include Rosso, Brunello, and Moscadello

di Montalcino, Sant'Antimo Colvecchio (Syrah), and Summus (Sangiovese, Syrah, and Cabernet Sauvignon). Among the other products on offer are an excellent oil (Banfi is part of the guild of oil-makers), grappas, plums, and honey. Two restaurants with different opening hours and price ranges complete the picture. The Taverna is open all day.

🍇 Fattoria dei Barbi

località Barbi
📞 0577 841111

Not so much a farm as a village for gourmets: this ancient hamlet southeast of Montalcino produces one of the most famous Brunello wines. Cheese and salumi are also made here. In the best years, as well as Brunello DOCG, an excellent special selection is produced: Brunello di Montalcino DOCG Vigna del Fiore. Other notable products are Rosso di Montalcino, Brigante from Sangiovese and Merlot grapes, Brusco, Grappa di Brunello, and extra-virgin olive oil.

🏛 Batignani Roberto

via Delle Caserme, 7
📞 0577 848444 ⏰ am

This family beekeeping business has honey from sunflowers, wild flowers, chestnut, and many others.

Barrels in the cellar of the Fattoria dei Barbi at Montalcino

🍇 Azienda Agricola Capanna

località Capanna, 333
📞 0577 848298

This small family-run vineyard has made a name with its Brunello di Montalcino Riserva and Rosso di Montalcino. Also available are Moscadello, Sant'Antimo, and grappa.

🍇 Tenuta Caparzo

località Caparzo
📞 0577 848390;
0577 847166 ⬛ Sat

The decision to make wine with Brunello grapes only in the best years has been rewarded by significant results, especially in the Brunello La Casa selection. Also excellent is the Rosso La Caduta and Ca' del Pazzo, from Sangiovese and Cabernet Sauvignon, a success since it was first made in 1982. Among the new generation of wines there is an outstanding Val d'Arbia Le Crete, made from Trebbiano, Malvasia, and Chardonnay.

🍇 Casanova di Neri

località Podere Fiesole
📞 0577 834455

This estate offers agriturismo-style accommodation with views over Montalcino. The wines produced include Brunello di Montalcino

Cerretalto and Tenuta Nuova, and Rosso di Montalcino. Also for sale are grappa and oil.

🍇 Fattoria del Casato

località Casato
📞 0577 849421

An integral part of Fattoria dei Barbi (see p141) until 1998, this estate, now run by Donatella Cinelli-Colombini, has become independent and is linked to the Fattoria del Colle in Trequanda (see p151), where the Rosso and Brunello di Montalcino produced here can be purchased. Its cellar will remain combined with the Barbi estate's until its own facilities are finished. The star wine is Brunello Prime Donne, made by an all-female staff.

🍇 Castello Romitorio

località Romitorio, 279
📞 0577 897220 ⬛ Sat

This estate is located in the castle belonging to artist Sandro Chia. It is worth a visit not just for the great view over the surrounding hills, but also for the park, which contains some works of art by Chia. They operate agriturismo facilities: there are two apartments at the Poggio di Sopra location, in Castelnuovo dell'Abate, and two at Molino di Sant'Antimo. Food is

COLLO RIPIENO

1¾ oz (50 g) parsley • 4 cloves garlic • 3½ oz (100 g) chicken livers • 3½ oz (100 g) breadcrumbs • 1 glass vegetable stock • 3 eggs • 3½ oz (100 g) grated pecorino • 6 chicken necks • 1 carrot, chopped • 1 stalk celery, chopped • 1 onion, chopped • 1 clove • 1 tomato, chopped • salt • pepper

Make a stuffing by chopping and mixing the parsley, garlic, chicken livers, breadcrumbs softened in the stock, eggs, and cheese. Season with salt and pepper. Clean and bone the necks and fill with the stuffing. Tie them at the ends. Make a stock with the carrot, celery, onion, clove, and tomato. Put the chicken necks in the stock and simmer for about 45 minutes. When cooked, allow to cool and serve cut into pieces with boiled potatoes and a green sauce.

supplied only if requested in advance. Among the wines made here are Romito del Romitorio, Sant'Antimo Rosso, Brunello and Rosso di Montalcino, Brio (Sangiovese). There is a fee for tastings.

🍇 La Cerbaiola

piazza Cavour, 19
📞 0577 848499

This estate produces a great Brunello and an excellent Rosso di Montalcino. The quality of the wine is very high but so, unfortunately, are the prices – without apparently discouraging the wine connoisseurs: there is always limited availability of this wine. The small amount of olive oil they produce is also excellent.

Harvesting Brunello grapes at the Tenuta Caparzo

Some of Hubert Ciacci's hives

Azienda Agricola Cerbaiona

località Cerbaiona
☎ 0577 848660

Diego Molinari, a former airline pilot, has successfully turned to the production of wines. His star wines are Brunello and Cerbaiona, based on Sangiovese grapes.

Hubert Ciacci

via Traversa dei Monti, 227a
☎ 0577 848640

Hubert Ciacci provides beekeeping of the highest quality. His great respect for the natural qualities of honey, combined with the practice of traveling to other parts of the country with the hives, has resulted in a wide variety of honeys (including bitter arbutus honey). Other delicacies on offer include jams made with honey, chestnuts preserved in honey, liqueurs, and traditional confectionery.

Another shop is located at via Ricosoli, 12 (0577 848019).

Ciacci Piccolomini d'Aragona

frazione Castelnuovo dell'Abate, via Borgo di Mezzo, 62
☎ 0577 835616

Housed in a 17th-century bishops' palace, this estate makes Sant'Antimo Fabius, Brunello di Montalcino Vigna di Pianrosso, Ateo (Sangiovese, Merlot, Cabernet Sauvignon), and Rosso di Montalcino Vigna della Fonte. Oil, grappa, and honey are also sold. Agriturismo-style accommodation is available.

Azienda Agricola Col d'Orcia

frazione Sant'Angelo in Colle
☎ 0577 808001
⬤ Sun pm

PICCHIO PACCHIO

extra-virgin olive oil
• *1 small onion, chopped*
• *3¼ lb (1.5 kg) ripe tomatoes, peeled*
• *vegetable or meat stock*
• *6 eggs • Tuscan bread, sliced • salt*

Heat the oil in a pan, add the chopped onion, and cook until softened. Add the tomatoes, lower the heat, and simmer for 30 minutes. Cover the mixture with plenty of stock. As soon as it boils, beat the eggs and add them to the soup, stirring briskly. Arrange the sliced bread in soup plates and ladle the soup on top of it. Drizzle a little extra-virgin olive oil over each dish and serve at once.

Many of the vines here carry a Brunello label and the estate's Poggio al Vento vineyard produces its finest Brunello. Equally good are the classic Brunello and Rosso di Montalcino. This estate is one of the few to produce Moscadello di Montalcino, offered in the "Vendemmia Tardiva" (late harvest) version of the Pascena selection. Olmaia, from Cabernet Sauvignon, is a "Super Tuscan." The Novello Novembrino is made from traditional Sangiovese. A member of the guild of oil-makers, Col d'Orcia also produces olive oil.

The Azienda Agricola Col d'Orcia at Montalcino

Azienda Agricola Collemattoni

località Sant'Angelo
in Colle, podere
Collemattoni, 100
☎ 0577 844127

*This family-run estate,
one of the smallest in
the area, produces
excellent Brunello and
an even finer Rosso di
Montalcino, as well as
oil and grappa.*

Costanti

località Colle
al Matrichese
☎ 0577 848195
⬤ Sat

*The vines on this estate
are carefully tended,
down to the rose bushes
planted at the ends of
the rows as a useful
indicator of any possible
disease in the vines.
The results are attractive:
the Brunello di
Montalcino is excellent
in the two versions,
regular and Riserva. Rosso
di Montalcino, Calbello,
Vermiglio, and Ardingo
are also worth trying.*

Enoteca La Fortezza

interno Fortezza
☎ 0577 849211
⬤ Mon

*Inside the fortress of
Montalcino, in what was
once the garrison tower,
there is a wine shop that,
together with the local
government, stocks
produce from all the
local producers. Hundreds
of firms are represented,
almost all wineries,
together with the few
major producers of
cheese and various
pecorini, salumi and
finocchiona, salami,
and cured ham suppliers.
The oil comes from the
few producers that
guarantee consistent
quality. There is a
charge for tasting.*

Drogheria Franci

piazzale Fortezza, 5
☎ 0577 848191

*This firm's apiary has
been one of the area's
best known for over three
generations. It has 10
types of honey, including
bitter arbutus honey,
dried fruit preserved in
honey and honey candies.
The shop has a wine section
that specializes in
Montalcino wines but also
has a pleasing selection
of other wines, not all of
them Tuscan. It also sells
various local gastronomic
specialties, with salumi
and cheeses to accompany
the wine tasting.*

Forno Lambardi

via Soccorso Saloni, 22
☎ 0577 848084
⬤ Wed pm

*On sale here are fresh
bread and traditional
cookies – ossi di morto,
morselletti, brutti e buoni,
and many others – made
from natural ingredients,
sold loose or prepackaged.*

Lisini

località Sant'Angelo in
Colle, podere Casanova
☎ 0577 844040

*Its favorable position
and the richness of the
soil make this estate one
of the finest in the area.
It produces a Brunello di
Montalcino of great body*

CAVOLO
SULLE FETTE

*2¼ lb (1 kg) black
cabbage • 12 slices of
Tuscan bread • 2 cloves
garlic • extra-virgin olive
oil • 2 tablespoons
vinegar • salt • pepper*

Wash the cabbage leaves
and remove the central
rib. Cook the leaves in
boiling water. Toast the
bread, halve the garlic
and rub the toast with
the cut surfaces. Place in
a soup tureen. When the
cabbage is cooked, put
the leaves on the bread
with a little cooking
water. Season with oil,
vinegar, salt, and pepper.

*and elegance. The Ugolaia
selection is interesting.*

Pasticceria Mariuccia

piazza del Popolo, 29
☎ 0577 849319
⬤ Mon

*Pasticceria Mariuccia
produces traditional
Montalcino cakes such
as* torta di Montalcino,
bacio di Montalcino *(a
cold dessert made from
a very old recipe), and*
pane coi santi.

Mastrojanni

frazione Castelnuovo
dell'Abate, podere
Loreto–San Pio
☎ 0577 835681 ⬤ Sat

Vineyards around Montalcino

Despite the fact that this estate is unable to satisfy the growing demand for its wine, it continues the policy of producing Brunello only in the best years. The result is an excellent Brunello, which has been appreciated for many years. The table wines combine Sangiovese and Cabernet Sauvignon grapes to make Rosso San Pio.

 Mocali

località Mocali
[0577 849485

This is a family-run estate in a panoramic location. The tastings take place in a 19th-century farmhouse. Among the wines are Rosso and Brunello di Montalcino, I Piaggioni (Sangiovese), and Moscadello di Montalcino. Grappa, brandy, and oil can also be purchased.

Osteria Osticcio

via Matteotti, 23
[0577 848271

This wine shop carries about 1,000 Tuscan, Italian, and international wines. A handful of them (usually the Tuscans) are available to be tasted, paired with Italian cheeses and salumi. Themed tastings and evenings are also organized.

Poggio Antico

località Poggio Antico
[0577 848044

The output is focused on Brunello, which in its best years achieves a notable level and also comes in a Riserva version. The estate's small wine shop contains a selection of its finest vintages, which are difficult to find even in specialty shops.

Il Poggione

località Sant'Angelo in Colle
[0577 844029
● Sat pm

The estate's best wine is definitely Brunello, but the Rosso di Montalcino is also of great interest. In addition, the estate produces Poggione (from Sangiovese) and San Leopoldo.

Talenti

frazione Sant'Angelo in Colle, località Pian di Conte
[0577 844064
● Sat pm

After years of careful selection in the vineyard, Pierluigi Talenti has created a great Brunello. There was nothing immodest in his dedication of a wine to himself: the Rosso Talenti, which is made from Sangiovese grapes combined with the

Tuscan Colorino and the French Syrah, is a great success.

Pasticceria Ticci

località Torrenieri, via Romana, 47
[0577 834146
● Thu, Sun pm

This is a great café and confectioner's with a wide range of excellent traditional cakes, including panforte *and* ciambelline *made with red Montalcino wine.*

MONTEFOLLONICO (SI)

Caseificio Putzulu

località Fattoria in Posto 1, 7
[0577 669744

Sheep are raised here and there is a dairy producing ricotta and a selection of other excellent ewe's milk cheeses which are aged for varying periods.

LESSO RIFATTO

1¼ lb (500 g) *leftover boiled meat (beef, veal, and chicken)*
• *extra-virgin olive oil* • 1 *onion, chopped*
• 1 *carrot , diced* • 1 *stalk celery, diced* • 2 oz (50 g)
pancetta, *diced* • 1 *glass red wine* • 12 oz (300 g)
tomatoes, pulped • 1 oz (30 g) *dried* porcini (cèpes)
• *salt* • *pepper*

Cut the beef and veal into slices and the chicken into strips. Heat the oil in a pan, add the onion, carrot, celery, and *pancetta* and fry gently until browned, then add the meat and wine. Add the tomatoes and season to taste with salt and pepper. Cover and simmer for 15 minutes. Meanwhile, soak the *porcini* in warm water for 15 minutes, then add to the pan. Continue to cook gently for 20 minutes. Arrange the meat on a serving dish, pour the sauce over it and serve.

MONTEPULCIANO (SI)

🍇 Avignonesi

Via di Gracciano
nel Corso, 91
📞 0578 724304
⬤ Sat

*This company has four
estates producing wine:
two at Montepulciano
and two at Cortona.
Its flagship wine is
the Vino Nobile di
Montepulciano, but
another wine that has
made a name for itself
is Desiderio, from pure
Merlot, Cabernet
Sauvignon, and Prugnolo
Gentile grapes. Other
pearls are the Vin Santo,
from white grapes, and
the Occhio di Pernice
from Prugnolo Gentile.
The careful selection of
grapes and the lengthy
aging of these dessert
wines inevitably means
that they will never be
cheap to buy. The extra-
virgin olive oil produced
by the company is also
excellent.*

🍇 Bindella

via delle Tre Berte, 10a
📞 0578 767777
⬤ Sat

*Located in the heart
of the most renowned
area for the production
of Vino Nobile, this estate
boasts a tasting room
with a splendid view.
Among the wines
produced here are Vino
Nobile di Montepulciano,
Dolce Sinfonia di
Vallocaia, Vin Santo
Colli dell'Etruria
Centrale, as well as
Rosso di Montepulciano
Fossolupaio and Vallocaia
(Prugnolo Gentile,
Cabernet Sauvignon).
The tasting (for which
there is a charge)
includes other local
products, such as oil
and grappa.*

🍇 Canneto

via dei Canneti, 14
📞 0578 757737
⬤ Sat

*This estate, which
features a modern
cellar, is located by the
Renaissance church of
San Biagio, about ⅗ mile
(1 km) from the historic
center of Montepulciano.
In production are Rosso
and Vino Nobile di
Montepulciano (also
Reserve), Vendemmia
Tardiva (Malvasia,
Trebbiano, Grechetto),
and extra-virgin olive oil.*

🍇 Le Casalte

via del Termine, 2
Sant'Albino
📞 0578 798246

*On a hill, with a view over
Cortona and the lakes of
Montepulciano and Chiusi,
is this estate housed in
a historic building. The
wines made here include
Rosso and Vino Nobile di
Montepulciano, Celius
(Chardonnay and other
white grapes), and Vin
Santo di Montepulciano.*

🍇 Fattoria del Cerro

località Acquaviva
📞 0578 767722
⬤ Sat

*This is probably the biggest
private producer of Vino
Nobile di Montepulciano.
Most of the vines, owned
by the Saiagricola group,
are reserved for the Vino
Nobile, on which the estate
is staking a lot, especially
on the Riserva, but it also
has a splendid Rosso di
Montepulciano. The white
wines are Braviolo, based
on Trebbiano, and Cerro
Bianco from Chardonnay.*

🍇 Azienda Agricola Contucci

via del Teatro, 1
📞 0578 757006

*The centuries-old cellars,
which have belonged
to the family since the
11th century, contain
large and small casks in
which the Vino Nobile
ages for the Pietra Rossa
label. Another wine
made here is Bianco
della Contessa, from
Malvasia del Chianti
and Trebbiano grapes.*

🍀 Caseificio Cugusi Silvana

strada statale per Pienza
via della Boccia, 8
📞 0578 757558

The Azienda Avignonesi at Montepulciano

ZUPPA DI LENTICCHIE CON FAGIANO

1¼ lb (500 g) lentils • 1 carrot • 1 onion, halved • 1 stalk celery, halved • 2 cloves garlic • 1 sprig of winter savory • 2 bay leaves • 1 pheasant • 4 oz (100 g) lardo (pork fat), finely sliced • 1 sprig of rosemary • 1 sprig of sage • extra-virgin olive oil • chicken stock • salt • pepper

Preheat the oven to 475°F (250°C). Put the lentils in a pan of water with the carrot, onion, celery, garlic, winter savory, bay leaves, a little oil, and salt. Cover and simmer over a moderate heat until the lentils are soft, adding more boiling water if necessary. Grease the inside of the pheasant with olive oil, tuck the sage and rosemary into the cavity, and season with salt and pepper. Lard it with the pork fat and tie with kitchen twine. Place in a greased roasting pan and roast for 30 minutes, turning and basting with the cooking juices from time to time. Remove the fat, return the pheasant to the oven, baste with the juices, and cook until golden. Remove the pheasant and chop the flesh. Deglaze the pan juices with a little oil and chicken stock. Drain the lentils, remove the vegetables, garlic, and bay leaves. Return the meat to the pan with the lentils. Warm through and serve.

Outstanding pecorino cheeses matured for varying periods, including the dark kind typical of Pienza, can be found at this dairy farm. The fresh pecorino is delectable, almost juicy in texture, somewhere between a caciotta and a mozzarella. Also unusual are the more mature types for grating which are always mellow and never dry. There are also excellent fresh cheeses with arugula or walnuts.

Dei

via di Martiena, 35
[📞] 0578 716878

At this small property, very respectable Vino Nobile di Montepulciano and Rosso di Montepulciano wines have been created. Recently the estate has introduced French vines which are used in its Sancta Catharina, a red made from Syrah, Cabernet Sauvignon, and Petit Verdot. Their Bianco di Martiena (from Malvasia, Grechetto, and Trebbiano) is also worth trying.

🍷 Il Frantoio di Montepulciano

piazza Pasquino
[📞] 0578 758732
[●] Wed pm

This is a cooperative olive mill producing fine extra-virgin olive oil, especially the product denominated IGP Toscano, which is made exclusively in this area from the output of the cooperative's 600 members.

🍇 Cantina Nottola

strada statale, 326, località Bivio di Nottola
[📞] 0578 707060
[●] Sat pm

In a panoramic spot, in a valley adjacent to Montepulciano, is this

estate. It features a cellar with a vaulted ceiling and wooden beams inspired by early 20th-century models. The Rosso and Vino Nobile di Montepulciano Vigna del Fattore, oil, and grappa are all worth trying. It is possible to rent apartments in a historic villa nearby.

🍇 Enoteca Oinochoè

via Voltaia del Corso, 82
[📞] 0578 757524
[●] Wed (Nov–May)

A wide range of the best Tuscan wines is sold in this wine shop, with most estates of the Montepulciano area represented. In addition to regional products, including dessert wines such as Moscadello and Vin Santo, there are classics from Piedmont, Friuli, the Veneto, and Lombardy. Tuscan oils and vinegars are also sold.

🍇 Poliziano

frazione Montepulciano Stazione, via Fontago, 1
[📞] 0578 738171 [●] Sat

This important estate lies between Gracciano and Montepulciano Stazione. Its aging cellar has a large room for barriques and there is also a new, technologically advanced fermentation cellar. There is a charge for visits and tastings. Try the Rosso and Vino Nobile di Montepulciano, and the excellent Vino Nobile di Montepulciano Asinone.

The winery at Fattoria Poliziano

The countryside around Pienza

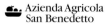

Romeo – Viticoltore in Montepulciano

strada statale, 326,
località Nottola,
podere Corsica, 25
☎ 0578 708599
⬤ Sat

Romeo's estate is located at the heart of the vineyards of Vino Nobile di Montepulciano. The cellar in Nottola is where vinification and aging happen; fining and selling take place in another cellar in the historic center. Among the products on sale are Rosso and Vino Nobile di Montepulciano, Vino Nobile di Montepulciano Riserva dei Mandorli, Lipitiresco (Prugnolo Gentile, Mammolo), Vin Santo, and oil.

Azienda Agricola San Benedetto

strada per
Chianciano, 25
☎ 0578 757649

This estate, set amid very beautiful hills, sells fruit (peaches, apricots, quinces, and grapes) and organically grown plums and figs, natural jams (some made without additional sugar), and wild flower honey.

Terra Toscana

via Ricci, 14a
☎ 0578 757708

Situated just 55 yards (50 meters) from Piazza Grande is this winery, representing 36 estates in the Montepulciano area. Many of them are essentially vineyards making only wine and grappa. The others have been chosen for the traditional quality of their regional produce: organically produced pasta, honey, truffles, and mushrooms from Monte Amiata, and excellent pecorino cheese. There is a charge for tastings.

Vecchia Cantina di Montepulciano

via Provinciale, 7
☎ 0578 716092

This winery is responsible for over half the volume of wine produced in the area. The extent of the vineyards, spread over a wide area, has made it possible to make some interesting wines, five or six altogether, that form a line of products marketed under the Cantina del Redi label. They include Vino Nobile and Rosso di Montepulciano, and a Vin Santo, while the greatest success of the Vecchia Cantina trademark is its Vino Nobile di Montepulciano.

MONTERONI D'ARBIA (SI)

Azienda Agricola Santa Margherita

località Ville di Corsano
via del Colle, 711
☎ 0577 377101

This farm makes fresh and matured goat's milk cheese, packaged French-style in various forms. The cheeses are produced organically, and some of them are flavored with fresh herbs.

MURLO (SI)

Apicoltura Quercioli Sonia

piazza Morviducci,
frazione Vescovado
☎ 0577 814255

All the local Sienese varieties of honey, including wild flower, arbutus, and sunflower are produced by this apiarist.

SUGO DI CHIOCCIOLE (SNAILS IN SAUCE)

extra-virgin olive oil • 1 stalk celery, sliced • 1 carrot, chopped • 1 onion, chopped • 2 cloves garlic, sliced • 1 chile, deseeded and chopped • sprig of rosemary • 1¼ lb (500 g) snails, prepared for cooking, boiled and removed from shells • 3½ lb (1.5 kg) tomatoes, peeled • ¾ lb (300 g) ground beef • chopped parsley • white wine • vegetable stock • salt

Heat some oil in a pan, add the vegetables, chile, garlic, and rosemary, then add the beef and fry until the meat is browned. Add the tomatoes and salt and cook for 30 minutes. Add the snails and parsley and cook for another hour, adding a little wine and stock from time to time.

PIENZA (SI)

 La Cornucopia

piazza Martiri
della Libertà, 2
0578 748150
Wed (winter)

*This wine store and
gourmet shop sells all
kinds of preserves from
Tuscany and other
Italian regions. It has a
wide range of wines,
mostly Tuscan labels but
with a good selection
from other regions. There
are also grappas, mainly
Tuscan, and various
other national and
international liquors.
The store also sells a
variety of vinegars and
Italian chocolate.*

 L'Enoteca
di Ghino

via del Leone, 16
0578 748057

*Since customers coming
from abroad would be
disappointed if they
found this wine shop
closed when they arrived,
owner Ghino Poggianini
decided to live over his
shop so he could always
be on call for his
customers. Poggianini
concentrates on wine
and has over 2,000 labels,
with wines ranging in
price from a few euros
up to several hundred a
bottle. He even has fine
old wines and collectors'
items. The shop also*

*stocks a fine selection
of extra-virgin olive oils
and balsamic vinegars.*

Forno
Sacchi Danilo

via delle Mura, 16/18
0578 748545
Wed pm

*This baker and pastry cook
is renowned for Tuscan
bread and traditional
cakes, especially* ricciarelli*,
made from coarsely
ground almonds. He also
makes* ossi di morto *from
almonds and egg whites,
and other confections
based on almond paste
enriched with dried fruits
and chocolate, such as*
pinolati, pizzicotti, *and*
serpe*. Tarts and*
ciambelloni *(ring-shaped
cakes) complete the
product line.*

Caseificio Solp

località Poggio
Colombo, 40
0578 748645

Pecorino *matured for
various periods is sold
here, plus* caciotta *from
a mix of cow's and ewe's
milk, and* raviggiolo *(see
page 133) made to order.*

SAN GIOVANNI D'ASSO (SI)

 La Canonica

podere La Canonica
0577 834338

The Enoteca di Ghino at Pienza

CAVALLUCCI

*10½ oz (300 g) sugar
• 10½ oz (300 g) plain
flour • 1¾ oz (50 g)
candied orange peel
• 3½ oz (100 g) walnuts,
crushed • ½ oz (15 g)
ground aniseed • a pinch
of ground cinnamon*

Preheat the oven to
300°F (150°C). Put
the sugar in a pan
with a glass of water and
heat until it forms a
thick, clear liquid. Off
the heat, stir in the flour,
candied orange peel,
walnuts, aniseed and
cinnamon. Roll out the
dough to the thickness
of a finger. Cut into
lozenge shapes and
bake in the oven for
about 30 minutes.

*This agricultural estate
offers wine from the new
DOC Orcia and Vin
Santo, in addition to
extra-virgin olive oil,
honey, fruit, and truffles.
It is located in an old
farmhouse made of
travertine stone, with
a splendid view over
the Sienese Crete. There
are also apartments
available to rent.*

SAN QUIRICO D'ORCIA (SI)

 Macelleria
Bassi Raffaello

piazza della Libertà, 1
0577 897057
Wed pm

*Raffaello Bassi chooses
his beef from small
farms which devote
special care to the
feeding of their animals.
He sells Chianina beef
and lamb from local
farms. His other meats,
like poultry and pork,
also come from trusted
breeders. Bassi makes
a variety of* salumi*,
sausages, and hams.*

RIVOLTI CON RICOTTA

extra-virgin olive oil • 2 cloves garlic • 1 handful parsley, chopped • 1 carrot, chopped • 1 onion, chopped • 1 stalk celery, chopped • ¾ lb (300 g) ground beef • 2 fresh sausages, chopped • 4 oz (100 g) prosciutto crudo, chopped • 2 glasses white wine • 1¼ lb (500 g) peeled, plum tomatoes • 1 egg • ¾ lb (300 g) plain flour • ¾ lb (300 g) cooked spinach, chopped • 8 oz (200 g) ricotta • 4 oz (100 g) grated Parmesan cheese • ground nutmeg • salt • pepper

In a large pan, heat some oil and fry the garlic, parsley, vegetables, and meat over a moderate heat until the meat is browned. Add the wine, cook until it evaporates, then add the tomatoes. Simmer gently for about 3 hours; stir frequently. Meanwhile, beat the egg and mix with 18 fl oz (500 ml) water and the flour to make a batter. Season with salt. Warm a pan that has been lightly greased with oil. Pour in a ladle of batter and smooth out to make a pancake. Cook on both sides until golden, then remove from the pan. Repeat until all the batter is used. Stir the spinach into the pan with some oil, the ricotta, half the Parmesan, and the nutmeg. Season. Use to fill the pancakes. Arrange in an ovenproof dish, cover with the meat sauce, sprinkle with the rest of the Parmesan, and cook in the oven at 350°F (180°C) until the cheese melts.

SARTEANO (SI)

La Bottegaccia Prodotti Tipici

via di Fuori, 73
☎ 0578 267020
⏺ Wed pm

All the traditional food specialties of the area encompassed between Montalcino to the west, Montepulciano to the east, and the Sienese Crete to the north can be purchased at this grocery. In particular, it stocks a wide range of pecorino cheese.

SINALUNGA (SI)

🐂 Barbieri

via Trieste, 102
☎ 0577 678256
⏺ Wed pm

Fresh meat, prosciutti, and pork sausages all from the firm's own pigs are sold here.

🍶 Frantoio Mazzarrini

frazione Rigomagno
☎ 0577 663624

Excellent extra-virgin olive oil, typical of the Colline Senesi, is produced here.

🌾 Pa. Ri. V.

frazione Guazzino, via XXV Luglio, 4
☎ 0577 624061
⏺ Sun am

There is a retail sales point for Tuscan bread and traditional Sienese cakes at this wholesale bakery.

SOVICILLE (SI)

🍇 Poggio Salvi

località Poggio Salvi
☎ 0577 349045

This winery is located in a 13th-century hospital. It produces an excellent and good-value-for-money Chianti Colli Senesi, as well as Campo del Bosco (Sangiovese), Vin Santo, Refola (Sauvignon), Val di Merse (Trebbiano), extra-virgin olive oil, and honey.

TREQUANDA (SI)

🐓 Azienda Agricola Belsedere

località Belsedere
☎ 0577 662307

Agriturismo *facilities are available at this farm. The lamb is certified organically produced, as is the* ricotta *and* pecorino, *made by hand from fresh milk. Belsedere also has excellent* pork *and* salumi *which, though not certified organic, are produced completely naturally.*

The Fattoria del Colle in Trequanda

In addition to Tuscan prosciutto *and* spalla, *there is excellent* buristo, mortadella, soppressata, lombo, finocchiona, *and other meat specialities which can be purchased in small quantities. All the products are also sold at the Pro Loco in Piazza di Trequanda.*

🍇 Fattoria del Colle

via Torta, 7
📞 0577 662108

The remarkable vivacity of one of Italy's leading oenologists (wine-makers), Donatella Cinelli-Colombini, guarantees quality and superior hospitality on this farm with its expanding agriturismo *facilities. The recently restored Fattoria del Colle dates back to at least 800 years ago and was once a residence of the future emperor Peter Leopold of Absburg. The farm is an exemplary leader in the* agriturismo *field. It distinguishes itself for its welcoming atmosphere, for the ingenuity and imagination devoted to the entertainment (especially for children), and for its extensive range of facilities. Donatella Cinelli-Colombini is renowned for devising the Movimento Turismo del Vino, which organizes Open Cellars – days when hundreds of the leading cellars all over Italy welcome visitors like guests to a party, with tastings, guided tours, and general pageantry. The brand-new* osteria *(inn) has tastings and sells excellent extra-virgin olive oil,* pecorino *cheeses, truffles,* Chianti DOCG, *Vin Santo, a white wine from Traminer grapes, and other wines. Donatella Cinelli-Colombini's policy is to produce everything in an environmentally friendly manner.*

ZUPPA DI CECI (CHICKPEA SOUP)

10 oz (300 g) chickpeas, soaked overnight • extra-virgin olive oil • 2 cloves garlic • rosemary • 1 dessertspoon tomato purée • 10 oz (300 g) Tuscan bread • salt

Preheat the oven to 200°C (400°F). Cook the chickpeas in a pan of water until tender, then press through a sieve to purée them, adding the cooking water. In an earthenware pan, heat some oil and lightly fry the garlic, rosemary, and the tomato purée diluted in half a glass of warm water. Add the chickpeas to the pan, season with salt, and stir for some minutes to absorb the flavors. Slice the bread into croutons and brown them in the oven. Put them into soup plates and pour in the chickpea purée. Drizzle with a little olive oil and serve.

🍷 Cooperativa Agricola Il Lecceto

via della Trove
località Castelmuzio
📞 0577 665358

This cooperative brings together 65 small olive growers from the village of Trequanda and the neighboring communes who produce an extra-virgin olive oil that is very typical of this area. The olive oil can also be purchased at the Pro Loco in Piazza di Trequanda.

🌾 Il Panaio di Cinzia e Roberto Mancini

via di Diacceto, 16
📞 0577 662288
⏺ Wed pm

Traditional Tuscan bread and cakes typical of this region are sold here. The cantucci, pinolata, panforte, *and* schiacciata di Pasqua *are all well worth trying.*

🐂 Macelleria Ricci

traversa dei Monti, 4
📞 0577 662252
⏺ Mon, Tue, Wed pm; Sun (winter)

A fine butcher's shop with scrupulous hygiene methods, Macelleria Ricci is run by the Azienda Agricola Trequanda.

It sells the estate's Chianina beef. The complete cycle for producing meat from birth to butchering is covered, following traditional methods. Also on sale are pecorino *cheeses from the estate of Sorano (near Grosseto), which raises sheep and has its own dairy farm.*

FRITTATA FINTA

2¼ lb (1 kg) potatoes, cut into cubes • 1 sprig of sage • 3 cloves garlic • extra-virgin olive oil • salt

Cook the potato cubes in salted boiling water until tender. Drain the potatoes, then purée them by passing them through a vegetable mill. Chop the sage and garlic in the vegetable mill. Heat some oil in a nonstick frying pan, add the sage and garlic, and fry briefly over a gentle heat. Add the puréed potatoes, stirring constantly to blend them with the sage and garlic. Using a fork, press the mixture to shape it into a flat, compact cake. Continue cooking, carefully turning the cake over a number of times until it is golden brown on both sides. The potato cake can be eaten hot or cold.

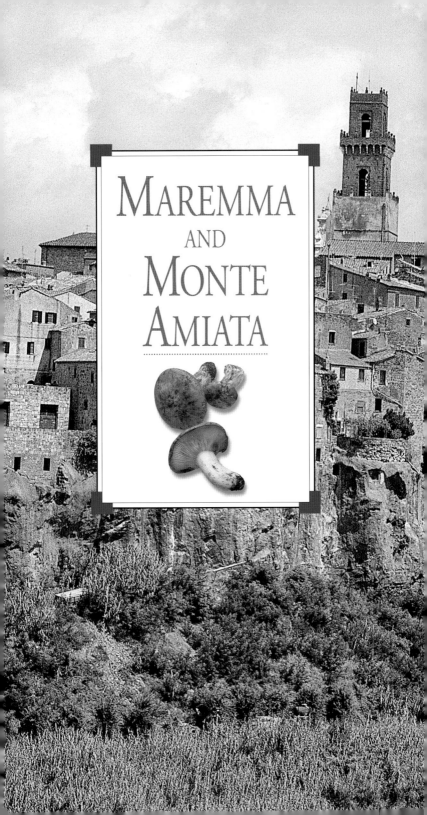

MAREMMA

AND
MONTE
AMIATA

Maremma and Monte Amiata

THE MAREMMA AND MONTE AMIATA region is the wildest part of Tuscany. Impenetrable scrub, crisscrossed by foresters following the wild boar tracks, alternates with the majestic forests of Monte Amiata and coastal pine woods studded with rosemary – especially those in the breathtaking park, Monti dell'Uccellina. The area covers the province of Grosseto, including Monte Amiata which is the highest mountain peak in southern Tuscany, and some communes from the province of Siena. For centuries human activities have been adapted to nature, which has bestowed rich gifts but which has equally been very hostile in the marshlands. Maremma cattle are raised here, looking like buffaloes with their wide horns. This is a land of strong flavors, with game a specialty on every restaurant menu and plenty of fresh fish in the fishing harbors of Porto San Stefano and Castiglione della Pescaia and the prolific lagoon of Orbetello. Old traditions endure, and it is a region of organic farming and farmhouse hospitality, in a land where there are still open spaces for men and animals.

Maremma cattle were mainly bred as draft animals, as they gave little milk or meat, though their meat tastes good. Some herds, tended by *butteri* (cowherds), graze half-wild on the edge of the stunningly beautiful Parco dell'Uccellina.

Monte Argentario, once an island, is now a promontory, rich in vegetation, with two ancient fishing ports, Porto Ercole and Porto San Stefano. It is joined to the coast by two strips of land enclosing the lagoon of Orbetello.

Massa Marittima

Roccastrao

Follonica

Montepescali

Vetulonia

Punta Ala

Castiglione della Pescaia

GROSSET

Marina di Grosseto

Ombrone

Mon dell'Uccel

Marina di Alberese

Talamone

0 kilometers   10

0 miles   10

A

Isola del Giglio

ORBETEL

Porto San Stefano

Giglio Castello

Monte Argentario

Giglio Campese

Giglio Porto

◁ **The medieval city of Pitigliano**

STAR ATTRACTIONS

- MASSA MARITTIMA (GR): Cathedral, **℃** 0566 902766
- PITIGLIANO (GR): Museo Palazzo Orsini, **℃** 0564 615568
- SOVANA (GR): Etruscan necropolis, **℃** 0564 414303
- ANSEDONIA (GR): Museo di Cosa, **℃** 0564 881421
- ALBERESE (GR): Uccellina National Park, **℃** 0564 407098

HERBS

The abundance of herbs, cultivated in most gardens and frequently found growing wild in thickets and along the coast, has influenced the cuisine of all Tuscany. In the Maremma, foods are nearly always flavored with herbs, particularly game dishes.

The wild boar, which is an indigenous variety, is the symbol of the Maremma. Its flesh is much prized. A Wild Boar Festival is held at Capalbio in September *(see pp158–9)*.

Monte Amiata's rugged sides are covered in chestnut woods rich with tasty mushrooms. The area is also famous for its fauna, especially the great variety of birds seen here.

Hare is a much-loved ingredient in many traditional Tuscan dishes. However, nowadays Italians usually have to import them as no hunters will give up the few hares they manage to shoot.

TOURIST OFFICES

- GROSSETO Viale Monterosa, 206 **℃** 0564 462611. **W** www.grosseto.turismo.toscana.it

- ORBETELLO Via Piazza della Repubblica, 1 **℃** 0564 860447. **@** croorcet@ouverture.it

- FOLLONICA Via Bicocchi, 57 **℃** 0566 41597. **@** koifon@tin.it

Places of Interest pp164–169
Restaurants pp190–191

Wines

THE MAREMMA USED to be considered a difficult area which produced rather lackluster wines. Today there is a growing appreciation of some of its wines, and the Maremma now appears to be a land whose winegrowing potential needs exploring. It is claimed, in fact, that the very first Sangiovese vines grew here, though some experts favor the Chianti area. Sangiovese is the main component of the area's reds, which may contain small amounts of local red grapes, including Canaiolo, Ciliegiolo, Malvasia Nera, Alicante, and even Montepulciano. White wines are nearly always based on Trebbiano Toscano mixed with Greco, Grechetto, Verdello, Malvasia del Chianti, and the local Ansonica. Imported vines are now grown here: Cabernet Sauvignon and Merlot for reds and Pinot, Chardonnay, Sauvignon, and Riesling for whites.

BIANCO DI PITIGLIANO

This wine is named after the picturesque town in the heart of the area of production. The wine is produced from Trebbiano Toscano plus numerous other white grapes which can make up to 50 percent of the grape quantity. It has a pleasant, slightly bitter flavor and is ideal with artichokes and savory vegetarian dishes. There are also Superiore and spumante versions.

The Morellino di Scansano Riserva is aged for at least two years and goes well with game.

MONTEREGIO DI MASSA MARITTIMA

The name refers to several different types of wine. The Bianco is made from Trebbiano Toscano with up to 50 percent of other white grapes, including Malvasia di Candia. The Vermentino has to contain at least 90 percent of the grape from which it gets its name. Both wines make good accompaniments for delicate fish and vegetable dishes. The Rosato, the Rosso Riserva, and Rosso Novello contain at least 80 percent Sangiovese, plus other red grapes. The Rosato goes well with white meats, the Rosso with red meats and game. The Vin Santo, in ordinary and Occhio di Pernice versions, is perfect with apple cakes and sweet dry cookies.

MORELLINO DI SCANSANO

The vines on the hills have the advantage of being exposed to cool breezes. Sangiovese grapes (here known as Morellino) from the hills are mixed with local grapes such as Alicante to produce this red wine. Its distinctive spicy perfume, full-bodied flavor and good acidity make the wine an ideal accompaniment for food in a spicy marinade. There is also a Reserve version.

ANSONICA COSTA DELL'ARGENTARIO

A recent appellation for a white wine from Ansonica grapes, this has subtle fruity scents. Light and fresh, it is suited to delicate fish *antipasti* or vegetable first courses. There is a sweet Passito wine, which is excellent with sweet dry cookies. The wine produced on the island of Giglio has a brinier taste and a higher alcohol content: ideal with fish baked or cooked in a sauce.

CORATA DI CINGHIALE

4 oz (100 g) lardo (lard), diced • extra-virgin olive oil • 1 onion, chopped • heart, spleen, lights, and liver of a wild boar • 1 sprig of calamint • 1 sprig of wild thyme • 1 chile, diced • 1¼ lb (600 g) ripe tomatoes, sliced • 4 fl oz (100 ml) red wine • salt

Put the *lardo* in a pan with some oil and the chopped onion. Cook until the onion is browned. Cut the heart, spleen, and lights into pieces and add to the pan with the calamint leaves, thyme, and chile. Cook until the meat is browned on all sides. Add the tomatoes and season with salt. Simmer briskly for 10 minutes. Chop the liver into small pieces and stir into the pan. Pour in the wine and cook over a brisk heat for another 5 minutes.

PARRINA ROSSO

This wine is produced from 80 percent Sangiovese with some Canaiolo and Montepulciano grapes. It goes well with white and red meats, roulades and medium-ripe cheeses.

The Riserva version is very good with traditional Tuscan roasted meats, especially roast guinea fowl.

PARRINA BIANCO

This white wine is made with at least 50 percent Trebbiano Toscano grapes, with some Malvasia del Chianti and Ansonica. It is good with *antipasti* and vegetable or egg dishes.

The Rosato version, made from at least 70 percent Sangiovese grapes, is drunk young. It is ideal with shellfish in sauce.

OTHER WINES WORTH TRYING

The **Montecucco** DOC wine was first marketed with the 1998 vintage. There are four types : **Bianco**, **Vermentino**, **Rosso**, and **Sangiovese**. The **Rosso di Sovana** DOC (Sangiovese or Ciliegiolo) was first marketed with the 1999 vintage.

WINE TYPE	GOOD VINTAGES	GOOD PRODUCERS
Red Wine		
Morellino di Scansano	98, 97, 95, 90	**Le Pupille di Magliano, Moris Farm di Massa Marittima**
Monteregio di Massa Marittima	98, 97, 90	**Massa Vecchia di Massa Marittima**
Super Tuscans *(see p130)*	98, 97, 95, 90	**Rascioni e Cecconello di Orbetello, La Stellata di Manciano, Moris Farm di Massa Marittima**

Wild Game

ONCE THE MAREMMA was so well known as "wild boar country" that the protected native Italian breed of boar was called the "maremmana." Its meat was not just an attraction in restaurants, but was commonly eaten in homes, and there was a flourishing business of making wild boar *salumi* to sell as a souvenir of the region. Wild boar was not the only game to populate the inaccessible undergrowth of this area, either – there were also deer, hares, and porcupines. The foresters, who for decades were also poachers, caught whatever came their way, cooking it over a wood or charcoal fire and creating the robust recipes that were the origins of the game cuisine of today, rich not only in flavor but also in imagination.

IL CINGHIALE (WILD BOAR)
A characteristic feature of Tuscan cooking, wild boar is now found all over Italy.

COSTOLETTE DI CINGHIALE (WILD BOAR CHOPS)
With wild boar chops, the gamey taste is not pronounced, so they appeal to those who prefer delicate flavors. They are excellent grilled and should be served rare.

SALSICCE (SAUSAGES)
Made from a mixture of finely ground boar meat and pig fat, these sausages are dried before they are eaten.

POLPA DI CINGHIALE (CUBED BOAR MEAT)
"*In scottiglia,*" a rich stew of meat in a sweet and sour sauce made with things like olives and apples, is a traditional Tuscan recipe. Leg or shoulder of wild boar, cut into cubes, is a popular ingredient for this sort of stew.

PROSCIUTTO DI CINGHIALE

Cured ham made from wild boar is drier and less fatty than the local *prosciutto* made from pigs, and is usually less salty and peppery. Traditionally, the fur was left on the skin, but EU regulations no longer allow this.

Small sausages (called cacciatorini*) are made from boar in the same way as from pork.*

SALAME DI CINGHIALE (WILD BOAR SALAME)

Salame made from lean boar's flesh and pig's fat (*pancetta* and *lardo*) is generally drier and has a stronger taste than pure pork salami.

Shoulder of venison is ideal for traditional Tuscan stews.

IL CAPRIOLO (VENISON)

Found all over Tuscany, venison was traditionally eaten only in a stew, *salmí*, or sauces for pasta. A newer idea is to grill the chops or pan-cook them with herbs, or roast a leg until rare.

OTHER GAME MEAT WORTH TRYING

Wild boar is also used to make **soppressate** (matured salami), often with chilli, **salt pork,** and **pork preserved in oil. Fallow deer** are common: they come from farms or graze in the open after being released into game reserves. The meat is usually stewed. A recent innovation is **salumi** (*salame, cacciatore, bresaoline*) made from **roe deer, red deer,** and **fallow deer.** These meats are also found preserved in oil with olives, garlic, chilli, and herbs. **Hare** is a basic ingredient of Tuscan cooking, but now, regrettably, it is impossible to find fresh hare. However, frozen ones are imported. Porcupine meat was once much prized, but it is now a protected animal.

Traditional Produce

THE LAGOON AT ORBETELLO adds wonderful variety to the foods produced in the province of Grosseto, making this region one of the richest in typical Tuscan foods. *Porcini* (cèpe mushrooms) can be found everywhere, especially on Monte Amiata, where picking them is a local industry. Amiata is one of the chestnut capitals of Italy. There is plentiful sea fish, with Porto San Stefano taking its catch mainly from the reefs called the Formiche di Grosseto and around the islands. With some of the Tuscany's largest olive presses in this area there is plenty of olive oil, and truffles, especially the March truffle *(see p18)*, are abundant along the coast.

TABLE OLIVES
Tuscany is not famed for its table olives, but the Santa Caterina variety, cured in brine while green, is sold throughout Italy. All the farmhouses still salt a small part of their olive crop, dry them in the oven to reduce the bitterness, and preserve them in oil, preferably Leccino oil. Olives are also an important ingredient in many of the traditional dishes of this area.

MAREMMA GROSSETANA OLIVE OIL
Practically the whole province makes this type of olive oil. Communes producing significant quantities are Orbetello, Capalbio, and Magliano in southern Tuscany, and Massa Marittima in the north. These are fruity oils of average intensity, with herbal and, at times, floral fragrances. They have excellent fluidity, firmly structured flavors and a pungent aftertaste, sometimes with a tinge of bitterness.

Carré (rib) of lamb is common in Tuscan restaurants. The chops are generally served in a mixed grill.

AGNELLO TOSCANO (TUSCAN LAMB)
The real Tuscan lamb comes from herds that move from pasture to pasture: they are driven from Maremma to Chianti, then Mugello and finally to Casentino. They are highly prized because the aromatic herbs they graze on flavors the meat.

WHAT TO SAMPLE
Large organically farmed estates, often offering farmhouse hospitality (*agriturismo*), make the Maremma one of the leading producers of **honey**, preserved **fruits**, and **vegetables**. The **pecorino** and **ricotta cheeses** are important, both in quantity and quality. The **table grapes** are excellent, as are the **peaches**, **pears**, and **yellow cherries** from Seggiano, and **walnuts** from Amiata. In addition to **game animals** there are numerous **wood pigeons** and **woodcock**.

ANGUILLA (EEL)
Excellent quality eels are abundant in the lagoon of Orbetello so there is no need to farm them in this area.

SCAVECCIO

2¼ lb 4 oz (1 kg) eels • flour • extra-virgin olive oil • 18 fl oz (500 ml) wine vinegar • 4 cloves garlic, sliced • 2 sprigs of rosemary • peppercorns • 1 chile, deseeded and chopped • salt

Clean the eels and cut them into smallish pieces. Roll the pieces in flour. Heat the oil, add the eel pieces, and fry until tender. Dry the pieces on absorbent paper towels and then pack them into a clean jar. Pour the vinegar into a pan, dilute it with a glass of water, and add the chile, the pepper, salt, garlic, and rosemary. Bring it to the boil, then pour it into the jar of eels, taking care to cover the pieces. Leave at room temperature for 3 or 4 days.

LE COPPIETTE (DRIED MEAT)
These are strips of meat salted, seasoned and hung up to dry on cords or slender sticks. The meat may be pork, beef, boar, mutton, donkey, or horse.

CEFALO OR MUGGINE (GRAY MULLET)
This fish is caught in the sea at the mouths of rivers and in lagoons. It is strongly associated with the resort of Orbetello in the middle of the Laguna di Orbetello, and is eaten both fresh and cured.

OTHER FISH WORTH TRYING
At Orbetello fish farms raise excellent **branzini** (sea bass) and **orate** (gilthead bream) in troughs fed either by warm subterranean waters or by seawater. **Latterini** (sand smelt), excellent fried or eaten raw with lemon and olive oil (*in carpione*), are caught in the sea, the lagoon of Orbetello, and the Lake of Chiusi. Fishing for **cieche** (elvers – eel's fry) is traditional at river mouths. **Anguilla sfumata** (smoked eel) is a Spanish dish adapted through the centuries to local tastes: the eels are marinated and then smoked. They are sautéed in extra virgin olive oil before eating. The **cefalo** (gray mullet) raised at Orbetello is smoked to a recipe of Spanish origin. For at least 1,000 years its roe has been dried and sold as **bottarga**, a custom that may be even older here than in Sardinia.

Wild Produce

LARDAIOLO ROSSO
(Hygrophorus russula)
In the late fall this white mushroom, with its burgundy-colored marbling and gills that are waxy to the touch, is very common under evergreen oak and Turkey oak. Foresters consider it one of the best mushrooms for preserving in oil.

SAMPHIRE
(Crithmum maritimum)
Samphire grows on cliffs. The narrow fleshy leaves, which have a distinct taste of iodine, are pickled before eating.

FUNGAGNELLO
(Lyophyllum fumosum)
Found in abundance in woods of broad-leaved trees, this mushroom often forms large tufts with numerous caps growing from a single base. It is much sought-after, despite the fact that it is very similar to a poisonous fungus. Firm and fleshy, it is eaten fried with garlic and parsley, in sauces and bottled in oil.

CICCIOLE
(Pleurotus eryngii and Pleurotus ferulae)
These winter mushrooms grow underneath eryngo and giant fennel. Widespread in Puglia, Sicily, and Sardinia, where they are the most common mushrooms, they are well-known to the foresters of Tuscany, who usually eat them grilled.

ACQUACOTTA CON I FUNGHI

extra-virgin olive oil • 2 cloves garlic, chopped • 2 stalks celery, sliced • 1¼ lb (600 g) mixed mushrooms, sliced • 14 oz (400 g) tomatoes, chopped • 1 small piece of chile, chopped • 1¾ pints (1 liter) boiling water • 12 slices Tuscan bread • 6 eggs • grated mature pecorino • salt

Heat some oil in a pan and fry the garlic and celery until soft. Leave to cool, then add the mushrooms, and season with salt. Return the pan to the heat and cook until the mushrooms have released their water and it has evaporated. Add the tomatoes and chile. Cook for 20 minutes. Pour in the boiling water and simmer for 10 minutes. Toast the bread and put it in a pan with the eggs and *pecorino*. Pour the boiling soup over them and serve.

ARISTA DI MAIALE ARROSTO

2¼ lb (1 kg) chine of pork • 2 cloves garlic, sliced • rosemary • fennel seeds • extra-virgin olive oil • salt • pepper

Make incisions in the meat, especially near the bone, and insert garlic, fennel seeds, and rosemary leaves. Tie sprigs of rosemary around the part opposite the bone. Season with salt and pepper and smear with oil. Leave for several hours. Preheat the oven to 325°F (160°C). Put the meat in a greased roasting pan containing a little water. Cook for about 1½ hours, turning frequently and basting with the juices.

CIAVARDELLO
(Sorbus torminalis)
The fruits of this tree are called sorbs. Smaller and less well-known than those of the domestic tree, they ripen on the plant and can be picked and eaten from the tree. They are excellent for making gelatin desserts and liqueurs. They were one of the ingredients of some ancient Celtic beverages.

CASTAGNOLO
(Tricholoma acerbum)
In the fall this mushroom can be found in the thick undergrowth and the chestnut woods of Monte Amiata. It has a distinctive yellowish cap with a flanged edge always turned downward. Tasting of unripe fruit, it is much in demand for preserving in oil.

RAMERINO (ROSEMARY)
(Rosmarinus officinalis)
Parts of the coastal scrub are overrun with wild rosemary, loved for its heady scent and robust flavor.

OVOLO BIANCO
(Amanita ovoidea)
Among the sand dunes and pine woods by the sea you can find this mushroom, which looks a large white ball. When it opens it turns into a sturdy white mushroom with a large bulb at the base of the stalk and a ring with the texture of butter. It is good fried with garlic and parsley. Always check with an expert before eating, as the genus includes some very poisonous species.

Places of Interest

THERE IS MUCH to explore in the wild Maremma region: great areas of woodland separate the villages and conceal farms of different sizes, often offering unusual gastronomic delights. The following establishments are all tried and tested, but if visiting the region you will probably be able to make other exciting discoveries of your own. Look out for handwritten notices offering agricultural produce. In this ideal setting, there is an increasing number of small properties run by enthusiasts of organic farming who breed cattle in the traditional way.

ALBINIA (GR)

 Tenuta La Parrina

località La Parrina
☎ 0564 862636

This farm produces a wide range of goods. Wine is an essential part of it, with the various types of Parrina including an enjoyable Bianco Podere Tinaro and Rosso Riserva. Among the other wines, there is an interesting Ansonica Costa dell'Argentario. The olive oil, honey, and cheese are very good. The farm has recently added agriturismo to its attractions.

Azienda Bioagricola La Selva

località San Donato
☎ 0564 885669
● Tue, Thu, Fri (winter)

Situated near the sea, this estate has agriturismo facilities and sells fresh vegetables, especially tomatoes, various kinds of preserves, and both classic sauces and a modern, creative range.

ARCIDOSSO (GR)

Agriturismo Sorripe

frazione Montelaterone
☎ 0564 964186

Agriturismo facilities with a restaurant are available at this estate. It produces and sells fresh and dried chestnuts, chestnut flour, and extra-virgin olive oil.

CASTEL DEL PIANO – MONTENERO D'ORCIA (GR)

Perazzeta

via Grandi
☎ 0564 954065

The farmhouse of the Tenuta La Parrina at Albinia

CALDARO

extra-virgin olive oil
• 1 onion, chopped •
1 chile, chopped • 1 glass white wine • ½–¾ lb
(250 g) tomatoes, peeled
• ¾ lb (300 g) octopus, ready prepared, rinsed, and cut into pieces • ¾ lb (300 g) squid, cleaned and sliced • 2 scorpion fish • 1 John Dory •
1 weever • 1 gurnard
• 1 sea bream • a few cockles • 6 shrimps •
¾ lb (300 g) sliced conger eel • ¾ lb (300 g) sliced moray eel • 1 stale loaf of bread • 2 cloves garlic, halved • chopped fresh parsley • salt

Heat some oil in a large pan, add the onion and chile, and cook until the onion has browned. Add the octopus and squid and cook until nearly tender. Stir in the wine, tomatoes, and a little water, cook briefly, then add the other fish and season with salt. Slice the bread and rub the slices with the garlic. Arrange the bread in soup plates. As soon as the soup is fairly thick, pour it over the bread slices to serve.

Located in the pretty village square, this estate offers extra-virgin olive oil, grappa, and various wines bearing the Montecucco DOC label. Free tastings with snacks are available.

CASTIGLIONE DELLA PESCAIA (GR)

Enoteca Castiglionese di Luciano Lenzi

piazza Orsini, 18
☎ 0564 933572
● Tue, Wed pm (winter)

A broad, carefully chosen range of the best Tuscan DOC and DOCG wines, including 200 types of Chianti, 70 of Brunello, and 20 of Vino Nobile can be found here. Practically all the producers of Bolgheri are represented, plus other significant Italian wines. There are also honey and local preserves in oil, and a selection of carefully chosen varieties of olive oil.

FOLLONICA (GR)

🍇 Ilia Enogastronomia

via Bicocchi, 83/85
📞 0566 40093
⏺ Wed pm

Traditional rustic soups, tortelloni maremmani, *and other stuffed pasta dishes are the specialities of this well-known delicatessen. It also offers a wide variety of Tuscan wines and liquors. The store has an interesting selection of its own fresh and preserved produce and some imported goods. Recently it has opened a wine-tasting room.*

🥫 Massai Drogheria e Pizzicheria

via Roma, 35
📞 0566 263269

This food shop has been in the same family certainly since 1867, when – as the proprietor likes to say – "round here it was all a swamp and the people lived in houses on stilts." Then, as now, it made its own classic Tuscan cakes and the recipes have not changed. Eugenio Massai selects the very best of the region's wines and foods. The delicatessen offers specialties made only from fresh produce and only to order.

 Pescheria Pallino

Mercato coperto di piazza XXIV Maggio
📞 0566 40322
⏺ Sat pm

Cellar of the Azienda Agricola Val delle Rose

This fish shop sells fresh fish from the nearby ports of Argentario and Castiglione della Pescaia as well as from its own fish farms.

GROSSETO

🐓 Fattoria Le Pupille

località Piagge del Maiano, Istia d'Ombrone
📞 0564 409517
⏺ Sat

The policy of this estate is research and innovation without neglecting the area's classic wine, Morellino di Scansano, *also produced in a Riserva version. One of their innovations is* Saffredi *(from Cabernet Sauvignon, Merlot, and Alicante). The estate's other produce includes various blends of extra-virgin olive oil and preserves bottled in the estate's own oil under the "Solo Maremma" brand name.*

🏛 Apicoltura Rossi

viale Caravaggio, 62
📞 0564 20459

A most original fragrant blackthorn honey is one of kinds of honey produced here. There are honey confectioneries in various flavors, including pine buds and woodland fruits. Another branch is located in via Tripoli.

🐓 Azienda Agricola La Tartaruga-Motta

località Banditella di Alberese
📞 0564 405105

The estate's main wine is Morellino di Scansano, *also available in a Riserva version. The other wines are based on local vines:* Giove, *a red made from Ciliegiolo grapes alone; and white* Tartaruga *from Trebbiano and Ansonica with a little Chardonnay. Its honey, made from blackthorn, sunflowers, and chestnut trees, is delicious.*

TOTANI RIPIENI

1 loaf of bread • white wine • extra-virgin olive oil • 1 egg • 6 squid, cleaned • fresh thyme leaves • fresh parsley • 1 onion • 2 cloves garlic • 1 chile • salt • pepper

Preheat the oven to 375°F (190°C). Mix a little wine and oil with the egg and season with salt and pepper, then soak the bread in it. Cut off the squid tentacles and chop together with the vegetables and herbs. Mix with the bread and use to stuff the squid. Close the opening with wooden toothpicks. Arrange in a dish, pour over a little more oil and wine, and bake for 20 minutes. Cool, then slice to serve.

A country estate in Maremma

🍇 Azienda Agricola Val delle Rose

località Poggio La Mozza
☎ 0564 409062
● Sat

This estate has been taken over by the Cecchi family, which has widened the production line with wines from other parts of Tuscany. In this case they have added Morellino di Scansano, both regular and Riserva. The wine tastings are accompanied by snacks.

MAGLIANO IN TOSCANA (GR)

🍇 Azienda Agricola Mantellassi

località Banditaccia
☎ 0564 592037

The very best wines here are Morellino di Scansano Riserva and Riserva Le Sentinelle. Also worth noting is the red Querciolaia, from Alicante grapes.

MANCIANO (GR)

🔻 Caseificio Sociale

località Piano di Cirignano, podere Fedeletto
☎ 0564 160941
● pm daily

Here you can find pecorino at various degrees of maturity from the Maremma's biggest cheese dairy.

🍇 Azienda Agricola La Stellata

via Fornacina, 18
☎ 0564 620190

Careful selection of the grapes guides the limited output of this small estate, which boasts one of the finest whites of the region, the Bianco di Pitigliano Lunaia. Also interesting is the Lunaia Rosso from Sangiovese, Ciliegiolo, and Montepulciano d'Abruzzo, as well as the Grappa Lunaia, distilled from the leftovers after white grapes have been pressed. Its agriturismo facilities include accommodation in apartments.

MANCIANO– MONTEMERANO (GR)

🍇 Enoteca Perbacco

via della Chiesa, 8
☎ 0564 602817
● Wed, Thu am

This wine shop is the sales point for the renowned Caino restaurant next door. It stocks all the wines that appear on the restaurant's very fine wine list, with about 900 labels and ample space devoted to Tuscany. Also for sale are cakes made in the restaurant kitchens, pickles and preserves in oil, coffees, and extra-virgin olive oil.

MASSA MARITTIMA (GR)

🍇 Azienda Agricola Massa Vecchia

località Rocche Podere Fornace
☎ 0566 904144

This estate has two lines of production: one is innovative, embodied in La Fonte di Pietrarsa, from Cabernet Sauvignon; the other uses traditional vines for Le Veglie di Neri from Aleatico and a good Terziere from Alicante. Wholemeal flour from an ancient local variety of grain is also produced.

SCOTTIGLIA (MEAT AND TOMATO STEW)

*extra-virgin olive oil • 3 stalks celery, chopped • 3 carrots, chopped • 2 onions, chopped • 3 cloves garlic, chopped
¾ lb (1.5 kg) mixed meat (chicken, duck, rabbit, pigeon, lamb), cut into large pieces
• 14 oz (500 g) tomatoes • 18 fl oz (500 ml) red wine • 1 fresh chile, chopped • salt*

Heat some oil in a pan, add the celery, carrots, onions, and garlic, and fry lightly. Add the meat and fry until browned. Stir in the tomatoes, wine, chile, and salt. Cover the pan and simmer until the meat is tender, adding hot water if it becomes too dry.

BUGLIONE

3¹/₄ lb (1.5 kg) mixed cuts of lamb (such as leg, shoulder, and loin), cut into pieces • 1 onion, chopped • 2 cloves garlic, chopped • 1 fresh chile, chopped • 1 sprig of rosemary, chopped • 1 glass Chianti • 1¹/₄ lb (600 g) peeled, plum tomatoes • 1 loaf of homemade bread • extra-virgin olive oil • salt • pepper

Put the meat in a pan with some oil and the chopped onion, garlic, chile, and rosemary. Brown the meat on all sides, then add the wine and cook until it evaporates. Add the tomatoes and dilute with a little hot water as the mixture cooks. When the meat is cooked, slice the bread and toast it. Dip the slices in the sauce and place them in a tureen. Pour the meat over them and serve.

Azienda Agraria Tesorino

località Valpiana
☎ 0566 55606

This farm's main product is an excellent, traditional extra-virgin olive oil. For tourists using the agriturismo facilities, there is no restaurant, only accommodation in houses and apartments and vegetables in season.

MONTENERO D'ORCIA (GR)

Frantoio Franci

via Grandi, 5
☎ 0564 954000

This olive mill produces a wide range of oils: a light, fruity oil for fish and salads; medium fruity oil for all uses; and Villa Magra, the estate's own blend, which is intensely fruity and ideal for typical Tuscan dishes. This last one comes only from the Montenero and Montalcino olive groves. Tuscan wines are available by the glass at the wine bar.

MONTEPESCALI SCALO (GR)

OLMA – Collegio Toscano Olivicoltori

località Madonnino, 3
☎ 0564 329090
Sat pm

This mill presses the olives from its 1,014 member estates in the Maremma. The Madonnino, an excellent, intensely fruity oil with a distinctive bitter tinge, is bottled here.

MONTEROTONDO (GR)

Suveraia

località Campopetroso
☎ 050 564428;
335 6211060

Situated on a hill, with sweeping views over vineyards and olive groves, this recently restored estate has maintained an older cellar with barriques for aging. The products include Monteregio di Massa Marittima Bacucco, Suveraia Rosso and Bianco, and extra-virgin olive oil. There is a charge for tastings.

ORBETELLO (GR)

Covitto Alfredo

via Volontari
del Sangue, 15
☎ 0564 862632
Sun pm

Excellent fresh fish from the Tuscan sea and the lagoon, purchased daily at local markets, is on sale here.

Danei

via Bolgia, 53
☎ 0564 863935

This family-run estate is beautifully located, offering views over the lagoon of Orbetello. Danei also owns Ansonica vineyards on the Island of Giglio. The wines produced include Morellino di Scansano and Vermentino. Also available are grappa, limoncino, and amaro.

The Azienda Agraria Tesorino at Massa Marittima

SPAGHETTI ALL'AMMIRAGLIA

4½ lb (2 kg) mussels, scrubbed • 1¼ lb (600 g) spaghetti • extra-virgin olive oil • 2 cloves garlic, chopped • ¾ lb (300 g) ripe tomatoes, sliced into strips • ½ fresh chile, deseeded and chopped • 1 oz (25 g) chopped fresh parsley • salt

Put the mussels in a pan with some water, cover and cook until they all open. Remove the mussels from their shells and strain the water. Cook the pasta. Meanwhile, heat plenty of oil in a large pan and fry the garlic. Add the tomatoes, chile, parsley, and ½ glass of the mussel water. Drain the spaghetti and add to the pan with the mussels plus more of the water. Sauté briskly, stirring.

✼ Pasticceria Ferrini

via Carducci, 8/10
☎ 0564 867265
● Tue

Rita Ferrini continues the family tradition in this quality patisserie, which sells classic fresh cakes and pastries, including fruit parcels, apple tarts, and ricotta cakes. Ice creams are also sold.

🐟 Orbetello Pesca Lagunare

via Leopardi, 9
☎ 0564 860288
● Sat pm

Fresh fish from both sea and lagoon is available here, as well as various preserved delicacies, like bottarga *(gray mullet roe), smoked fillets of gray mullet, and smoked eel.*

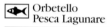 Azienda Agricola Rascioni e Cecconello

località Poggio Sugherino
☎ 0564 885642

The estate's owners deserve praise for bringing out the best in two traditional Tuscan vines: Sangiovese (Poggio Capitana) and Ciliegiolo (Poggio Ciliegio). A recent innovation is Ildono (Sangiovese and Ciliegiolo).

PAGANICO (GR)

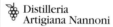 Distilleria Artigiana Nannoni

Fattoria Aratrice
☎ 0564 905204
● Sat pm

This distillery works for outside customers and

---

also specializes in making its own grappa from Fragolino, a strawberry-scented grape. However, its most appealing products are fruit vinegars (plum, woodland berries, pear, orange) matured in small oak casks with the addition of small amounts of a distillate of the same fruit and beech shavings.

PITIGLIANO (GR)

 Cantina Cooperativa di Pitigliano

via Nicola Ciacci, 974
☎ 0564 616133

This cooperative winery has about 700 members producing the grapes for the Bianco di Pitigliano and Duropersico, a white from an ancient local vine. It also makes a kosher wine for Jewish communities.

🐂 Macelleria Polidori

via Roma, 139
☎ 0564 616108
● Wed pm

Fresh local meats are sold here, as well as their own salumi – the one made from wild boar is very popular. Other specialties include dried boar's meat (coppiette), *which is*

The Castle of Montepò near Scansano

called "carne secca" here; schiacciata, *also from boar; and turkey ham, a specialty of Jewish origin.*

ROCCALBEGNA (GR)

Tistarelli

Aia della Colonna, località Santa Caterina
[0564 986110

This organic farm raises Maremma cattle, sheep, and Cinta Senese pigs. It is located on the slopes of Monte Amiata, and includes a beautiful forteto, *that is, an area of maquis devoted to the replenishment of the number of game birds.* Agriturismo *and B&B accommodation are available; food is supplied only when requested in advance. Among the products on sale are* salumi *from Cinta pork, fresh Maremmana beef (minimum purchase 110 lb/50 kg), and fresh lamb (this needs to be booked ahead). Homemade cakes are also available.*

SATURNIA (GR)

Macelleria Vito Passalacqua

via Ciacci, 4
[0564 601269
[Mon–Thu only am; Fri, Sat all day

This butcher's shop sells high quality beef and lamb exclusively from local breeders. The firm's own hams and salumi *are also extremely good.*

SCANSANO (GR)

Fratelli Andreini

frazione Poggioferro, via Provinciale
[0564 511067

POLLO ALLA CACCIATORA (HUNTER'S CHICKEN)

extra-virgin olive oil • 2 onions, chopped • 3 cloves garlic, chopped • 3 spring chickens, each cut into 8 pieces • 1 glass white wine • 10 oz (300 g) tomatoes, peeled • chopped fresh chile to taste • salt

Heat the oil in a pan and lightly fry the onions and garlic. Add the chicken and brown on all sides. Pour in the wine and cook until it evaporates, then add the tomatoes, chile, and salt. Simmer until the chicken is cooked, adding hot water if the sauce starts to dry out.

The Mignola extra virgin olive oil, exclusively from local olive groves, is an excellent oil with a medium fruity bouquet, fairly versatile and well suited to all local dishes.

Castello di Montepò

località Pancole
[0564 580326 ● Sat

The winery is set in a 16th-century castle perched on an imposingly rugged hill top and surrounded by vines. The estate has been actively producing wine only since the 1995 vintage. It immediately made its name due to the quality of its Morellino di Scansano and Schidione Oro Millennio. It also produces fine meat from its select breed of Apennine sheep.

Erik Banti

località Fosso dei Molini
[0564 508006
● Sat (winter)

This is one of the leading producers of Morellino di Scansano in the Ciabatta, a wine of excellent texture. The Aquilaia '95, made from Alicante and Morellino grapes, is also of interest.

SEMPRONIANO (GR)

Flamini Flaviano

via Toscana, 12
[0564 986346
● Wed pm

This patisserie uses only natural ingredients for its products. Also for sale here are bread and a savoury cookie typical of the area. It is made with extra-virgin olive oil and enriched with eggs.

SORANO (GR)

Azienda Agricola Sassotondo

località Pian di Conati, 52
[0564 614218

Set amid meadows and attractive woods, this organically farmed estate offers agriturismo with bedrooms and a shared kitchen. It is a new wine producer (its first wine was the 1997 vintage), but already it guarantees a product of good quality. The underground cellar, hewn out of tufa, holds a Bianco di Pitigliano, a Rosso Franze (Sangiovese) matured in barriques, *and a Rosso which, since the 1999 vintage, qualifies for the new DOC Rosso di Sovana label. The estate also produces good oil.*

TRAVELERS' NEEDS

Restaurants

THE ADDRESSES THAT FOLLOW include the most celebrated restaurants in the region, as well as less well-known ones that are recommended for their careful presentation of the region's cuisine and its wines, in keeping with the philosophy of a gourmet guide. The list is based on such factors as the quality of the food and wine in relation to the kind of restaurant, the general standard of the food, and the exclusivity of the produce or the setting. For the price guide, ©, see the inside back cover. The following criteria in each restaurant have been rated on a scale of 1 to 5.

Cellar: variety, quality, and originality of the wine list.
Comfort: level of service, space between tables, the view, location, ease of parking, standard and cleanliness of the restrooms.
Tradition: conformity to local traditions and skill in choosing local ingredients.
Q/P: quality:price ratio (value for money).
○ **Cooking pot:** a special merit for restaurants offering classic regional dishes cooked to perfection, and for the quality of the preparation and faithfulness to local traditions.
Ⓖ **Gourmet rosette:** a special merit mark for the quality of the cuisine, character of the dishes (authentically Italian), courteous staff, and good service.

FLORENCE, AREZZO AND CASENTINO

ANGHIARI (AR)

Locanda Castello di Sorci

località San Lorenzo
☎ 0575 789066
● Mon. ©

This restaurant is run by Primetto, a friend of various well-known people, such as the political cartoonist Forattini, who drew the amusing wine labels. It is a must if you want to eat well and spend little. The tagliatelle is splendid, cut from enormous sheets of dough worked by the skillful chefs in a kitchen in full view of the customers.

CELLAR	●				
COMFORT	●				
TRADITION	●	●	●	●	●
Q/P	●	●	●	●	●

AREZZO

Antica Osteria L'Agania   ○

via Mazzini, 10
☎ 0575 295381
● Mon. ©

Home-style cooking covering all the regional traditions, with the emphasis on game, can be found at this restaurant in the center of Tuscany (don't miss the grifi con polenta*). The restaurant shows great flair in its use of wild herbs and the host is a great connoisseur of mushrooms (available from spring to winter).*

CELLAR	●	●			
COMFORT	●	●			
TRADITION	●	●	●	●	●
Q/P	●	●	●	●	

Il Saraceno

via Mazzini, 6a
☎ 0575 27644
● Wed. ©

You can enjoy authentic Arezzo cuisine at this small rustic restaurant. There is genuine Chianina beef, dishes of the local pork, game, mushrooms, and classic soups. Everything is made on the premises. The cellar has a fascinating selection of all the best Tuscan wines.

CELLAR	●	●	●		
COMFORT	●	●	●		
TRADITION	●	●	●	●	●
Q/P	●	●	●	●	

BADIA TEDALDA (AR)

L'Erbhosteria del Castello

frazione Rofelle
☎ 0575 714017
● Wed. ©

This charming trattoria is in a village high in the Apennines between Tuscany and Emilia Romagna. Its specialties are mushrooms and truffles and dishes based on wild herbs, such as omelettes with borage, or pastry cakes with alpine yarrow or thyme. There are good first and second courses of game and excellent beef from local pastures. The desserts are homemade, and there are unusual wild herb and fruit liqueurs.

CELLAR	●	●			
COMFORT	●	●	●		
TRADITION	●	●	●	●	●
Q/P	●	●	●		

Sottobosco

località Svolta del Podere
☎ 0575 714031
● Wed. ©©

This restaurant is located on the Apennines between Tuscany and Emilia

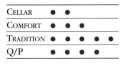

◁ **The interior of La Locanda at Volpaia near Radda in Chianti**

Romagna, at an altitude of over 2,624 ft (800 m). It features simple, rustic décor and cooking, with numerous dishes based on porcini *mushrooms* and truffles, white or black according to the season. Also on the menu are fresh boar and deer meat and guaranteed Chianina beef. The meats that constitute the mixed roast are also from local animals. A large section of the menu is devoted to fresh pasta dishes, while the dessert section includes only one (excellent) house specialty.

CELLAR	●	●			
COMFORT	●	●	●		
TRADITION	●	●	●	●	
Q/P	●	●	●	●	

BORGO SAN LORENZO (FI)

Ristorante degli Artisti

piazza Romagnoli, 1
055 8457707
Wed. €€

Here, in an elegant late 19th-century ambience, Tuscan dishes feature on the richly traditional menu. There is Chianina beef from Cecchini and Cinta Senese pork from Massanera. Note the tortelli di patate al ragù, *a specialty of the Mugello. All the food is prepared on the premises.*

CELLAR	●	●		
COMFORT	●	●	●	
TRADITION	●	●	●	●
Q/P	●	●	●	

CAPOLONA (AR)

Acquamatta

piazza della Vittoria, 13
0575 420999
Sun, Mon.
€€€€

This restaurant is run by three friends, all of them chefs. After working abroad, they have returned to Tuscany with a menu that has an international touch, but that relies on the typical products of the Casentino and Tuscany and reinterprets them in a new way. This traditional-looking establishment facing the Arno river boasts a good fish menu. In terms of meat, the most popular are pigeon, duck, and Chianina beef. Everything is prepared on the spot, from first-class ingredients. They also have themed evenings, the most entertaining of which are the one devoted to cherries (in spring) and the one based on boiled meats (in winter). The interesting wine list contains over 700 labels.

CELLAR	●	●	●	●	●
COMFORT	●	●	●	●	
TRADITION	●	●	●		
Q/P	●	●	●		

CAPRESE MICHELANGELO (AR)

Buca di Michelangelo

via Roma, 51
0575 793921
Thu.
€

Real Tuscan mountain cuisine – unpretentious but with all the authentic flavors – is offered at this simple restaurant. The desserts merit a special mention: they are very simple, but utterly delicious. The restaurant offers accommodation in a number of hotel rooms.

CELLAR	●	●			
COMFORT	●	●			
TRADITION	●	●	●	●	
Q/P	●	●	●		

CARMIGNANO (PO)

Biagio Pignatta

località Artimino
via Papa Giovanni XXIII
055 8718086
Wed, Thu midday.
€€€

Fairly traditional Tuscan cooking is served at this restaurant, with the meat grilled over a wood fire. It also serves some fish dishes. The fresh pasta and delicious pastries are all made on the premises. The restaurant's wine list is good and fairly comprehensive, with a careful selection of local vintages from which to choose.

CELLAR	●	●	●	
COMFORT	●	●	●	
TRADITION	●	●	●	
Q/P	●	●	●	

Da Delfina

località Artimino
via della Chiesa, 1
055 8718074
Mon, Sun eve.
€€€€

This restaurant offers traditional Tuscan cuisine with some occasional variations on the basic theme. The classic dishes are all here, from ribollita to pigeon. It is one of the few restaurants to make real panzanella. *There are also good desserts. The wine list has a large selection of premium Carmignano wines. In the summer you can eat outside on the attractive terrace with a wonderful view over the nearby Tuscan hills.*

CELLAR	●	●	●		
COMFORT	●	●	●	●	
TRADITION	●	●	●	●	
Q/P	●	●	●	●	●

CORTONA (AR)

Tonino

piazza Garibaldi, 1
☎ 0575 630500
● Wed, Mon eve
(always open in summer).
€€€

*Elegant in Art Nouveau
style, this restaurant
serves a rich range of
antipasti, first courses of
pasta, and more or less
classic second courses. The
pasta, bread, and desserts
are all homemade.*

CELLAR	●	●	●	
COMFORT	●	●	●	●
TRADITION	●	●	●	
Q/P		●	●	●

FLORENCE

Caffè Concerto

lungarno Cristoforo
Colombo, 7
☎ 055 677377
● Sun. €€€€

*Gabriele Tarchiani's
eclectic décor and the
"Nouvelle Cuisine" here
are a distinct innovation
compared with the
traditional style found in
other restaurants in the
area. The view of the river
Arno from the veranda
alone makes a visit
worthwhile. Meat and fish
are skillfully combined
with seasonal vegetables in
a choice of dishes. Their
desserts are especially
tempting.*

CELLAR	●	●	●	●
COMFORT	●	●	●	
TRADITION	●	●	●	●
Q/P		●	●	●

Cibreo

via Andrea del Verrocchio
(corner with via dei Macci)
☎ 055 2341100
● Sun, Mon. €€€€€

*This famous, elegant
restaurant belongs to
Fabio Picchi, who is very
skillful at enhancing quite
simple, traditional Tuscan
dishes with his own
special touch (there is
no printed menu). The
wide-ranging and richly
inventive Tuscan dishes
are made on the premises
from quality ingredients.
Note the cuttlefish and
other seafood dishes.
The desserts are especially
attractive. There is an
international wine list
with plenty of Tuscan
wines. The restaurant's
annex, the Vineria del
Cibreino, is popular and
always crowded due to
its very reasonable prices
(though the cooking is
of the same standard).*

CELLAR	●	●	●	●
COMFORT	●	●	●	
TRADITION	●	●	●	●
Q/P		●	●	●

Cinghiale Bianco

borgo San Jacopo, 43 r
☎ 055 215706
● Wed. €€

*This small restaurant is
near the Ponte Vecchio on
the Arno's "rive gauche."
Try the first courses dressed
with vegetables and good
quality olive oil. The
bistecca alla fiorentina
and tagliata di manzo
are both excellent. If you
plan to go with someone
special, book the table in
the romantic niche on the
second floor.*

CELLAR	●	●		
COMFORT	●	●		
TRADITION	●	●	●	●
Q/P		●	●	●

Del Carmine　　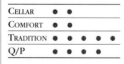

piazza del Carmine, 18
☎ 055 218601
● Sun. €

*All the classic Florentine
dishes, with occasional
detours to other Italian
provinces, are served here.
The ribollita is notable,
as are the various other
soups. There are first
courses of pasta, and
fish is served on Friday.
Don't miss the Florentine-
style tripe.*

CELLAR	●	●		
COMFORT	●	●	●	
TRADITION	●	●	●	●
Q/P		●	●	●

Il Latini

via dei Palchetti, 6 r
☎ 055 210916
● Mon. €€

*The setting here is a
typical old-fashioned
trattoria with Florentine
and Chianti dishes, such
as ribollita, pappa col
pomodoro, spelt soup,
pork, rabbit, and
Chianina steaks. Some of
the ingredients come from
local suppliers, and the
wine and oil come from
the owners' estate. The
wine list has a selection
of good Tuscan labels,
and there is a house
wine served in flasks.*

CELLAR	●	●		
COMFORT	●	●	●	
TRADITION	●	●	●	●
Q/P		●	●	●

Le Mossacce

via del Proconsole, 55 r
☎ 055 294361
● Sat, Sun. €

*The menu prices are not
excessive when you think
of the delicious Florentine
food being served here.
The restaurant only seats
35 at a time, and its name
alludes to the rapid
rotation of diners as they
give up their places to
others waiting their turn.
A good house wine
(Chianti Colline
Fiorentine) is served in
flasks and other Chianti
labels are also available.*

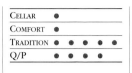

CELLAR	●				
COMFORT	●				
TRADITION	●	●	●	●	●
Q/P	●	●	●	●	

Pane e Vino

via San Niccolò, 70, a/r
☎ 055 2476956
⬤ Sun, midday.
€€€

As the name suggests, the wine here is particularly good. The restaurant has a wide range of very attractive regional dishes that are far from predictable. There is a choice selection of cheeses and the desserts are all prepared on the premises.

CELLAR	●	●	●	●	
COMFORT	●	●	●		
TRADITION	●	●	●		
Q/P	●	●	●		

Enoteca Pinchiorri

via Ghibellina, 87
☎ 055 242777
⬤ Sun, Mon, Tue lunch.
€€€€€

Giorgio Pinchiorri and Annie Feolde fully deserve their worldwide fame for this restaurant. Every detail of the setting and service – its elegance, quality, and sheer cachet – put it at the very top of the class in Italy and the rest of Europe. The cuisine is delectable and full of character, the ingredients are the very best the market offers, the cellar is among the finest in Europe. And the bill will reflect this.

CELLAR	●	●	●	●	●
COMFORT	●	●	●	●	●
TRADITION	●				
Q/P	●				

Ruggero

via Senese, 89 r
☎ 055 220542
⬤ Tue, Wed. €

A classic Florentine trattoria in both the décor and the menu, which includes traditional crostini with regional salumi, various soups and minestroni, ribollita and pappa col pomodoro, with old-fashioned stews.

CELLAR	●				
COMFORT	●	●			
TRADITION	●	●	●	●	●
Q/P	●	●	●		

FUCECCHIO (FI)

Le Vedute

frazione Ponte a Cappiano,
via Romana Lucchese, 121
☎ 0571 297498
⬤ Mon. €€€€

Quality fish dishes are the backbone of the menu, alternating with meat, and in particular game, all following the cycle of the seasons – mushrooms and truffles come in October, spring brings fresh vegetables, and so on. There is a careful selection of salumi – a wider choice in winter – and cheese. Pasta and desserts are homemade.

CELLAR	●	●	●		
COMFORT	●	●	●		
TRADITION	●				
Q/P	●	●	●		

LASTRA A SIGNA (FI)

Sanesi

via Arione, 33
☎ 055 8720234
⬤ Mon, Sun eve.
€€

This historic restaurant in a lovely rustic setting has been in the same family for 170 years. It serves classic Tuscan home cooking, especially meat grilled over charcoal, such as bistecca alla fiorentina accompanied by beans.

CELLAR	●	●			
COMFORT	●	●			
TRADITION	●	●	●	●	●
Q/P	●	●	●	●	

MARRADI (FI)

Cucina il Camino

viale Baccarini, 38
☎ 055 8045069
⬤ Wed. €€€

Lovers of quality home cooking will enjoy this restaurant. The dishes are not always strictly Tuscan because geographically this is in Romagna. Worthy of note are the mushrooms in season, fresh pasta, meat roasted in the wood-burning oven, and tasty desserts made with the celebrated local chestnuts.

CELLAR	●	●			
COMFORT	●	●	●		
TRADITION	●	●	●	●	●
Q/P	●	●	●		

PALAZZUOLO SUL SENIO (FI)

Locanda Senio

via Borgo dell'Ore, 1
☎ 055 8046019
⬤ Tue, Wed, midday on weekdays. €€€

Sample traditional dishes of wild herbs and fruits, as well as ancient recipes handed down from memory by the old folks of the town, in this very interesting and original restaurant. Set in a 14th-century town in the Mugello, it uses local ingredients and the basic dishes are creatively assembled. There are some pleasant rooms available.

CELLAR	●	●	●		
COMFORT	●	●	●	●	
TRADITION	●	●	●	●	●
Q/P	●	●	●		

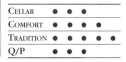

PRATO

Enoteca Barni

via Ferrucci, 22
☎ 0574 607845
● Sun, Sat midday.
€€€

This pleasant, cheerful restaurant grew out of the success of a delicatessen, which at first offered meals only at midday. For several years now it has opened in the evenings as well and has retained its lively atmosphere. Three young chefs create tasty meat and fish dishes using plenty of fresh ingredients (including some unusual game). Everything is made on the premises, including the bread, fresh pasta, and desserts. There is an international wine list.

CELLAR	●	●	●	●
COMFORT	●	●	●	●
TRADITION	●	●		
Q/P	●	●	●	

Il Borbottino

via Fra Bartolomeo, 13
☎ 0574 23810
● Sun, Sat midday,
Mon eve. €€€

This subtly elegant establishment offers an innovative surf-and-turf menu. They use good-quality ingredients, some from outside the region, but mostly local. Many of the dishes are inspired by traditional Tuscan recipes. The desserts are delicious.

CELLAR	●	●	●	
COMFORT	●	●	●	
TRADITION	●	●		
Q/P	●	●	●	

Il Piraña

via Valentini, 110
☎ 0574 25746
● Sun, Sat midday.
€€€€

Fish dishes are the specialty of this popular restaurant. The simple Mediterranean-style dishes rely on high-quality fresh ingredients for their excellent flavor. The homemade desserts are equally good.

CELLAR	●	●	●
COMFORT	●	●	●
TRADITION	●		
Q/P	●	●	●

PRATOVECCHIO (AR)

Gliaccaniti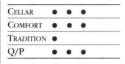

via Fiorentina, 14
☎ 0575 583345
● Tue. €

This is one of the rare restaurants with the courage to offer porcini *exclusively when they are found locally. The home-style cooking uses local ingredients, prepared in a way that maintains the wholesome quality.*

CELLAR	●	●			
COMFORT	●	●	●		
TRADITION	●	●	●	●	●
Q/P	●	●	●	●	

Quattro Cantoni

via Uffenheim, 10
☎ 0575 582696
● Mon.
€

This trattoria *serves good traditional cooking. There is a wide choice of first course dishes, including* tagliatelle, tortelli di patate, *and* tortelli di carne, ravioli di magro *(ravioli stuffed with spinach and ricotta),* gnocchi, *and* strozzapreti. *On Sundays there is a set menu option.*

CELLAR	●	●		
COMFORT	●	●		
TRADITION	●	●	●	●
Q/P	●	●	●	

SANSEPOLCRO (AR)

Balestra

via dei Montefeltro, 29
☎ 0575 735151
● Mon, Sun eve.
€

This is a classic Tuscan restaurant in a modern setting. The restaurant gets its name from the fact that all the members of the family who own it are expert marksmen with crossbows. Creative cooking enhances the regional ingredients (plus a few from neighboring Umbria and Marche). The pasta is handmade and fresh Italian mushrooms and truffles are served when they are in season.

CELLAR	●	●	●
COMFORT	●	●	●
TRADITION	●	●	●
Q/P	●	●	●

Da Paola e Marco Mercati all'Albergo Oroscopo

località Pieve Vecchia,
via Togliatti, 68
☎ 0575 734875
● Sun, midday.
€€€

Set in a lovely 19th-century building, this small restaurant has a rustic yet elegant quality. The fine cuisine consists partly of regional dishes and partly of innovative modern recipes. The desserts are excellent, and there is a choice wine list, which includes some notable wines. The restaurant also has some attractive rooms available.

CELLAR	●	●	●	●
COMFORT	●	●	●	●
TRADITION	●	●		
Q/P	●	●	●	

Da Ventura

via Aggiunti, 30
📞 0575 3425560
🍽 Sat.
€€

*Reflecting influences
from three different
regions – Tuscany,
Romagna, and Umbria –
this restaurant serves
simple, tasty traditional
dishes from all their
cuisines. Alongside
Chianti beef there is
suckling pig and shin
of pork, freshly made
pasta (wonderful tagliolini
with truffles), and good
desserts. The restaurant
has accommodation in
six bedrooms.*

CELLAR	●	●		
COMFORT	●	●	●	
TRADITION	●	●	●	●
Q/P	●	●	●	●

TERRANUOVA BRACCIOLINI (AR)

Ristorante Pin Rose

località Cicogna,
via La Pineta, 38
📞 055 9703833
🍽 Mon, Tue.
€€€

*The owner belongs to a
family of fish wholesalers,
and this restaurant
specializes in Tuscan
fresh fish dishes. The
huge restaurant is
situated in an enormous
wood of ancient pine
and oak trees. The
fish comes mostly from
Porto Santo Stefano,
Piombino, and Viareggio.
The cellar has a good
selection of wines from
the Veneto, Friuli, Alto
Adige, Tuscany, and
Sardinia.*

CELLAR	●	●		
COMFORT	●	●	●	
TRADITION	●			
Q/P	●	●	●	

LUNIGIANA, GARFAGNANA AND VERSILIA

CAMAIORE (LU)

Ristorante Emilio e Bona

località Lombrici, 22
📞 0584 989289
🍽 Mon. €€€

*In an old olive mill by a
mountain stream, Tuscan
and classic Italian dishes
are served. The food is
prepared with a light touch,
and the meals finish with
a few carefully chosen
homemade desserts. The
wine list is Tuscan and
Italian with some French.*

CELLAR	●	●	●
COMFORT	●	●	●
TRADITION	●	●	●
Q/P	●	●	●

Ristorante Vignaccio

località Santa Lucia,
via della Chiesa
📞 0584 914200
🍽 Wed. €€

*Flavorsome traditional
dishes are served at this
restaurant in the hills. Local
specialties are combined
with other dishes made
from quality Italian and
international ingredients.
A rich selection of Italian
and French cheeses and
excellent desserts follows.
The cellar has many
delightful regional wines.*

CELLAR	●	●	●
COMFORT	●	●	●
TRADITION	●	●	●
Q/P	●	●	●

CAPANNORI (LU)

La Cecca

località Coselli
📞 0583 94130
🍽 Mon, Wed eve. €€

*Here, the dishes take
their theme, in rotation,
from Garfagnana and
Lucchesia, with rustic
dishes like biroldo (blood
pudding) or a polenta of
chestnut flour and other
more elaborate dishes.
There is meat grilled over
charcoal, good salumi, and
rural desserts. The wines
are mainly regional.*

CELLAR	●	●		
COMFORT	●	●	●	
TRADITION	●	●	●	
Q/P	●	●	●	●

CARRARA

Ninan

via Lorenzo Bartolini, 3
📞 0585 74741
🍽 Sun. €€€€

*This husband-and-wife
team worked for Gualtiero
Marchesi and the cooking
is influenced by his
culinary style. Meat and
fish are offered in an
unusual, personal way.
Local tradition receives
a nod in the use of lardo
di Colonnata, aromatic
herbs, and the extremely
sweet onion of Treschetto.
The wine list favors Italian
labels. The restaurant is
fairly small so it is wise
to book in advance.*

CELLAR	●	●	●	
COMFORT	●	●	●	●
TRADITION	●	●	●	
Q/P	●	●	●	

Da Venanzio

località Colonnata
📞 0585 758062
🍽 Thu, Sun eve. €€

*The cuisine here is mainly
regional and confined to
seasonal produce.
Everything is made in the
kitchens, including a rich
selection of desserts. The
cellar is mostly Tuscan
with various notable
Italian or foreign wines.*

But Venanzio is above all the undisputed king of lardo: *his* lardo di Colonnata, *seasoned with herbs is world famous. Venanzio cures his beef for the* carpaccio *in brine left over from the* lardo.

CELLAR	●	●	●	●	
COMFORT	●	●	●		
TRADITION	●	●	●	●	
Q/P		●	●	●	●

CUTIGLIANO (PT)

Trattoria da Fagiolino

via Carega, 1
☎ 0573 68014
● Wed, Tue eve. €€

Classic Tuscan mountain dishes are served here, with mushrooms and game in season, plus kid and steak. There are first courses with homemade pasta and various soups. The menu finishes with a wide range of desserts.

CELLAR	●	●			
COMFORT	●	●			
TRADITION	●	●	●	●	
Q/P		●	●	●	●

FIVIZZANO (MS)

Il Giardinetto

via Roma, 155
☎ 0585 92060
● Mon (exc summer). €

This historic restaurant-cum-hotel in a small town in the Lunigiana has been in the same family since 1882. On offer are many vegetable dishes as well as regional food using local ingredients. Everything is homemade, including the ice cream. There is also a good list of local wines.

CELLAR	●	●			
COMFORT	●	●	●		
TRADITION	●	●	●	●	
Q/P		●	●	●	

FORTE DEI MARMI (LU)

Lorenzo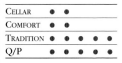

via Carducci, 61
☎ 0584 84030
● Mon. €€€€€

This elegant restaurant, run by Lorenzo Viani, is a shrine to Tuscan and Italian gourmets. All the ingredients are exceptional, especially the fish which Viani gets twice daily from trusted sources. The chef, who does not lack creativity when needed, often holds back to keep things simple to highlight the freshness and quality of the food. There are specialties like "bavette sul pesce," *spaghetti with tiny squid scented with sage, or* bocconcini di pescatrice *with slivers of artichokes. For meat-lovers there is equally good fare. The wine list is one of the finest in Italy.*

CELLAR	●	●	●	●	●
COMFORT	●	●	●	●	●
TRADITION	●	●	●		
Q/P		●	●	●	

LUCCA

Buca di Sant'Antonio

via della Cervia, 1/3
☎ 0583 55881
● Mon, Sun eve. €€€

There was an inn on this site as long ago as the 18th century. Nowadays it is an elegant rural restaurant featuring regional specialties with certain innovations. The meat and vegetable dishes are imaginative, and the desserts reflect the town's gastronomic traditions. There is a good choice of wines at reasonable prices.

CELLAR	●	●	●	●	
COMFORT	●	●	●	●	
TRADITION	●	●	●	●	
Q/P		●	●	●	

Da Giulio - in Pelleria

via delle Conce, 45
☎ 0583 55948
● Sun, Mon. €

The menu here features the classic dishes of Lucca, starting with antipasti of crostini, salumi, *and other rustic specialties, and continuing with local* minestre *and soups, meat and game, almost all in rustic style.*

CELLAR	●	●			
COMFORT	●	●			
TRADITION	●	●	●	●	●
Q/P		●	●	●	●

MONTIGNOSO (MS)

Il Bottaccio

via Bottaccio,1
☎ 0585 340031
€€€€€

An enchanting Relais & Châteaux (historic hotel), set in an old oil mill, has a restaurant which is acquiring an increasingly leading role thanks to the quality and character of the cuisine. The menu includes fresh seafood, good meat (especially the game), and extremely good cakes and pastries.

CELLAR	●	●	●	●	
COMFORT	●	●	●	●	●
TRADITION	●	●			
Q/P		●			

PESCIA (PT)

Cecco

viale Forti, 96
☎ 0572 477955
● Mon. €€

This restaurant has always been a shrine to the green asparagus of Pescia, the most prized in all of Tuscany – but only

in springtime. The rest of
the year try the local
mushrooms, truffles,
Sorana beans, and
whatever else the season
offers. Everything is made
on the premises and there
is a marked preference for
local produce. The house
specialty is chicken "al
mattone." The wine list is
largely Tuscan with some
whites from Friuli.

CELLAR	●	●			
COMFORT	●	●	●		
TRADITION	●	●	●	●	●
Q/P	●	●	●	●	

PIETRASANTA (LU)

L'Enoteca Marcucci

via Garibaldi, 40
📞 0584 791962
🍴 Mon, midday daily.
€€

This is somewhere half-
way between a wine bar
and a restaurant. It
presents simple country
and seafood dishes with
a regional accent, chosen
especially to accompany
the excellent wines in
the cellar.

CELLAR	●	●	●	●	●
COMFORT	●	●			
TRADITION	●	●	●		
Q/P	●	●	●	●	

PISTOIA

Trattoria dell'Abbondanza

via dell'Abbondanza, 10/14
📞 0573 368037
🍴 Wed, Thu lunch. €

Here you will find Tuscan
cuisine prepared the old
way – no cream or frozen
foods, and only seasonal
produce fresh from the
kitchen garden. Among
the regular dishes are
bollito misto, chicken
and fried vegetables with

good oil, and fish (on
Fridays). The desserts are
homemade. There is no
wine list, just the house
red and white.

CELLAR	●				
COMFORT	●	●	●		
TRADITION	●	●	●	●	●
Q/P	●	●	●	●	●

Il Castagno di Pier Angelo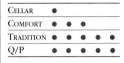

località Piteccio
via del Castagno, 46/b
📞 0573 42214 🍴 Mon,
midday on weekdays.
€€€

Set in a glade of chestnut
trees, this restaurant
provides good service with
its three menus, featuring
meat, fish, and creative
dishes. They are all based
on traditional cuisine, but
with innovative touches.
The imagination shown
in the fish cuisine is truly
admirable, as is the
originality shown in
finding ingredients from
Tuscany and the rest of
Italy. The wine list prices
are reasonable.

CELLAR	●	●	●	●	
COMFORT	●	●	●	●	●
TRADITION	●	●	●		
Q/P	●	●	●	●	

PODENZANA (MS)

La Gavarina d'Oro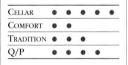

via Castello, 13
📞 0187 410021
🍴 Wed. €

This is the right place to
sample the famous
panigacci, once a simple
dish of Lunigiana, now a
traditional delicacy:
focaccine cooked between
two testi (earthenware
pans) and flavored with
pesto or mushrooms.
There is also chargrilled
meat, testaroli, and other
fresh pasta and simple
traditional dishes.

CELLAR	●				
COMFORT	●				
TRADITION	●	●	●	●	●
Q/P	●	●	●	●	●

PONTE A MORIANO (LU)

La Mora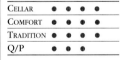

via Sesto di Moriano
📞 0583 406402
🍴 Wed. €€€

La Mora means "the
stopover," and this is the
place to stop if you want
to eat good Tuscan food
or simply eat and drink
well. The well-established
restaurant is Sauro
Brunicardi's jewel (his
family has run it since
1867). He is a passionate
lover of his region and
of good wine. This is
apparent in the excellent
cellar which has
everything from the
Lucca area and much
from the other regions
of Italy and the world,
as well as a distinctive
choice of liquors and
liqueurs. The Garfagnana
cuisine – modernized
where necessary – is
equally good and the
restaurant has an elegant,
hospitable atmosphere.
Try the gran farro and
local porcini.

CELLAR	●	●	●	●	
COMFORT	●	●	●	●	
TRADITION	●	●	●	●	
Q/P	●	●	●		

UZZANO (PT)

Mason

via Parri, 56
📞 0572 451363
🍴 Wed, midday Sat.
€€€

The chef's skill is displayed
to best advantage in the
fish and game bird dishes
in this restaurant, which

is tucked away in the hills between Pescia and Montecatini. The cuisine is traditional, local Tuscan but it has a very distinctive personal touch that serves to show off the produce at its best.

CELLAR	●	●	●	
COMFORT	●	●	●	
TRADITION	●	●	●	●
Q/P	●	●	●	

VIAREGGIO (LU)

Gusmano

via Regia, 58
📞 0584 31233
🔴 Tue, lunchtime on weekdays in summer.
€€€

Situated in the heart of Viareggio, this pleasant restaurant is distinguished by its excellent fish cuisine. Importantly for a seafood restaurant, fresh fish is delivered twice a day thanks to the good rapport between the restaurant owner and the fishermen who cast their nets in the waters off Viareggio.

CELLAR	●	●	●	
COMFORT	●	●	●	●
TRADITION	●	●	●	
Q/P	●	●	●	●

Oca Bianca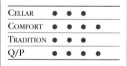

via Coppino, 409
📞 0584 388477
🔴 Tue, lunchtime.
€€€€

Upstairs with a view over the sea and the harbor, in a luxurious setting with a very distinctive décor, is a traditional restaurant. The cuisine is mainly seafood with a tried and tested menu. The fish is local, the cellar huge (2,000 wines) and excellent. Downstairs at

the Bistrot dell'Oca (0584 388477) the mood changes. There are wines by the glass, great dishes of oysters and other French-style raw shellfish, steam-cooked seafood, Catalan-style lobsters, soups according to the season, and a choice of over 100 international cheeses, all at very reasonable prices.

CELLAR	●	●	●	●
COMFORT	●	●	●	●
TRADITION	●	●	●	
Q/P	●	●	●	

Romano Ⓖ

via Mazzini, 120
📞 0584 31382
🔴 Mon.
€€€€€

This is one of the best seafood restaurants in Italy. Romano and Franca Franceschini cook wonderful dishes from high-quality fresh fish. Their menu is a stunning mixture of simplicity and creativity, with harmonious colors, aromas, and accompaniments. Trying to choose between stuffed baby squid, sparnocchi (mantis shrimp) with honey, or cacciucco alla viareggina (Viareggio-style fish soup) is hard because all the dishes are an inspiration. The excellent extra-virgin olive oil and perfectly fresh vegetables only serve to enhance the dishes. The style of the desserts is just as good, and the quality and variety of the cellar puts it on the same level. Try the Montecarlo wine from the restaurant's own vineyard, a white well above average.

CELLAR	●	●	●	●	●
COMFORT	●	●	●	●	
TRADITION	●	●	●		
Q/P	●	●	●		

BIBBONA (LI)

La Pineta

località Marina di Bibbona, via dei Cavalleggeri, 27
📞 0586 600016
🔴 Mon.
€€€

The owners of this seafront restaurant have no fewer than three fishing boats in the family, which augurs well for the fresh fish which is its staple fare. The fish comes to the table perfectly fresh in simple dishes, accompanied by equally fresh vegetables. Other dishes on the menu are either made on the premises or by local producers – even the mayonnaise is made on the spot with extra-virgin olive oil. The cellar contains a wide selection of mostly Italian wines with the odd French label.

CELLAR	●	●	●	
COMFORT	●	●	●	
TRADITION	●	●	●	
Q/P	●	●	●	

CAPOLIVERI – ELBA (LI)

Il Chiasso ☯

vicolo Sauro, 13
📞 0565 968709
🔴 Tue, lunchtime.
🔲 Apr–Oct. €€€

The layout of this restaurant is unusual. Situated in a small street in the town, it has tables set outside and two rustic dining rooms at the side. The affable host, Luciano, serves octopus with potatoes (minestrone di polpo), Livorno-style mullet in a pot, spaghetti with amberjack roe or served alla Chiasso (with sea urchins, prawns, and *tomatoes), and other seafood dishes, with both local and regional recipes.*

CELLAR	●	●	●	
COMFORT	●	●	●	
TRADITION	●	●	●	●	●
Q/P	●	●	●	●	

Da Pilade

località Marina di Mola
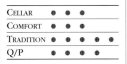 0565 968635
◯ Easter–Oct. €€

Tuscan fish and meat dishes are served here – grilled meat, game in season, fresh fish, and the island's mushrooms. Desserts include sorbets and schiacciunta *(fruit bread). This is a hotel as well as a restaurant.*

CELLAR	●	●	●
COMFORT	●	●	●
TRADITION	●	●	●
Q/P	●	●	●

CASTAGNETO CARDUCCI (LI)

Ristorante Da Ugo

via Pari, 3
● 0565 763746
● Mon. €€

This restaurant offers traditional Tuscan and Maremma cooking with particular emphasis on mushrooms and game. Wood pigeon, pork, and rabbit are served, plus some seafood, especially in summer. The owner also runs the Enoteca Il Borgo opposite the restaurant.

CELLAR	●	●	●	
COMFORT	●	●		
TRADITION	●	●	●	●	●
Q/P	●	●	●	

Zi' Martino

località San Giusto, 264
● 0565 763666
● Mon. €

This inexpensive rustic trattoria-cum-hotel is typically Tuscan. You can find wild boar, lamb, and grilled meats and tortelli *on the menu.*

CELLAR	●	●		
COMFORT	●	●	●	
TRADITION	●	●	●	●	●
Q/P	●	●	●	●	

CECINA (LI)

Antica Cecina

via Cavour, 17
● 0586 681528
● Sun lunch. €€€€

Owner Marcello Nenci runs this small restaurant that offers authentic regional cuisine based on locally sourced ingredients. His Chianina beef, for example, comes from Foiano della Chiana, and for his fish recipes, he uses sea water brought to him by fishermen who gather it in open sea. Nenci also makes his own butter and cheeses. The desserts are made by Nenci's wife. The cellar holds 500 wines, all of them Tuscan.

CELLAR	●	●	●	●
COMFORT	●	●	●	
TRADITION	●	●	●	●
Q/P	●	●	●	

LARI (PI)

Castero

località Lavaiano,
via Galilei, 2
● 0587 616121
● Sun eve, Mon. €€

A must for its meat dishes grilled over charcoal, this pleasant family-run restaurant features typical, simple Tuscan cuisine. The pork, beef (not Chianina), lamb, and much else are all choice quality, and the ingredients (especially the salumi*) are local.*

CELLAR	●	●	●	
COMFORT	●	●	●	
TRADITION	●	●	●	●
Q/P	●	●	●	●	●

LIVORNO

Antico Moro

via Bartelloni, 59
● 0586 884659
● Wed.
€€

The classic local fish dishes – the usual grilled fish and fritto misto *– are available here, but there is also steak for dedicated meat-eaters.*

CELLAR	●	●	
COMFORT	●	●	
TRADITION	●	●	●
Q/P	●	●	●

La Barcarola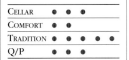

viale Carducci, 39
● 0586 402367
● Sun.
€€

The family that owns this restaurant has run it for over 60 years, so they have built up a close relationship with their suppliers. This ensures good-quality local fish, which is the mainstay of the menu. Cacciucco is one of the traditional dishes found all year round. There is a good choice of first and second courses, which are exclusively seafood.

CELLAR	●	●	●
COMFORT	●	●	●
TRADITION	●	●	●
Q/P	●	●	●

Ciglieri

frazione Ardenza,
via Franchini, 38
● 0586 508194
● Wed.
€€€€€

This elegant restaurant uses good-quality regional ingredients (including fresh vegetables, pigeons, and Chianina beef) to produce creative traditional recipes. The bread, pasta, and pastry are all homemade.

CELLAR	●	●	●	●
COMFORT	●	●	●	●
TRADITION	●	●		
Q/P	●	●		

MARCIANA – ELBA (LI)

Publius

località Poggio, piazza XX Settembre
[0565 99208
● Mon. ☐ Mar–Nov.
€€

Fine regional cooking and courteous service can be found here. Many of the dishes are based on fresh fish, such as stoccafisso all'elbana, *but there are also meat and game dishes. The restaurant is good value for money, and the terrace has a fine sea view.*

CELLAR	●	●	●
COMFORT	●	●	●
TRADITION	●	●	●
Q/P	●	●	●

MARCIANA MARINA – ELBA (LI)

Capo Nord

località La Fenicia
[0565 996983
● Mon.
☐ April–Dec. €€€€

Elba's classic dishes, such as stock fish with potatoes, are alternated with fresh fish cooked very simply in salt at this seafront restaurant. There are plenty of creative ideas for using the produce from the island and nearby

areas. The desserts, presented in a separate menu, are good. There is an international wine list.

CELLAR	●	●	●
COMFORT	●	●	●
TRADITION	●	●	●
Q/P	●	●	●

Rendez Vous – Da Marcello

piazza della Vittoria, 1
[0565 99251;
0565 99298
● Wed. ☐ Jun–Sep.
€€

At this restaurant fish and other seafood are cooked both in simple, tasty dishes and in more sophisticated forms, including potato stuffed with a mixture of polpa di pesce *(filleted fish)* and shellfish roasted in a wood-burning oven (along with other kinds of fish).

CELLAR	●	●	
COMFORT	●	●	
TRADITION	●	●	
Q/P	●	●	●

MONTOPOLI VAL D'ARNO (PI)

Quattro Gigli

piazza Michele, 2
[0571 466878
● Mon, Sun eve.
(Jan 10–Mar 31). €€

Here flavor is wedded to culture. Many of the traditional dishes are taken from ancient – mostly Renaissance – Florentine recipe books, the fruit of careful historical research. The results are some excellent savory dishes with fruit as one of the ingredients. More recent tradition is not neglected: there is ribollita, *classic Tuscan meat dishes, and also stock fish and salt cod. In season there are truffles*

and mushrooms from San Miniato. The wine list has a good selection of Tuscan labels. The restaurant has some bedrooms available.

CELLAR	●	●	●
COMFORT	●	●	●
TRADITION	●	●	●
Q/P	●	●	●

PISA

Artilafo

via Volturno, 38
[050 27010
● Sun.
€€€

International cuisine – revisited and revised in some cases – and simple but creative meat and fish courses are on the menu at this tasteful restaurant. There is no printed wine list but the cellar contains about 300 wines from all over Italy.

CELLAR	●	●	
COMFORT	●	●	
TRADITION	●		
Q/P	●	●	

Bruno

via Bianchi, 12
[050 560818
● Tue, Mon eve.
€€

Enjoy typical Pisan cooking at this rustic family-run restaurant. Dishes include salt cod with leeks, Pisan-style stock fish, and seppie in zimino (cuttlefish soup).

CELLAR	●	●		
COMFORT	●	●		
TRADITION	●	●	●	●
Q/P	●	●		

Cagliostro

via del Castelletto, 26
[050 575413
● Tue. €€

This highly unusual trattoria *is in an ancient monastery which has been renovated in a modern, airy style and is also used for art exhibitions. The creative seasonal cuisine is based on produce from the land. Traditional Tuscan dishes are not listed on the menu but can be ordered on special evenings. The desserts are homemade, and the chocolate ones deserve a special mention, especially the steamed chocolate pudding. The wine bar has about 300 Italian wines. There are selections of Italian and foreign cheeses and* salumi *from the Marches.*

CELLAR	●	●	●	
COMFORT	●	●	●	
TRADITION	●			
Q/P	●	●	●	

Osteria dei Cavalieri

via San Frediano, 16
 050 580858
● Sun, Sat lunchtime. €

Interesting Tuscan cuisine offers very good value for money here. Ingredients are fresh, seasonal, and mostly local. The cellar has a good selection of Italian wines and the extra-virgin olive oil comes from a small producer nearby. The restaurant offers three "tasting menus": fish, meat, and vegetarian.

CELLAR	●	●	●	
COMFORT	●	●	●	
TRADITION	●	●	●	●
Q/P	●	●	●	

PONTEDERA (PI)

La Polveriera

via Marconcini, 54
 0587 54765
● Sun. €€

This restaurant is rich in character and culinary intuition, producing interesting seafood dishes combined with the region's herbs and vegetables.

CELLAR	●			
COMFORT	●	●	●	
TRADITION	●			
Q/P	●	●	●	

PORTOFERRAIO – ELBA (LI)

La Barca

via Guerrazzi, 60
 0565 918036
● Wed. €€

This small restaurant on the seafront offers high-quality dishes made with fresh ingredients, all at reasonable prices. The cuisine is mainly seafood, grilled over a wood fire.

CELLAR	●	●		
COMFORT	●	●		
TRADITION	●	●	●	●
Q/P	●	●	●	●

RIO MARINA – ELBA (LI)

La Canocchia

via Palestro, 3
 0565 962432
● Mon (except summer).
○ Apr–Oct. €€

For some years this has been the premier restaurant on Elba, one not to miss. The menu features local recipes plus original ideas based on fresh seafood. There is a broad range of first courses and a good selection of the island's wines.

CELLAR	●	●		
COMFORT	●	●		
TRADITION	●	●	●	●
Q/P	●	●	●	●

SAN MINIATO (PI)

Il Convio

località San Maiano
 0571 408114
● Wed. €€

This elegantly rustic restaurant is deep in the countryside. The cuisine is traditional with regional recipes. It specializes in both classic and modern, creative dishes made with the local white truffles.

CELLAR	●	●	●	
COMFORT	●	●	●	
TRADITION	●	●	●	
Q/P	●	●	●	

SANTA CROCE SULL'ARNO– STAFFOLI (PI)

Da Beppe

via Livornese, 35/37
 0571 37002
● Mon, Sun eve. €€€€

Located in the hills, this restaurant traditionally offered a meat-based menu when the present owner's father ran it. Nowadays, fish is favored on the menu, but there is still a small space for the style of the past. The dishes are based on local produce, with ideas from other regions and countries. There is a good wine list with an eye to the whites.

CELLAR	●	●	●	●
COMFORT	●	●	●	●
TRADITION	●	●		
Q/P	●	●	●	

SAN VINCENZO (LI)

Il Bucaniere

viale Marconi
 0565 705555
● Tue. ○ Summer. €€

In a wooden cabin on stilts by the sea, Fulvietto Pierangelini, son of the well-known restaurateur Fulvio, who owns the Gambero Rosso (see p184), runs this restaurant. Open only in the evenings, it offers real seafood delicacies. There are one-course meals, antipasti and first courses, and both traditional and creative modern dishes, all using good quality ingredients. The cheese trolley has fine Tuscan cheeses, the desserts are interesting, and the wine list (only Tuscan and French) is small but carefully chosen.

CELLAR	•	•			
COMFORT	•	•	•		
TRADITION	•	•			
Q/P	•	•	•	•	

Gambero Rosso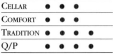

piazza della Vittoria, 13
☎ 0565 701021
⬤ Mon, Tue in winter.
€€€€€

Fulvio Pierangelini is the owner and chef of this splendid, unforgettable, small restaurant – one of the most famous in Italy – serving fine food. He has an unerring instinct for flavors and scents, and a quite exceptional ability to improvise. Everything at the Gambero Rosso is perfect: carefully chosen raw materials from all over Europe combined with fresh meat and fish from his own region. The dishes are light and full of flavor, with the cooking beautifully timed. Tasteful tables are laid under the watchful eye of Emanuela, the padrona di casa*. The cellar, which contains an international range of wines, is one of the most outstanding in Italy. Even the price:quality ratio is very good if you choose the "tasting menu."*

CELLAR	•	•	•	•	•
COMFORT	•	•	•	•	•
TRADITION	•	•			
Q/P	•	•	•		

SUVERETO (LI)

Eno-oliteca Ombrone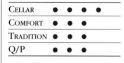

piazza dei Giudici, 1
☎ 0565 829336
⬤ Mon.
€€€€

This restaurant is in a renovated 14th-century olive mill. Giancarlo Bini was one of the first – if not the first – to provide in his restaurant (formerly at Grosseto) an informative list of types of olive oil and combine each dish with the right oil. In his new premises he has continued along the same lines, offering a choice of no fewer than 168 kinds of extra-virgin olive oil from all over Italy. The cuisine is excellent and definitely regional. Note particularly the wild boar (in the traditional recipe alla bracconiera*) and the game. The restaurant's* salumi *and desserts are excellent.*

CELLAR	•	•	•	
COMFORT	•	•	•	
TRADITION	•	•	•	
Q/P	•	•	•	

TIRRENIA (PI)

Dante e Ivana

via del Tirreno, 207/c
☎ 050 32549
⬤ Sun, Mon lunchtime.
€€€€

This fish restaurant offers shellfish from the markets at Viareggio and Livorno. The dishes, which reflect the day's catch, do full justice to the fish.

CELLAR	•	•	•	•	
COMFORT	•	•	•		
TRADITION	•				
Q/P	•	•	•		

ULIVETO TERME (PI)

Osteria Vecchia Noce

località Noce Est
☎ 050 788229
⬤ Sun evening.
€€

Set in an 18th-century olive mill in a medieval town, this atmospheric restaurant also boasts a pretty garden. It serves creative Tuscan cuisine as well as traditional dishes, such as the classic ribollita. Fish must be booked in advance, which ensures the freshness of the product. The wines are Italian – mainly Tuscan – with the occasional foreign wine.

CELLAR	•	•	•	
COMFORT	•	•	•	
TRADITION	•	•	•	•
Q/P	•	•	•	•

VADA (LI)

Il Ducale

piazza Garibaldi, 33
☎ 0586 788600
⬤ Mon.
€€€

Situated in an elegant 19th-century building, this restaurant serves its customers traditional seafood cuisine. Its fish is supplied almost exclusively by local fishermen. The homemade bottarga *(dried, salted fish roe) uses roe from various kinds of fish.*

CELLAR	•	•	•	
COMFORT	•	•	•	
TRADITION	•	•	•	
Q/P	•	•	•	•	•

VOLTERRA (PI)

Vecchio Mulino

Saline di Volterra,
via del Molino, 23
☎ 0588 44060;
0588 44238
⬤ Mon, Sun eve (winter).
€€

The setting for this delightful restaurant is a renovated old mill. The restaurant's sophisticated cuisine is based on meat (game in the fall and winter), with plenty of fresh vegetables in season, and mushrooms depending on the time of year. The dishes have a regional flavor with some added personal touches. There are some rooms available for people to stay.

CELLAR	●	●	●		
COMFORT	●	●	●		
TRADITION	●	●	●	●	
Q/P	●	●	●		

CHIANTI AND SIENA

CASTELLINA IN CHIANTI (SI)

Antica Trattoria La Torre

piazza del Comune, 15
☎ 0577 740236
⬤ Fri. €€

The tables and chairs at this restaurant are set out in the attractive medieval piazza, and the food is cooked on an open spit. The cuisine is typical of Chianti with ribollita, *homemade pasta,* crostini, *Chianina beef and pigeon, plus a good choice of homemade desserts. The restaurant's cellar stocks a good range of the top Tuscan wines plus a selection of other wines from northern Italy.*

CELLAR	●	●	●		
COMFORT	●	●	●		
TRADITION	●	●	●	●	
Q/P	●	●	●	●	

Pietrafitta

località Pietrafitta
☎ 0577 741123 ⬤ Thu. €

This hospitable small restaurant with its period furnishings serves a few classic Tuscan dishes, such as local salumi *and* bistecca alla Fiorentina. *Everything is homemade.*

CELLAR	●	●	●		
COMFORT	●	●	●		
TRADITION	●	●	●	●	
Q/P	●	●	●		

CASTELNUOVO BERARDENGA (SI)

Antonio

via del Chianti, 32
☎ 0577 355321
⬤ Mon–Tue lunchtime.
€€€€

This fine restaurant is celebrated for its excellent seafood dishes. The menu is rewritten each morning, after the dawn purchases at the meat, fruit, and vegetable markets. The host, Antonio Farina, has an excellent cellar with prestigious wines from all over the world.

CELLAR	●	●	●	●	
COMFORT	●	●	●		
TRADITION	●				
Q/P	●	●			

Bottega del 30

località Villa a Sesia,
via Santa Caterina, 2
☎ 0577 359226
⬤ Tue, Wed, lunchtime on weekdays. €€€€

This small restaurant is set in a 17th-century farmyard above an ancient monastery and is surrounded by vines. Elegant without being too formal, it offers interesting, creative cooking based on old Tuscan recipes. The versatile "tasting menu" includes some of their specialties. They also offer cooking lessons, a small museum, and a 250-label cellar.

CELLAR	●	●	●	●	
COMFORT	●	●	●		
TRADITION	●	●	●		
Q/P	●	●			

Poggio Rosso

località San Felice Nord Ovest
☎ 0577 359260
€€€€€

Set in the farming hamlet of San Felice, where there is also a fascinating historic hotel with well-appointed rooms, this is a stylish restaurant. It serves good, fairly creative, meat-based dishes with special emphasis on the farm's own produce, especially the excellent extra-virgin olive oil. The restaurant also serves some seafood dishes.

CELLAR	●	●	●		
COMFORT	●	●	●	●	●
TRADITION	●	●			
Q/P	●				

COLLE DI VAL D'ELSA (SI)

Arnolfo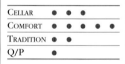

via XX Settembre, 50
☎ 0577 920549
⬤ Tue, Wed.
€€€€€

This restaurant is housed in a 500-year-old building in a charming village. There are two menus – one is traditional and the other innovative modern – both featuring excellent, tasty dishes.

The service reflects great courtesy and professionalism. The dishes range from fish to local meat, as well as a choice selection of ingredients from other areas of Tuscany. The pastries are not to be missed. The markups on the wine list are very reasonable. There is accommodation available in five bedrooms, which all have a pleasant, relaxed atmosphere.

CELLAR	●	●	●	●	●
COMFORT	●	●	●	●	●
TRADITION	●	●			
Q/P	●	●	●		

GAIOLE IN CHIANTI (SI)

Ristorante Badia a Coltibuono

località Badia
a Coltibuono
☎ 0577 749031
€€

A splendid medieval abbey is the setting for this restaurant, which is run by the Stucchi Prinetti family (their mother, Lorenza de' Medici, is in charge of the kitchen). As a showcase for their wines, the restaurant's owners serve traditional Tuscan dishes, which are sometimes enriched with modern personal touches. Dishes are made with choice ingredients such as Cinta Senese pork and fresh produce either from their own market garden, or supplied by small local growers. The interesting wine list includes fine wines from the family estate together with a selection of other Tuscan and Italian wines.

CELLAR	●	●			
COMFORT	●	●	●	●	
TRADITION	●	●	●	●	
Q/P	●	●	●		

GREVE IN CHIANTI (FI)

Da Padellina �

via Chiantigiana,
corso del Popolo
☎ 055 858388
● Thu.
€€

This pleasant country trattoria in Chianti serves purely classical cuisine. The ribollita and bistecca alla fiorentina are excellent, while the peposo alla fornacina, an old Impruneta recipe for meat stew, is worth trying. Desserts are homemade and include a traditional zuccotto.

CELLAR	●	●	●		
COMFORT	●	●	●		
TRADITION	●	●	●	●	●
Q/P	●	●	●		

SAN CASCIANO IN VAL DI PESA (FI)

La Tenda Rossa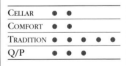

località Cerbaia,
piazza del Monumento,
9/14
☎ 055 826132
● Sun, Mon lunchtime.
€€€€€

A busy family team runs this stylish, but very friendly restaurant, which offers innovative versions of the Tuscan classics as well as new ideas for fish and meat. The starting point is the local market, as reflected in the menu, which is rewritten almost daily. Everything is homemade, including the bread, the service is impeccable, and there is a fine cellar.

CELLAR	●	●	●	●	●
COMFORT	●	●	●	●	●
TRADITION	●	●			
Q/P	●	●			

SIENA

Botteganova

via Chiantigiana, 29
☎ 0577 284230
● Mon. €€€

The Sicilian chef at this chic restaurant knows how to get hold of perfect ingredients. He adapts the local cuisine to produce his own personal version of Mediterranean dishes, with an especially creative approach to seafood. The desserts are skillfully prepared, and there is a choice selection of cheeses.

CELLAR	●	●	●	●
COMFORT	●	●	●	
TRADITION	●	●		
Q/P	●	●	●	

Osteria La Chiacchiera

via Costa di Sant'Antonio, 4
☎ 0577 280631 €

This old-fashioned wine bar in a historical building in the center of Siena offers Tuscan food or, more precisely, "poor Sienese food". The dishes include tripe, legumes, soups, homemade pasta, meat. Everything is made on the premises. The wine list includes local wines. No coffee or strong alcoholic drinks are available.

CELLAR	●	●			
COMFORT	●	●			
TRADITION	●	●	●	●	●
Q/P	●	●	●		

Osteria da Divo

via Franciosa, 25
☎ 0577 284381 €€€

This restaurant is located partly in Etruscan tombs dug out of tufa and partly in medieval cellars. It offers Tuscan cuisine made using local products, including fish. Pasta and bread are made on the premises.

CELLAR	•	•	•	
COMFORT	•	•	•	•
TRADITION	•	•	•	
Q/P	•	•	•	

Enzo

via Camollia, 49
📞 0577 281277
⬤ Sun. €€€€

Located in a 12th-century building, this welcoming restaurant is devoted to both surf and turf. There is also a traditional menu. Everything is homemade. The cellar holds many national labels.

CELLAR	•	•	•	
COMFORT	•	•	•	
TRADITION	•	•		
Q/P	•	•	•	

Grotta del Gallo Nero

via del Porrione, 65/67
📞 0577 284356 €€

This restaurant in a medieval building features an old cellar. It specializes in medieval cuisine – the dishes were rediscovered after thorough historical research. There is a wide selection of Sienese wines.

CELLAR	•	•			
COMFORT	•	•	•		
TRADITION	•	•	•	•	•
Q/P	•	•	•		

Le Logge

via del Porrione, 33
📞 0577 48013 ⬤ Sun, lunchtime on Mon. €€€

Set in the oldest palace in Siena, Palazzo Piccolomini, next to t he Logge del Papa, this restaurant is popular with artists. It offers typical Tuscan cuisine (plus some fish dishes) with plenty of traditional recipes and homemade fresh pasta. The wines are mainly regional.

CELLAR	•	•	•	
COMFORT	•	•	•	
TRADITION	•	•	•	
Q/P	•	•	•	

Antica Trattoria Papei 🍴

piazza del Mercato, 6
📞 0577 280894
⬤ Mon. €

This is probably the only trattoria in town with a real family atmosphere. The sauces and the pasta are made on the premises: the pappardelle with hare is really special. The dishes are authentic Sienese cuisine – nothing is frozen or prepackaged.

CELLAR	•	•	•		
COMFORT	•	•			
TRADITION	•	•	•	•	•
Q/P	•	•	•	•	

MONTALCINO AND THE SIENESE CRETE

BUONCONVENTO (SI)

Osteria di Duccio

via Soccini, 76
📞 0577 807042
⬤ Wed. €

There is a very welcoming family atmosphere at this restaurant. The food is typical Sienese cuisine with numerous rustic dishes, including crostini and salumi, tagiolini ginestrati (with local chicken and saffron), ravioli of potatoes, ribollita seasoned with oil and onion, pappardelle sulla lepre (only in the open season for hare), faraona in crosta tartufata (guinea fowl in a crust), saddle of rabbit with herbs, purée of chickpeas, patate alla fattoressa (country-style potatoes), porcini specialties (in summer and early fall), and

---

homemade desserts. The produce is always fresh with ingredients bought in daily. There is house wine or Tuscan labels.

CELLAR	•	•		
COMFORT	•	•		
TRADITION	•	•	•	•
Q/P	•	•	•	

CETONA (SI)

Frateria di Padre Eligio

convento di San Francesco
📞 0578 238015
⬤ Tue. €€€€€

Intriguingly situated in a medieval monastery, this restaurant is surrounded by a park housing a community of young people who work in the restaurant and hotel. The traditional Italian cuisine, with a personal touch, is very good. Most of the ingredients are produced by the community. The menus are hand-painted. Prices are steep, however – think of them as a contribution to this community.

CELLAR	•	•	•	•	
COMFORT	•	•	•	•	•
TRADITION	•	•			
Q/P	•				

CHIUSI (SI)

Zaira

via Arunte, 12
📞 0578 20260
⬤ Mon (except summer). €€

This simple pleasant family-run restaurant in the town center serves classic local cuisine, which is closely linked to the seasons. It has a fascinating cellar (20,000 bottles) that stretches into Etruscan tunnels hewn out of the rock.

CELLAR	●	●	●		
COMFORT	●	●	●		
TRADITION	●	●	●	●	●
Q/P	●	●	●		

MONTALCINO (SI)

Osteria del Vecchio Castello

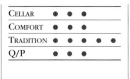

località Poggio
alle Mura
☎ 0577 816026
⬤ Tue. €€€€

*The little convent of the
13th-century Pieve di
San Sigismondo housed
a restaurant of the same
name until March 2000.
Now, in its place Susanna
Fumi (in the kitchen) and
her husband Alfredo
Sibaldi (sommelier) have
taken over, bringing with
them all the history and
experience of the Osteria
del Vecchio Castello di
Roccalbenga which they
used to run. Despite the
change of location – no
longer among the woods
at the foot of Monte
Amiata but amid the
celebrated vines of
Montalcino – there are
still only 16 covers and
the food is as wonderful
as ever. The cooking serves
only to enhance the
excellent regional and
seasonal ingredients in
harmonious flavor
combinations. The wine
lists have been increased
from two to three: Italian,
regional, and foreign.
Adjacent to the restaurant
are a wine store and six
large suites.*

CELLAR	●	●	●	●	●
COMFORT	●	●	●	●	●
TRADITION	●	●	●		
Q/P	●	●	●	●	

Poggio Antico

località i Poggi
☎ 0577 849200
⬤ Mon, Sun eve.
€€€€

---

*Diners have a panoramic
view of the countryside at
this charming restaurant.
The regional cuisine is
adapted intelligently, as
in the fried vegetables
and the* gnocchetti di ragù
bianco di cinghiale. *There
are excellent desserts.*

CELLAR	●	●	●	
COMFORT	●	●	●	●
TRADITION	●	●	●	
Q/P	●			

Porta al Cassero

Rocca della Fortezza
☎ 0577 847196
⬤ Wed. €

A small osteria *offering
Montalcino cuisine, with
classic* pinci *(or* pici*) and
traditional dishes, from*
pappa col pomodoro
*(bread and tomato soup)
to a purée of chickpeas
and* zuppa alla scottiglia
di cinghiale *(wild boar
stew), with the occasional
dish from other regions.*

CELLAR	●	●			
COMFORT	●	●	●		
TRADITION	●	●	●	●	●
Q/P	●	●	●		

Il Pozzo

località Sant'Angelo in
Colle ☎ 0577 844015
⬤ Tue. €

*Nestled in the hills ten
minutes from Montalcino,
this traditional* trattoria *is
run by two sisters. They
offer typically Sienese and
Maremman dishes, such
as* pici, *soups, handmade*
tagliatelle, *and many meat-
based dishes, including the
traditional* fiorentina, *from
locally reared cattle. The
desserts are homemade;
the wine list is limited to
a few local classics.*

CELLAR	●	●			
COMFORT	●	●			
TRADITION	●	●	●	●	●
Q/P	●	●	●		

Taverna dei Barbi

località Pordenoni
☎ 0577 841111
⬤ Tue, Wed eve.
€€

*This restaurant is
situated next door to
the famous Barbi wine
store. The décor is rustic
yet elegant and the
food served is typical
Montalcino cuisine.*

CELLAR	●	●			
COMFORT	●	●	●		
TRADITION	●	●	●	●	
Q/P	●	●	●		

MONTEPULCIANO (SI)

Diva e Maceo

via di Gracciano
nel Corso, 90/92
☎ 0578 716951
⬤ Tue.
€

*This simple restaurant
is very popular with locals
and visitors alike, who
enjoy its Tuscan dishes.
These range from classic
antipasti to* pappardelle
al cinghiale, pici
all'aglione *(considered
the best in the area),
and grilled or roasted
meat. The desserts are
homemade.*

CELLAR	●	●			
COMFORT	●	●			
TRADITION	●	●	●	●	●
Q/P	●	●	●	●	

La Grotta

località San Biagio, 15
☎ 0578 757607
⬤ Wed.
€€€

*This restaurant, opposite
the church of San Biagio,
is renowned for its meat,
especially the* tagliata di
Chianina *and* bistecca
alla fiorentina. *The rest
of the menu offers*

regional specialties such as antipasti with bruschetta *and* crostini, *homemade pasta, and second courses such as duck, stuffed pigeon, and rabbit. Everything is delicious. The wine list has some French wines.*

CELLAR	●	●	●		
COMFORT	●	●	●	●	
TRADITION	●	●	●	●	●
Q/P		●	●	●	

PIENZA (SI)

La Taverna di Moranda

frazione di Monticchiello, via di Mezzo, 17
🗲 0578 755050
⬤ Mon.
€€

About 6 miles (10 km) from Pienza, toward Monte Amiata, you can find real Tuscan cuisine at this restaurant. The pasta is made by hand and the menu changes depending on the seasons. The antipasti *are based on local* salumi; *the first courses are* pici *served with simple tomato sauces, or richer meat sauces; and the second courses are meat, including stuffed pigeon, the house specialty,* agnello a scottadito, *rabbit with olives, and steak dishes.*

CELLAR		●	●	●	
COMFORT		●	●	●	
TRADITION	●	●	●	●	●
Q/P		●	●	●	

SAN QUIRICO D'ORCIA – BAGNO VIGNONI (SI)

Antica Osteria del Leone

piazza del Muretto
🗲 0577 887300
⬤ Mon.
€€

This attractive restaurant in the center of town is made up of four rooms and set in a 14th-century building with exposed beams, a terracotta floor, and a pleasant garden. It offers some typically Sienese dishes, but has recently expanded its focus to include Tuscan recipes and other dishes with only a subtle regional hint. Occasionally the menu includes fish dishes. The homemade desserts are also good.

CELLAR		●	●	●	
COMFORT		●	●	●	
TRADITION	●	●	●		
Q/P		●	●	●	

Osteria della Parata

via del Moretto, 40
🗲 0577 887559
⬤ Wed.
€

A 15th-century barn with a fine panoramic garden is the attractive setting for this restaurant. Grilled food is its specialty. The pecorino *cheeses are excellent, as is the* lombo bagnato *(loin) with balsamic vinegar. Fresh vegetables are widely used in the first courses.*

CELLAR		●	●		
COMFORT		●	●		
TRADITION	●	●	●	●	
Q/P		●	●	●	●

SINALUNGA (SI)

Locanda dell'Amorosa

località Amorosa
🗲 0577 677211
⬤ Mon, Tue lunchtime.
€€€€€

This is one of the most important and fascinating Tuscan restaurants, situated in a 400-year-old town. The excellent

cuisine draws on tradition but is also innovative. The menu gives a lot of space to meat dishes but there is no lack of fish. The desserts are very good. The cheeses from the Crete are noteworthy, as is the salumi *produced by a local firm. Splendid suites and rooms in the medieval town's towers and walls are available.*

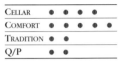

CELLAR		●	●	●	●
COMFORT		●	●	●	●
TRADITION	●	●			
Q/P		●	●		

Osteria delle Grotte

via Matteotti, 33
🗲 0577 630269.
⬤ Wed.
€€

Set in an old lemon grove, this restaurant has a fixed-price "tasting menu" (including Tuscan wine) with seasonal produce, meat, game, and excellent handmade fresh pasta.

CELLAR		●	●		
COMFORT		●	●	●	
TRADITION	●	●	●	●	
Q/P		●	●	●	

SOVICILLE (SI)

Trattoria Cateni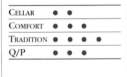

via dei Pratini, 19
🗲 0577 342028
⬤ Wed.
€

This restaurant has a panoramic terrace overlooking Siena. The arched interior and antique furniture give it a traditional feel. The scottiglia *is excellent, as are the specialties based on wild boar* (pappardelle, cinghiale alla cacciatora) *and mushrooms* (zuppa, vitella). *The pasta and desserts are homemade.*

CELLAR	●			
COMFORT	●			
TRADITION	●	●	●	●
Q/P	●	●	●	●

TORRITA DI SIENA – MONTEFOLLONICO (SI)

La Chiusa

via della Madonnina, 88
☎ 0577 669668
◐ Tue.
€€€€€

Situated in an ancient farmhouse, this is one of the most celebrated restaurants in the region. Dania Masotti presents regional food in a cuisine that is full of character but inspired by tradition. There are charming, but very expensive, rooms too.

CELLAR	●	●	●
COMFORT	●	●	●
TRADITION	●	●	●
Q/P	●		

TREQUANDA (SI)

Locanda del Colle ☕

via Torta, 7
☎ 0577 662108
◐ Wed in the low season.
€

The dining room of this restaurant is painted with floral frescoes, reminiscent of the old verandas on Sienese country houses a century ago. The décor is Art Nouveau with original period furniture. Here you can taste simple dishes, such as picchio-pacchio, homemade lunghetti with nana (muscovy duck), zuppa Trequanda, Chianina beef, or beef in Brunello wine. The homemade jams turn up in excellent tarts. To sample the food,

you are set a task – a farm chore, or a guided tasting of oil or wine.

CELLAR	●			
COMFORT	●	●	●	
TRADITION	●	●	●	●
Q/P	●	●	●	●

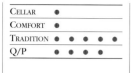

MAREMMA AND MONTE AMIATA

ARCIDOSSO (GR)

Aiuole

località Aiole
☎ 0564 967300
◐ Mon.
€€

This restaurant-cum-hotel belongs to a sommelier who offers traditional recipes typical of the Amiata area. Some of them date back to the Middle Ages. Everything is homemade, including the pasta, and the menu contains many vegetable-based dishes. There is an interesting selection of Tuscan grappa.

CELLAR	●	●	●
COMFORT	●	●	●
TRADITION	●	●	●
Q/P	●	●	●

La Tagliola

località Bagnoli,
via di Centro
☎ 0564 967351
◐ Mon. €

The best features of this restaurant are the large fireplace (on which the meat is grilled) and the underground cellars. It is possible to visit the cellars and to buy wine, oil, salumi, and other products. The dishes are typical of the Amiata area (with lots of porcini mushrooms) and the atmosphere is warm and welcoming.

CELLAR	●	●	●	
COMFORT	●	●	●	
TRADITION	●	●	●	●
Q/P	●	●	●	

CAPALBIO (GR)

Maria

via Comunale, 3
☎ 0564 896014
◐ Tue.
€€

Politicians and media personalities can often be found among the tourists sampling Maurizio Rossi's Maremma specialties. While wild boar dominates the menu, the tortelli with truffles, the acquacotta (soup), and the fried vegetables are noteworthy.

CELLAR	●	●	●	
COMFORT	●	●	●	
TRADITION	●	●	●	●
Q/P	●	●	●	

CASTIGLIONE DELLA PESCAIA (GR)

Osteria del Buco

via del Recinto, 11
☎ 0564 934460
◐ Mon.
€

This restaurant is located in an opening in the ancient walls surrounding the medieval town. The cuisine, like the décor, is pure Maremma. Dishes include bruschette (some with long-forgotten toppings), vegetable and pulse soups, game, and very good fish (including some little-known kinds unusual in a restaurant).

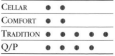

CELLAR	●	●		
COMFORT	●	●		
TRADITION	●	●	●	●
Q/P	●	●	●	●

GROSSETO

Buca di S. Lorenzo

viale Manetti, 1
📞 0564 25142
⬤ Sun, Mon. €€

*This restaurant serves
fish cuisine when local
fish is available. At other
times it offers traditional
Tuscan dishes, including
homemade pasta.*

CELLAR	●	●	●	
COMFORT	●	●	●	
TRADITION	●	●	●	●
Q/P	●	●	●	

ISOLA DEL GIGLIO (GR)

La Margherita

località Giglio Porto,
via Thaon de Revel, 5
📞 0564 809237
⬤ Mon.
◻ Easter–Sept. €

*Good home-cooked
simple fresh fish dishes
are served at this
restaurant. Note the
delicious first course
dish* cavatelli *(pasta) with*
mazzancolle *(mantis
shrimp) and pecorino.*

CELLAR	●	●		
COMFORT	●	●		
TRADITION	●	●	●	
Q/P	●	●	●	

Trattoria Da Maria ○

località Giglio Castello
📞 0564 806062
⬤ Wed.
◻ Mar–Dec.
€€

*This family restaurant
is set in the hills with a
delightful view over the
Baia di Campese. The
restaurant serves a choice
of fine fish and meat
dishes, including the
island's traditional
rabbit recipe.*

CELLAR	●	●	●	
COMFORT	●	●	●	
TRADITION	●	●	●	
Q/P	●	●	●	

Da Santi

località Castello
via Marconi, 20
📞 0564 806188
⬤ Mon (except summer).
€€

*In this restaurant, you
can enjoy excellent
fish cuisine with the
type of fish dependent
on availability. Classic
Tuscan dishes are given
the personal touch by
skillfully incorporating
fresh vegetables.*

CELLAR	●	●		
COMFORT	●	●		
TRADITION	●	●	●	
Q/P	●	●	●	

MANCIANO – MONTEMERANO (GR)

Da Caino ⓖ

via Canonica, 3
📞 0564 602817
⬤ Wed, Thu midday.
€€€€€

*This is one of the most
important, up-and-
coming restaurants in
Italy, renowned for its
quality. Although it is
off the beaten track
and the prices are high,
this is one not to miss.
It serves a cuisine that
mirrors the territory to
a small number of
patrons each night.
The* salumi *and extra-
virgin olive oil are from
the restaurant's own
estate. The desserts,
liquors, and selection
of coffees are very good.*

CELLAR	●	●	●	●	●
COMFORT	●	●	●	●	
TRADITION	●	●	●	●	
Q/P	●	●	●		

MASSA MARITTIMA (GR)

Bracali ⓖ

località Ghirlanda,
via di Perollo, 2
📞 0566 902318
⬤ Tue, Mon
(except August).
€€€€€

*At this family-run
restaurant visitors will
find creative cooking
that is inspired by the
regional tradition of light,
well-balanced meat and
fish dishes. Among the
best dishes on the menu
is a masterly, innovative
Tuscan lamb recipe
consisting of two halves:
one dish is cold, the other,
made from leg and ribs
of lamb, is served hot.
The pastries are also
extremely good and
well worth sampling.*

CELLAR	●	●	●	●	●
COMFORT	●	●	●	●	
TRADITION	●	●			
Q/P	●	●	●		

SEGGIANO (GR)

Silene ○

località La Pescina Est
📞 0564 950805
⬤ Mon. €€

*Set in the mountains,
this excellent and
welcoming restaurant
offers Tuscan home
cooking with particular
emphasis on woodland
produce – mushrooms
and truffles when in
season, as well as wild
boar and venison. The
meat is mostly grilled over
charcoal. The pasta is
homemade. There are
some rooms available.*

CELLAR	●	●	●		
COMFORT	●	●	●		
TRADITION	●	●	●	●	●
Q/P	●	●	●		

Accommodation

Tuscany is probably the region of Italy with the most charming inns and small country hotels offering wonderful hospitality and comfort in settings of great natural beauty. The guide below takes into account, as far as possible, the price quality ratio, so this means it excludes some of the world's finest and most luxurious hotels – such as Villa San Michele at Fiesole, for example – because the average price of a room goes well beyond the limits set for this guide.

Most of the inns listed here are situated deep in the hills, surrounded by breathtaking countryside. The rooms are furnished with typical Tuscan country furniture, and the food offered is the traditional local cuisine.

BAGNI DI LUCCA (LU)

Locanda Maiola

località Maiola di Sotto
C FAX 0583 86296
● Nov–Feb.
€€

This is a 17th-century Tuscan house, set in the green hills near Lucca, that has been converted to a welcoming family inn. In the kitchen, Signora Simonetta makes exquisite dishes reflecting the cuisine of Lucca and Garfagnana, such as her zuppa di farro with vegetables, or the homemade pasta with chickpeas or beans. The five tastefully renovated rooms are furnished with dark wood furniture. The panoramic view is magnificent.

BALBANO (LU)

Villa Casanova

via di Casanova, 1600
C 0583 548429
FAX 0583 368955
Villa ❍ Mar–Oct.
Annexe ❍ all year. €€

Nestling in the green hills between Lucca and Pisa, this 18th-century villa offers good value for money. The rooms, some very spacious, have terra-cotta floors, some fine period furniture, and a splendid view over the Valle del Serchio. Next to the villa the Antica Foresteria (annexe), dating back to the 15th century, accommodates guests in smaller rooms, some of

them extremely pleasant. The restaurant, which is open from April to November, serves wholesome home cooking. There is a good swimming pool, which is open to guests from June to September.

BORGO SAN LORENZO (FI)

Casa Palmira

località Feriolo,
via Faentina Polcanto
C FAX 055 8409749
● Jan–Feb. €€

A small rural building has been converted into this delightful hotel deep in the green hills between the Mugello and Florence. It has six rooms, each one different, but all furnished in good taste and with objects belonging to the family to give a personal touch. Eat at the nearby restaurant Il Feriolo, set in a 14th-century monastery, which specializes in good home cooking based on mushrooms and game.

BUCINE (AR)

Le Antiche Sere

località Sogna
C FAX 055 998149
● Nov.
€€€€

A medieval village called Sogna ("dream") is the setting for this fascinating inn. The owners' idea is to

let guests isolate themselves from the outside world and lose themselves in the relaxing atmosphere. The old stables have been converted into the restaurant, which serves an imaginative cuisine with lots of interesting dishes made with fresh produce. The menu changes two or three times a week and there is a good selection of wines. There are four suites with country-style furniture, fireplaces, and, above all, no telephone. The hotel has a park, a swimming pool and tennis courts.

CASTELLINA IN CHIANTI (SI)

Belvedere di San Leonino

località San Leonino
C 0577 740887
FAX 0577 740924
● Nov 15–Mar 15.
€€€

Set in a tiny rural village, this is a cluster of adjoining houses providing accommodation in 28 rooms, all spacious and pleasantly furnished. There is a lovely garden with a lawn and swimming pool with a great view over the valley. The restaurant serves good, imaginative Tuscan cuisine.

Il Colombaio

via Chiantigiana, 29
C 0577 740444
FAX 0577 740402
❍ all year. €€

You come across this hotel with its inviting name set in a 15th-century farmhouse at the entrance to the village. The rooms, all with 19th-century furniture, have wooden beams and terra-cotta floors. There is a lovely garden with a swimming pool and a view over the village and valley. Eat at the nearby restaurant Le Tre Porte, run by the hotelier's son, where real Tuscan food, such as crostini, *pasta*, and ribollita *is served.*

CASTIGLIONE D'ORCIA (SI)

Cantina Il Borgo

località Rocca d'Orcia
C **FAX** 0577 887280
● Jan, Feb.
€€

In this little medieval village overlooking the Val d'Orcia, these are three delightful rooms set in one of the fine houses of light-colored brick. The walls are whitewashed, there are wrought-iron bedsteads, and typical Tuscan country furniture. The restaurant offers real local cooking, with exquisite pecorino *from Pienza. Do not miss the excursion to the splendid spa, the* Bagno Vignoni, *which can be visited in the evening when the hot bath in the middle of the piazza exhales vapors reminiscent of a scene from Dante's* Inferno.

CERTALDO (FI)

Osteria del Vicario

via Rivellino, 3
C 0571 668228
FAX 0571 668676
☐ all year. €€

In the Middle Ages this inn was the residence of the vicar of Certaldo Alto. Set in the depths of the Val

d'Elsa, between Siena and Florence, it has 11 rooms, each very different, very romantic, and with fine Tuscan furnishings. The skilled restaurant chef presents a creative cuisine based on beautifully fresh produce – meat, poultry, mushrooms, and truffles.

CORTONA (AR)

Relais Il Falconiere

località San Martino, 370
C 0575 612616
FAX 0575 612927
☐ all year. €€€€€

This splendid 17th-century country house, now converted into a hotel, part of the Relais & Châteaux group, has a stunning hill-top location amid vines and olives facing Cortona. There are 19 rooms, all spacious and filled with period furniture and attractive wall hangings. As well as wooden beams and parquet floors, some rooms have a fireplace. The two suites overlook the garden and swimming pool. The restaurant is renowned for its very fine cuisine, based on genuine local produce. There are also helicopter-landing facilities.

Locanda del Molino

località Montanare
C 0575 614192
FAX 0575 614054
● Jan 15–Mar 15.
€€€

Situated a few miles from Cortona, this pleasant, small inn, deep in the countryside, is famed for its authentic cuisine and courteous hospitality. The ground floor restaurant's specialties, like the torte al testo *(griddle cakes), reflect Umbrian influence. The rooms on the first floor are all furnished with fine local antiques. There are antique furnishings in some of the rooms.*

FIESOLE (FI)

Pensione Bencistà

via Benedetto da Maiano, 4
C **FAX** 055 59163
● Dec–Jan.
€€€€ with half board

This calls itself a modest pensione *but is actually a pleasant villa situated in the hills of Fiesole and, in fact, looks more like a small inn. The living areas are very attractive – there are intimate lounges with fireplaces, and there is a small library. The comfortable bedrooms are furnished with period furniture. The restaurant offers good Tuscan cuisine, and there is a pleasant garden and terrace with a view over Florence.*

FLORENCE

Villa Montartino

via G. Silvani, 151
C 055 223520
FAX 055 223495
☐ all year. €€€€€

You can find this corner of paradise just a few miles from Florence on the road from Certosa to Impruneta. Montartino was originally an 11th-century watchtower guarding the valley of the Ema, where goods were brought from Chianti to Florence. The tower was later converted into a charming and graceful mansion. The enormous rooms with four-poster beds and the original terra-cotta floors contain elegant Tuscan craft furniture. Some rooms have a terrace with splendid views over the surrounding hills. Guests can use the lovely swimming pool. The food is refined but wholesome, using all local produce, including the excellent extra-virgin olive oil and

the local red wine –
Chianti. The favorite
Tuscan beef steak dish,
bistecca alla fiorentina,
which a small butcher in
Impruneta supplies to the
villa, is truly wonderful.

GAIOLE
IN CHIANTI (SI)

Relais San Sano

località San Sano
☎ 0577 746130
FAX 0577 746156
● Mar.
€€€

This cluster of stone
farmhouses overlooking
the Chianti hills nestles in
an ancient hamlet. Each
of the rooms has a name
suggesting its character:
for instance, "Il nido"
(The nest) is isolated and
romantic, while "Camera
con vista" (Room with a
view) has a view over the
gently rolling Tuscan hills.
The food served each
evening in the restaurant
is the local cuisine.

LUCCA

Locanda L'Elisa

via Nuova per Pisa
at 3 miles (5 km), 1952
☎ 0583 379737
FAX 0583 379019
● Jan 7–Feb 11.
€€€€€

This beautiful mauve-
colored villa was restored
in the early 19th century
by a steward of Princess
Elisa Baiocchi. It has two
rooms and eight suites,
all of them graciously
furnished with 19th-
century mahogany
furniture, four-poster beds,
and fine damask fabrics.
The spectacular park has
a swimming pool in it and
a myriad of geraniums,
trees, and water plants.
The veranda-gazebo
housing the restaurant
overlooks the park.

MANCIANO (GR)

Il Poderino

strada statale Maremmana
at 19 miles (30 km)
☎ FAX 0564 625031
● 2 weeks in Jan.
€€

This ancient converted
farmhouse at the gates of
Manciano has 11 spacious,
well-furnished rooms. This
is a very friendly, well-run
hotel with a splendid
panoramic view across
to Monte Argentario. The
restaurant serves Maremma
cuisine with the addition of
some interesting new dishes.

PIENZA
(SI)

Dal Falco

piazza Dante Alighieri, 3
☎ FAX 0578 748551
□ all year. €€

Visitors to this attractive
Tuscan town can find
inexpensive family
accommodation at this
small inn situated in the
center. The restaurant's
cuisine is good; specialties
include excellent pici
all'aglione, handmade
ravioli, ribollita, and meat
grilled over charcoal. The
simple, comfortable rooms
all have TV and bathrooms
with furnishings in "arte
povera" style.

ORBETELLO
(GR)

Locanda d'Ansedonia

via Aurelia toward
Ansedonia at 87 miles
(140 km), 500
☎ 0564 881317
FAX 0564 881727
● Feb. €€€

This strategically placed
inn has a wonderful view
overlooking the fascinating
lagoon of Orbetello, a few
miles from Argentario and

the Etruscan citadel of
Ansedonia. The 12 rooms
are whitewashed and
furnished in Maremma
style with fine wrought-iron
bedsteads. The restaurant
cuisine is typical of the
area, with Maremma
dishes and seafood – try the
famous acquacotta as well
as excellent Orbetello eel.

PITECCIO (PT)

Villa Vannini

Villa di Piteccio, 6
☎ 0573 42031
FAX 0573 42551
□ all year.
€€

Surrounded by a pleasant,
quiet garden, this lovely
villa is set just above
Pistoia. Friendly, family
hospitality is extended
by Signora Vannini who
oversees every detail,
from furnishing the
rooms to the homemade
produce served at
breakfast and dinner.

RADDA IN CHIANTI
(SI)

Podere Terreno

road to Volpaia,
☎ FAX 0577 738312
□ all year.
€€€ with half board

This farm is on the road
to the village of Volpaia,
famous for its Chianti
Classico and olive oil. The
owners, Sylvie Heniez
(who is French) and her
husband Roberto Melosi,
see to every last detail from
furnishing the farmhouse
with genuine rustic
furniture to organizing the
kitchen. The seven rooms
are full of charm and very
relaxing. At mealtimes
everyone eats together
around a single large table
and it is common to hear
two or three languages
spoken by diners from
different continents.

La Locanda

località Montanino
☎ 0577 738833
FAX 0577 739263
● Dec–Mar.
€€€€

This fascinating inn in the splendid Chianti hills was a 17th-century farmhouse. The seven rooms, all very different, are furnished with handsome country furniture and each has a different color scheme. They have chests and wardrobes in dark wood, and bedsteads with Viennese woven rush headboards. Particularly interesting is the arched bedroom and a suite with a loggia and a magnificent view. For dinner, there is a set menu.

RADICOFANI (SI)

La Palazzina

località Le Vigne
☎ FAX 0578 55771
● Nov–Mar.
€€€

This vacation farm in the hills of the Alta Valle d'Orcia is in an area rich in spas. The 18th-century Medici villa has bright, spacious rooms, all very tastefully furnished. There is a swimming pool on the grounds. The cuisine is based on the revival of ancient Medici recipes and uses the same fresh local produce as in the past. The villa is a good starting point for various sightseeing excursions.

ROCCALBEGNA (GR)

Dimora del Baccinello

fattoria di Baccinello
☎ 0564 982013
FAX 0564 982016
☐ all year.
€€€

At this evocative residence in an old restructured farm overlooking the Maremma it is possible to relax or have a sporting holiday thanks to the many facilities on Mount Amiata. The rooms and apartments are in an original and rustic style, with some contemporary furnishings. Modern comforts and services are provided, including a swimming pool and child-minders. The menu offers Tuscan and international dishes, all made with organic products.

SIENA

Certosa di Maggiano

strada di Certosa, 82
☎ 0577 288180
FAX 0577 288189
☐ all year.
€€€€€

This splendid 14th-century Charterhouse is just outside the center of Siena. The building is laid out around a courtyard and comprises six rooms and 11 suites, luxuriously and tastefully furnished in a choice of fabrics and colors. In the inner rooms are prized Sienese paintings and antique furniture. The restaurant's cuisine is of a high level, using plenty of fresh ingredients. In summer the tables are laid in the cloister portico. There is a park with a swimming pool and tennis courts.

SINALUNGA (SI)

Locanda della Bandita

località Bettolle,
via Bandita, 72
☎ FAX 0577 624649
● Dec 1–Feb 28.
☐ Christmas. €€€

This small farmhouse in Val di Chiana has just seven rooms, all furnished with wrought-iron beds, country furniture, and

curtains in shades of blue. The restaurant cuisine is outstanding: it offers local salumi *and specialty meats, Tuscan* crostini, *homemade pasta and excellent Chianina beef steaks. There is a good choice of Tuscan wines. A swimming pool is available.*

SORANO – SOVANA (GR)

Taverna Etrusca

piazza del Pretorio, 16
☎ 0564 616183
FAX 0564 614193
● Jan 1–Feb 10. €€

This charming inn is housed in a 13th-century building in this Etruscan village in the Maremma. It has eight air-conditioned rooms with fine dark wooden furnishings and parquet floors. The restaurant, which has a mezzanine and a ceiling with wooden beams, offers typical Maremman dishes like acquacotta, *nettle soup, and* pici all'agliata, *as well as modern ideas, such as tomato with marjoram and* ravioli *with* caciotta.

VOLTERRA (PI)

Villa Nencini

borgo Santo Stefano, 55
☎ FAX 0588 86571
☐ all year. €€

You can find this small rustic-style hotel – a real oasis of peace and quiet – just below Volterra's medieval quarter. The rooms are simple and tastefully furnished; some face the fine swimming pool. Surrounding the hotel is a private park, with trees providing shady spots, and lots of nooks and crannies where you can relax or read a book in peace. The genuine Tuscan cuisine is very reasonably priced and the hotel staff are obliging.

Practical Information

TRAVELING TO TUSCANY is most easily done by air, but although planes arrive from European airports, there are no direct intercontinental flights, and visitors from outside Europe have to transfer. The nearest intercontinental airports are Milan and Rome. Tuscany's main airport is in Pisa; it receives both domestic and European flights as well as most charter traffic. Florence's airport is smaller and is located slightly north of the city, a short bus ride away from the center. Almost exclusively, it deals with scheduled flights. Florence is also the main arrival point for the far-reaching European train and bus network, and Pisa has good international rail connections. Once in Tuscany, travel around the region is straightforward by train, bus, or car. In the cities, it is best to visit the sights on foot wherever possible.

TRAVELLING BY AIR

Useful Numbers

Alitalia
National Flights
📱 8488 656 41
International Flights
📱 8488 656 42
Information
📱 8488 656 43
🌐 www.alitalia.it

British Airways
☎ 1997 122 66
🌐 www.britishairways.com

Meridiana
☎ 055 230 23 34
🌐 www.meridiana.it

Ryanair
☎ 050 503 770
🌐 www.ryanair.com

CIT Viaggi
Florence ☎ 055 28 41 45
London ☎ 020 8686 0677
Sydney ☎ (2) 267 12 55

American Express
Via Dante Alighieri, 22 r
Florence ☎ 055 509 81

Airport Information
Florence ☎ 055 306 15
🌐 www.safnet.it
Pisa ☎ 050 50 07 07
🌐 www.pisa-airport.com

Direct flights connect Pisa and Florence to London, Paris, and Frankfurt all year round. There are also flights to Florence from Barcelona and Brussels. In the summer months, Pisa can be reached directly from Madrid, Manchester, and Glasgow. There are no direct inter-continental flights to Pisa or Florence, but you can transfer in Rome or Milan.

Alitalia also runs a fast (though expensive) train link between Rome's Fiumicino airport and Florence. You may find it cheaper to get a budget flight to London, Paris, or Frankfurt and transfer to another carrier.

Daily scheduled flights to Pisa are operated by British Airways, Ryanair, Alitalia, Air France, and Lufthansa from London, Paris, Munich, and Frankfurt. During the summer, Viva Air flies from Madrid.

Meridiana operates scheduled flights to Florence from London Gatwick, Amsterdam, Barcelona, and Paris, and has a wide range of domestic flights to Pisa and Florence from points all over Italy. Generally speaking, the further in advance you are able to book your ticket, the lower your fare will be.

Pisa Airport

Trains run directly from Pisa's Galileo Galilei airport to Florence's Santa Maria Novella station. To reach the trains, turn left as you leave the airport arrivals hall. Train tickets can be bought from the information kiosk at the airport. The journey to Florence takes an hour and the service runs once an hour, but is less regular or frequent in the early morning and late evening. There is also an infrequent train serving Lucca and Montecatini. The through train to Florence stops at Pisa Centrale, and Empoli,

where you can change on to the local line for Siena.

The No. 7 bus runs from Pisa airport to the town center. Buy tickets before you get on the bus from the airport information kiosk. There is also a taxi stand at the front of the airport. Buy some euros before landing, as there are no facilities for changing money in the baggage claim hall.

Florence Airport

Florence's Amerigo Vespucci airport, often known as Peretola, is very small. The local SITA bus to the city center leaves from the front of the airport building. The bus goes to and from the airport every 30 minutes. The bus to the airport leaves from the SITA station at Via di Santa Caterina di Siena, 15 r.

Only take a taxi from the official stand. They will charge a supplement for coming from the airport plus another for luggage. There is also an extra charge on Sundays and holidays. Most drivers are honest, but check that the meter is switched on and showing the minimum fare before setting off.

Car Rental

All the major car rental firms have offices at both airports. However, it is wise to make a booking well in advance, because it will be cheaper than renting after you arrive in Italy.

Leaving Pisa airport by car it is easy to get on to

the divided highway linking Pisa and Florence.

At Florence airport, it might be easier to take public transportation into the city center and pick up your rental car there.

Airport Car Rental Companies

Avis
Florence Airport 📞 055 31 55 88
Pisa Airport 📞 050 420 28
🔲 www.avis.com

Hertz
Florence Airport 📞 055 30 73 70
Pisa Airport 📞 050 432 20
🔲 www.hertz.com

Maggiore
Florence Airport 📞 055 31 12 56
Pisa Airport 📞 050 425 74

TRAVELING BY TRAIN

Traveling by train is a pleasurable way of getting to and around Tuscany. Italy's state railway (Ferrovie dello Stato, or FS) has a train for every type of journey, from the quaintly, maddeningly slow locali (stopping trains) through various levels of rapid intercity service, to the luxurious, superfast Eurostar, which rushes between Italian cities at a speed to match its ticket price. The train network between large cities is very good, but journeys to towns on branch lines may be quicker by bus.

Arriving by Train

Florence and Pisa are the main arrival points for trains from Europe. The Galilei from Paris and the Italia Express from Frankfurt travel direct to Florence. Passengers from London have to change in Paris or Lille.

From Florence, there is also a direct Alitalia train link with Pisa's Galileo Galilei airport, which can be very useful.

Europe-wide train passes, such as EurRail (US) or InterRail for those under 26 (Europe), are accepted on the FS network. You may have to pay a supplement to travel on fast trains. Always check first before using any private rail lines.

Train Travel in Italy

Trains from all over Italy arrive at and depart from Pisa Centrale and Florence's Santa Maria Novella station, while the Eurostar uses Florence's Rifredi station. If you are planning to travel around, there are passes which allow unlimited travel on the FS network for a determined period of time, such as the Italy Rail Card and the Italy Flexi Rail Card. Available only to nonresidents, the cards can be purchased from the station. There is a biglietto chilometrico which allows 20 trips totaling no more than 1,865 miles (3,000 km) for up to five people. This is available from international and Italian CIT offices, and from any travel agent selling train tickets. There are facilities for disabled travelers on some intercity services.

Booking and Reservations

Booking is obligatory on the Eurostar and on some other intercity services, indicated on the timetable by a black R on a white background. The booking office is at the front of Florence station.

Alternatively, you can book on the FS website (www.fs-on-line.com). Users must first register on the site, then follow the instructions on how to book and pay for seats. Tickets booked online can be delivered by courier for an additional charge, or picked up for free at a self-service ticket machine in stations offering this

service, but bring the booking code (PNR) you receive via email after completing the transaction online. Travel agents can book tickets free of charge.

Booking is advisable if you wish to travel at busy times: during the high season or on weekends. Buying your intercity ticket at least five hours before traveling entitles you to a free seat reservation. For a small fee, you can reserve a seat on any train, except local trains.

For further information, visit www.trenitalia.it or call 892021.

Booking Agents

CIT Viaggi
Piazza della Stazione, 51 r, Florence
📞 055 28 41 45

Palio Viaggi
Piazza Gramsci, Siena
📞 0577 28 08 28

Train Tickets

Always buy a ticket before you travel: if you purchase your ticket on the train, you will be surcharged a percentage of the ticket price. You can upgrade to first class or sleeper by paying the conductor.

If the ticket office is busy, try one of the self-service ticket machines found at most stations. They accept coins, notes, and credit cards. The instructions are easy to follow and come in six European languages. If you are traveling no more than 124 miles (200 km), you can buy a short-range ticket (biglietto a fasce chilometriche) from a station newsstand. The name of your station of departure will usually be stamped on the ticket, but if it is not, write it on the back. You must then validate the ticket by stamping it in one of the gold-colored machines situated at the entrance to most platforms. These machines must also be used to time stamp the return portion of a ticket.

Both the outward and return portions of a return ticket must be used within three days of purchase. Singles are issued in 124-mile (200-km) bands and are valid according to band: for example, a ticket for 124 miles (200 km) lasts for a day, one for 248 miles (400 km) lasts for two days, and so on.

On all intercity trains you will be charged a supplementary fee (supplemento) *even if you have an InterRail card.* This includes the Eurostar and Eurocity services. The cost depends on how far you are traveling.

TRAVELING BY BUS

Florence is linked by bus to most major European cities and local companies operate an extensive network of services within Tuscany. Buses are quicker where there is no direct train link, especially in the countryside. The train is faster for long journeys, but the bus may be cheaper. To plan trips around Tuscany by bus, maps and timetables are available from all the bus companies' offices, which are usually situated near city railway stations.

Arriving by Bus

Santa Maria Novella railway station in Florence is Tuscany's main arrival and departure point for all long-distance coach journeys, and the hub of the extensive local coach network. The Lazzi company runs coach links with major European cities from Florence and sells tickets for Eurolines coaches. Book tickets at their office by Santa Maria Novella station. Express services to Rome are run by Lazzi from Florence and TRA-IN from Siena.

Florence

Florence has four main bus companies. Lazzi serves the region north and west of Florence and SITA the southern and eastern region. The COPIT bus company connects the city with the Abetone/Pistoia region and CAP links Florence to the Mugello area north of the city. All these companies have ticket and information offices near Santa Maria Novella railway station.

Lazzi
Piazza della Stazione
055 21 51 55 (all services)
www.lazzi.it

SITA
Via di Santa Caterina da Siena, 15 r
800 373760 (Tuscany);
055 29 49 55 (national)
www.sita-on-line.it

COPIT of Pistoia
Piazza San Francesco
0573 36 30

CAP
Largo Fratelli Alinari 9
055 21 46 37
www.capautolinee.it

Siena

Siena's main bus company is TRA-IN, which runs urban, local, and regional services. Local services leave from Piazza Antonio Gramsci and regional buses from Piazza San Domenico. There is an information/ticket office in both squares. TRA-IN operates buses to most parts of Tuscany, as well as a direct bus to Rome twice daily.

TRA-IN
Piazza Antonio Gramsci
0577 20 42 46 (local)
Piazza San Domenico
0577 20 42 45 (regional).

Pisa

The city bus company CPT also serves the surrounding area, including the towns of Volterra, Livorno, San Miniato, and Pontedera. Buses leave from Piazza Sant'Antonio. Lazzi runs a service to Viareggio, Lucca, and Florence from Pisa, departing from Piazza Vittorio Emanuele II, which has a Lazzi ticket office.

CPT
Piazza Sant'Antonio, 1
050 50 55 11

Lazzi
Piazza Vittorio Emanuele II
050 462 88 www.lazzi.it

GETTING AROUND ON FOOT AND BY BUS

Tuscan cities are compact enough to get around fairly comfortably on foot, and the city buses are relatively cheap, regular and wide-ranging. A single ticket will take you up to 10 miles (15 km) out of town, making the bus ideal for trips from the city center to outlying areas of Florence, Pisa, or Siena. The buses get very hot in the summer and are popular with pickpockets (especially Florence's No. 7 bus), so be aware.

Walking

Sightseeing on foot in Tuscan cities is made all the more pleasurable by the fact that there are plenty of squares in which to rest and watch the world go by, or cool churches to pop into when the heat gets too much. Moreover, there are limited-traffic zones in the center of most towns, which make life slightly easier for pedestrians.

Signs for sights and landmarks are usually quite clear, especially those in Siena. In Florence it is easy to pick out the Duomo and the river and orientate yourself in relation to them. A gentle stroll around the main sights of Florence can take just a couple of hours. The Duomo, Santa Maria

Novella, Ponte Vecchio, and the Accademia are all within 10 minutes' walk of each other. The main sights in Pisa are all in the same square. Siena is also compact but hilly, so wear comfortable shoes.

The cities can, however, be unbearably hot in the summer. Plan your day so that you are inside for the hottest part. Recuperate Italian-style with a leisurely lunch followed by a siesta. Shopping is more pleasant in the early evening when it is cooler and the streets start to come alive.

Crossing Roads

Use the sottopassaggio (underpass) wherever possible. The busiest roads also have signals to help you cross: the green avanti sign gives you right of way, in theory, but never expect drivers to recognize this as a matter of course. Seize your opportunity and walk out slowly and confidently, glaring at the traffic and maintaining a determined pace: the traffic should stop, or at least swerve. Take extra care at night: traffic lights are switched to flashing amber and the road crossings become free-for-alls.

City Buses

Florence's city bus company is called ATAF, Pisa's is CPT, and Siena's TRA-IN. All the buses are bright orange. Most lines run until at least 9:30pm, with the most popular running until midnight or 1am in Florence.

In Pisa and Florence, buses run near the main sights. Useful Florentine routes for visitors are the No. 12 and the No. 13 (they make hour-long clockwise/counterclockwise circuits of the city), the No. 7 to Fiesole, and the new "eco-routes" A, B, C, and D which are electric or eco-diesel-fueled minibuses.

Using Local Services

Florence does not have a main terminus, but most buses can be picked up alongside Santa Maria Novella station. In Pisa, most buses stop at the railway station and Piazza Vittorio Emanuele II; in Siena, at Piazza Antonio Gramsci, and Piazza San Domenico. There are bus information kiosks at all these points, but they are not always open. Tourist information offices can usually help.

Enter the bus at the front or back and get off through the middle doors. However, when the bus is full, you have to struggle on and off wherever you can.

The four low seats at the front of the bus are meant for the elderly, the disabled, and people with children.

Fare dodging is common, but so are inspectors. The fine is at least 50 times the cost of a ticket.

Bus Tickets

Tickets for city buses must be bought before you travel. Buy them from newsstands, bars displaying the bus company sign (ATAF, APT, TRA-IN), tobacconists, or at the bus terminal. If you are likely to make a few trips, buy several tickets at once; they become valid when you time stamp them in the machine in the bus. There are also ticket vending machines in the streets, which take any coins and low-value notes.

Ticket prices and validity vary from town to town. You can usually buy a ticket valid for one, two, or sometimes four hours' unlimited travel. The time limit starts when you stamp your ticket on the first bus. You can also buy daily passes, or a tesserino consisting of one or four tickets, each valid for a number of rides. A tesserino is slightly cheaper than the same number of single tickets. You just

stamp it as and when needed until you have made the permitted number of trips.

Long-Term Passes

If staying for a long time in one town, a monthly pass for unlimited travel is a good idea. You will need an identity card with your photograph. These are available for a small charge from the ATAF Ufficio Abbonamenti located in Piazza della Stazione. In Siena, photocards are available from the TRA-IN office in Piazza San Domenico. Monthly passes can be bought wherever bus tickets are on sale.

In Florence, the best bus ticket for visitors is the plurigiornale, from the ATAF office, newsstands, bars, and tobacconists. These are valid for two, three, or seven days. The ATAF also sells a ticket called an abbonamento plurigiornaliero, valid for between 2–25 days. These are nontransferable.

You can also buy a carta arancio, valid for seven days on trains and bus lines within the province of Florence. You can buy it from any train or bus company ticket office.

Useful Addresses

ATAF
Ufficio Informazioni & Abbonamenti,
Piazza della Stazione, Florence
C 800 424 500 **W** www.ataf.net

CPT
Ufficio Informazioni,
Piazza Sant'Antonio, 1, Pisa
C 050 505 511
W www.cpt.pisa.it

EUROLINES
UK **C** 01582 404511
W www.eurolines.co.uk

Taxis in Tuscany

Official taxis are white in Tuscan cities, with a "Taxi" sign on the roof. Only take taxis at official stands, not offers from freelancers at the stations. There are supplements for baggage, for rides between 10pm and 7am, on Sundays and on public holidays, and for journeys to and from the airport. If you phone for a taxi, the meter starts to run from the moment you book the taxi; by the time it arrives there could already be several euros clocked up. Generally, taxis are costly. Taxi drivers are usually honest, but make sure you know what any supplements are for. Italians give very small tips or nothing at all, but 10 percent is expected from visitors.

In Florence, there are ranks at Via Pellicceria, Piazza di Santa Maria Novella, and Piazza di San Marco. In Siena, taxis can be found in Piazza Matteotti and Piazza della Stazione. In Pisa, they can be found at the Piazza del Duomo, Piazza Garibaldi, and Piazza della Stazione.

Booking Numbers

Florence Radiotaxi
C 055 47 98 or 055 42 42 or 055 43 90

Siena Radiotaxi
C 0577 492 22

Pisa Radiotaxi
C 050 54 16 00

DRIVING IN TUSCANY

A driving tour of Tuscan vineyards makes a memorable vacation, if you are prepared for high fuel costs and erratic Italian driving. If you are staying in Siena or Florence, with no plans to travel around, there is little point in having a car: both are small enough to walk around and parking is difficult and expensive. If you are staying in the countryside and visiting towns by car, it is best to park on the outskirts and walk or take a bus into the center.

Arriving by Car

Drivers from Britain need a Green Card for insurance purposes and the vehicle's registration document. EU nationals who intend to stay for more than six months and do not have the standard pink license will need an Italian translation of their license, available from most automobile organizations and Italian tourist offices.

The ACI (Automobile Club d'Italia) provides excellent maps and invaluable help. It will tow anyone free, and offers free repairs to members of affiliated associations, such as the AA or RAC in Britain, ADAC in Germany, the AIT in France, the RACE in Spain, and ANWB in Holland. SOS columns on highways allow instant access to the emergency services.

Car Rental

Car rental in Italy is expensive and, ideally, should be organized through a travel agent before leaving for Tuscany. Cars can be prebooked through any rental firm with branches in Italy. If you rent a car when in Tuscany, a local firm such as Maggiore may be cheaper. Book well in advance, especially for weekend outings.

To rent a car you must be over 21, and have held a license for at least a year. Visitors from outside the EU need an international license. Make sure the rental includes collision damage waiver, breakdown service, and insurance against theft.

Bike and Moped Rental

A day spent cycling out in the countryside can be a healthy and relaxing pastime, and a moped or scooter makes lighter and swifter work of the Tuscan hills. Bicycles can be rented

for around 3 per hour; moped prices start at about 25 per day. Helmets are mandatory on mopeds. Bicycles can also be rented from the main paying parking areas of Florence for a cheaper price.

Rules of the Road

Drive on the right and, generally, give way to the right. Seat belts are compulsory in the front and the back, and children should be properly restrained. You must carry a warning triangle in case of breakdown.

In town centers, the speed limit is 30 mph (50 km/h); on ordinary roads 55 mph (90 km/h); and on highways 70 mph (110 km/h) for cars up to 1099cc, and 80 mph (130 km/h) for more powerful cars. Penalties for speeding include fines on the spot and license points, and there are strict drunk-driving laws as elsewhere in the EU.

Driving in Town

City centers are usually fraught with one-way systems, limited-traffic zones, and erratic drivers, and are only recommended to the confident driver. In Lucca, Siena, and San Gimignano, only residents and taxis may drive inside the city walls. Visitors may go in to unload at their hotel but must then park outside the walls.

Pisa has limited-traffic zones around the Arno, and the rule for tourists unloading also applies in Florence, with its zona traffico limitato or zona blu, which covers most of the center. There is a pedestrian zone around the Duomo, although pedestrians here should be prepared to step aside for taxis, mopeds, and bicycles. The latter two often do not comply with the traffic-light instructions.

Parking

Official parking areas are marked by blue lines, usually with meters or an attendant nearby. There are three large underground parking lots in Florence: at Santa Maria Novella station; at the Parterre, northeast of Piazza della Libertà; and below the Central Market. They are open 24 hours a day. Some hotels have their own parking, or have agreements for reduced rates with private garages.

If you park illegally, your car could be towed away. In Tuscany, one day a week is set aside for street cleaning, when parking is forbidden. This is indicated by signs saying zona rimozione *with the day and time. Beware of residents-only parking areas (*riservato ai residenti*).*

If your car is towed away, phone the Vigili, *the municipal police, to find out where it has been taken.*

Driving in the Countryside

Driving on the quiet Tuscan country roads can be a pleasure. Distances can be deceptive. What may look like a short trip on the map could actually take much longer because of winding roads. Some back roads may not be paved, so beware of flat tires. You may also find driving at night disorientating as roads and signs are generally poorly lit.

Tolls and Gasoline

Tolls operate on highways, but there are some free divided highways. Toll-booths take cash or prepaid magnetic "swipe" cards called Viacards, *available from tobacconists and ACI. Highway service stations occur at irregular intervals, and there are fewer gas stations in the countryside than the cities. Hardly any*

outside the cities take credit cards. Many close at noon and reopen about 3:30pm until 7:30pm; few open on Sundays. Many in the countryside close in August.

At gas stations with self-service pumps, put notes or credit cards in the machine. Lead-free gas is senza piombo.

City Car Rental

Avis
Borgo Ognissanti, 128 r, Florence
📞 055 21 36 29
c/o de Martino Autonoleggi,
Via Simone Martini, 36, Siena
📞 0577 27 03 05
🅦 www.avis.com

Hertz
Via Maso Finiguerra, 33 r, Florence
📞 055 239 82 05
🅦 www.hertz.com

Maggiore
Via Maso Finiguerra, 31 r, Florence
📞 055 21 02 38

Cycle and Moped Hire

Ciclo Posse
Via Matteotti, 45, Montepulciano
📞 0578 71 63 92
🅦 www.cicloposse.com

Happy Rent
Borgo Ognissanti 153 r, Florence
📞 055 239 96 96

DF Bike
Via Massetani, 54, Siena
📞 0577 27 19 05

DF Moto
Via dei Gazzani, 16, Siena
📞 0577 28 83 87

Breakdown

Automobile Club d'Italia
Viale G. Amendola, 36, Florence
📞 055 24 861
Via Cisanello, 168, Pisa
📞 050 95 01 11
Viale Vittorio Veneto, 47, Siena
📞 0577 490 01

Emergencies 📞 116

Towing Away

Vigili (Municipal Police)
Florence 📞 055 32 831
Pisa 📞 050 91 03 78
Siena 📞 0577 29 25 58

24-Hour Gas Stations, Florence

AGIP
Viale dei Mille
📞 055 58 70 91
Via Senese
📞 055 204 97 85

Disabled Travelers

Facilities for the disabled traveler in Tuscany are fairly limited. If you book a package tour, representatives can assist in organizing help at airports and ensure that you are given the most convenient hotel room.

Some intercity trains have special facilities for wheelchair users. There are lifts at some stations, such as Santa Maria Novella, to help those with wheelchairs on and off trains, but they must be booked 24 hours in advance (for more details, visit www.trenitalia.it).

The organization CO.IN also provides information for disabled tourists traveling to Italy.

CO.IN
Via E. Gioglioli 54a, Rome
📞 06 712 90 11
🅦 www.coinsociale.it

Visiting Estates

Wine-makers welcome visitors, and it is usually quite easy to arrange a visit to an estate. They vary considerably, but many offer tours and wine tastings and sell produce. They are commercial enterprises: estate owners cannot spend all day chatting to visitors, so it is best to telephone to make an appointment. Agriturismo (farm and vineyard estate vacations) are becoming increasingly popular and there is a wide choice of farm houses, apartments, and rooms in villas to rent, but many of them need booking well in advance.

General Index

Acknowledgments

DORLING KINDERSLEY would like to thank the following associations and people whose contributions and assistance have made the preparation of this book possible.

Donatella Cinelli Colombini, president of Movimento Turismo del Vino; Sylvie Heiniz, agriturismo Podere Terreno alla Volpaia; Flavio Zaramella, president of Oil Masters Corporation; journalists Stefano Tesi (Firenze) and Marzia Tempestini (Prato); Sauro Brunicardi, Ristorante La Mora; Romano Franceschini, Ristorante Romano; Fulvio Pierangelini, Ristorante Gambero Rosso; Lorenzo Totò, Osteria Da Totò, Lucignano; Ristorante La Torre del Mangia, Milano; Loris Bocconi, fishmarket wholesaler in Milan; Sandro Carelli, SAMA, Milan; Azienda agricola Belsedere, Trequanda; Hubert Ciacci, Montalcino; Pa.Ri.V., Sinalunga; Silvana Cugusi, Montepulciano; butchers shops: Franco Scarpelli in Lucignano, Cecchini in Panzano in Chianti, Falorni in Greve in Chianti, Porciatti in Radda in Chianti, Chini in Gaiole in Chianti, Pollo San Marco in Arezzo; Moris Farms, Massa Marittima; Fattoria di Celaja di Crespina; Aziende agricole Danei (Giglio), Acquabona and La Chiusa (Elba).

PICTURE CREDITS
Guido Stecchi (mushrooms, herbs and fruits, typical products, farms), Paolo Liverani (herbs and fruits), Giuseppe Masciadri (pp 71, 85, 169); many pictures come from Image Bank, APT of Versilia, Livorno and Arcipelago toscano, and from Comune di Montespertoli (Florence).

JACKET
Front – DK PICTURE LIBRARY: John Heseltine cl; Guido Stecchi bl; ROBERT HARDING PICTURE LIBRARY: M. Short main image.
Back – DK PICTURE LIBRARY: John Heseltine t; Guido Stecchi b; TIPS IMAGES, London: c.
Spine – ROBERT HARDING PICTURE LIBRARY: M. Short.

Phrase Book

IN EMERGENCY

Help!	**Aiuto!**	eye-**yoo**-toh
Stop!	**Fermate!**	fair-**mah**-teh
Call a doctor.	**Chiama un medico.**	kee-**ah**-mah oon **meh**-dee-koh
Call an ambulance.	**Chiama un' ambulanza.**	kee-**ah**-mah oon am-boo-**lan**-tsa
Call the police.	**Chiama la polizia.**	kee-**ah**-mah lah pol-ee-**tsee**-ah
Call the fire department.	**Chiama i pompieri.**	kee-**ah**-mah ee pom-pee-**air**-ee
Where is the telephone?	**Dov'è il telefono?**	dov-**eh** eel teh-**leh**-foh-noh?
The nearest hospital?	**L'ospedale più vicino?**	loss-peh-**dah**-leh pee-**oovee**-**chee**-noh?

COMMUNICATION ESSENTIALS

Yes/No	**Sì/No**	see/**noh**
Please	**Per favore**	pair fah-**vor**-eh
Thank you	**Grazie**	**grah**-tsee-eh
Excuse me	**Mi scusi**	mee **skoo**-zee
Hello	**Buon giorno**	bwon **jor**-noh
Good-bye	**Arrivederci**	ah-ree-veh-**dair**-chee
Good evening	**Buona sera**	**bwon**-ah **sair**-ah
morning	**la mattina**	lah mah-**tee**-nah
afternoon	**il pomeriggio**	eel poh-meh-**ree**-joh
evening	**la sera**	lah **sair**-ah
yesterday	**ieri**	ee-**air**-ee
today	**oggi**	**ob**-jee
tomorrow	**domani**	doh-**mah**-nee
here	**qui**	kwee
there	**la**	**lah**
What?	**Quale?**	**kwab**-leh?
When?	**Quando?**	**kwan**-doh?
Why?	**Perchè?**	pair-**keh**?
Where?	**Dove?**	**dob**-veh?

USEFUL PHRASES

How are you?	**Come sta?**	**kob**-meh stah?
Very well, thank you.	**Molto bene, grazie.**	**moll**-toh **beb**-neh **grah**-tsee-eh
Pleased to meet you.	**Piacere di conoscerla.**	pee-ah-**chair**-eh dee coh-**nob**-shair-lah
See you later.	**A più tardi.**	ah pee-oo **tar**-dee
That's fine.	**Va bene.**	va **beb**-neh
Where is/are ...?	**Dov'è/Dove sono ...?**	dov-**eh**/doveh **sob**-noh?
How long does it take to get to ...?	**Quanto tempo ci vuole per andare a ...?**	**kwan**-toh **tem**-poh chee voo-**ob**-leh pair an-**dar**-eh ah ...?
How do I get to ...?	**Come faccio per arrivare a ...?**	koh-meh **fab**-choh pair arri-**var**-eh ah..?
Do you speak English?	**Parla inglese?**	**par**-lah een-**gleb**-zeh?
I don't understand.	**Non capisco.**	non ka-**pee**-skoh
Could you speak more slowly, please?	**Può parlare più lentamente, per favore?**	pwoh par-**lab**-reh pee-**oo** len-ta-**men**-teh pair fah-**vor**-eh?
I'm sorry.	**Mi dispiace.**	mee dee-spee-**ab**-cheh

USEFUL WORDS

big	**grande**	**gran**-deh
small	**piccolo**	**pee**-koh-loh
hot	**caldo**	**kal**-doh
cold	**freddo**	**fred**-doh
good	**buono**	**bwob**-noh
bad	**cattivo**	kat-**tee**-voh
enough	**basta**	**bas**-tah
well	**bene**	**beb**-neh
open	**aperto**	ah-**pair**-toh
closed	**chiuso**	kee-**oo**-zoh
left	**a sinistra**	ah see-**nee**-strah
right	**a destra**	ah **dess**-trah
straight ahead	**sempre dritto**	**sem**-preh **dree**-toh
near	**vicino**	vee-**chee**-noh
far	**lontano**	lon-**tab**-noh
up	**su**	**soo**
down	**giù**	**joo**
early	**presto**	**press**-toh
late	**tardi**	**tar**-dee
entrance	**entrata**	en-**trab**-tah
exit	**uscita**	oo-**shee**-ta
lavatory	**il gabinetto**	eel gah-bee-**net**-toh
free, unoccupied	**libero**	**lee**-bair-oh
free, no charge	**gratuito**	grah-**too**-ee-toh

MAKING A TELEPHONE CALL

I'd like to place a long-distance call.	**Vorrei fare una interurbana.**	vor-**ray far**-eh oona in-tair-oor-**bab**-nah
I'd like to make a collect call.	**Vorrei fare una telefonata a carico del destinatario.**	vor-**ray far**-eh oona teh-leh-fon-**ab**-tah ah **kar**-ee-koh dell dess-tee-nah-**tar**-ree-oh
I'll try again later.	**Ritelefono più tardi.**	ree-teh-**leh**-foh-noh pee-oo **tar**-dee
Can I leave a message?	**Posso lasciare un messaggio?**	**poss**-oh lash-**ab**-reh oon mess-**sab**-joh?
Hold on.	**Un attimo, per favore**	oon **ab**-tee-mob, pair fab-**vor**-eh
Could you speak up a little please?	**Può parlare più forte, per favore?**	pwoh par-**lab**-reh pee-oo **for**-teh, pair fab-**vor**-eh?
local call	**la telefonata locale**	lah teh-leh-fon-**ab**-ta loh-**kab**-leh

SHOPPING

How much does this cost?	**Quant'è, per favore?**	kwan-**teb** pair fab-**vor**-eh?
I would like ...	**Vorrei ...**	vor-**ray**
Do you have ...?	**Avete ...?**	ah-**veb**-teh.. ?
I'm just looking.	**Sto soltanto guardando.**	stoh sol-**tan**-toh gwar-**dan**-doh
Do you take credit cards?	**Accettate carte di credito?**	ah-chet-**tab**-teh **kar**-teh dee **creb**-dee-toh?
What time do you open/close?	**A che ora apre/ chiude?**	ah keh **or**-ah **ab**-preh/kee-**oo**-deh?
this one	**questo**	**kweb**-stoh
that one	**quello**	**kwell**-oh
expensive	**caro**	**kar**-oh
cheap	**a buon prezzo**	ah bwon **pret**-soh
size, clothes	**la taglia**	lah **tab**-lee-ah
size, shoes	**il numero**	eel **noo**-mair-oh
white	**bianco**	bee-**ang**-koh
black	**nero**	**neb**-roh
red	**rosso**	**ross**-oh
yellow	**giallo**	**jal**-loh
green	**verde**	**vair**-deh
blue	**blu**	bloo
brown	**marrone**	mar-**rob**-neh

TYPES OF STORES

antique dealer	**l'antiquario**	lan-tee-**kwab**-ree-oh
bakery	**la panetteria**	lah pah-net-tair-**ree**-ah
bank	**la banca**	lah **bang**-kah
bookstore	**la libreria**	lah lee-breh-**ree**-ah
butcher's	**la macelleria**	lah mah-chell-eh-**ree**-ah
cake store	**la pasticceria**	lah pas-tee-chair-**ee**-ah
pharmacy	**la farmacia**	lah far-mah-**chee**-ah
delicatessen	**la salumeria**	lah sah-loo-meh-**ree**-ah
department store	**il grande magazzino**	eel **gran**-deh mag-gad-**zee**-noh
fish store	**la pescheria**	lah pess-keh-**ree**-ah
florist	**il fioraio**	eel fee-or-**eye**-oh
vegetable stand	**il fruttivendolo**	eel froo-tee-**ven**-doh-loh
grocery	**alimentari**	ah-lee-men-**tah**-ree
hairdresser	**il parrucchiere**	eel par-oo-kee-**air**-eh
ice cream parlor	**la gelateria**	lah jel-lah-tair-**ree**-ah
market	**il mercato**	eel mair-**kab**-toh
news-stand	**l'edicola**	leh-**dee**-koh-lah
post office	**l'ufficio postale**	loo-**fee**-choh pos-**tab**-leh
shoe store	**il negozio di scarpe**	eel neh-**gob**-tsioh dee **skar**-peh
supermarket	**il supermercato**	su-pair-mair-**kab**-toh
tobacco store	**il tabaccaio**	eel tab-bak-**eye**-oh
travel agent	**l'agenzia di viaggi**	lah-jen-**tsee**-ah dee vee-**ad**-jee

SIGHTSEEING

art gallery	**la pinacoteca**	lah peena-koh-**teb**-kah
bus stop	**la fermata dell'autobus**	lah fair-**mab**-tah dell ow-toh-booss
church	**la chiesa**	lah kee-**eb**-zah
	la basilica	lah bah-**seel**-i-kah
closed for the public holiday	**chiuso per la festa**	kee-**oo**-zoh pair lah **fess**-tah
garden	**il giardino**	eel jar-**dee**-no
library	**la biblioteca**	lah beeb-lee-oh-**teb**-kah
museum	**il museo**	eel moo-**zeb**-oh
railroad station	**la stazione**	lah stah-tsee-**ob**-neh
tourist information	**l'ufficio turistico**	loo-**fee**-choh too-**ree**-stee-koh

STAYING IN A HOTEL

Do you have any vacant rooms?	**Avete camere libere?**	ab-**veh**-teh **kab**-mair-eh lee-bair-eh?
double room	**una camera doppia**	oona **kab**-mair-ah **dob**-pee-ah
with double bed	**con letto matrimoniale**	kon **let**-toh mab-tree-moh-nee-**ah**-leh
twin room	**una camera con due letti**	oona **kab**-mair-ah kon **doo**-eh **let**-tee
single room	**una camera singola**	oona **kab**-mair-ah **sing**-goh-lah
room with a bath, shower	**una camera con bagno, con doccia**	oona **kab**-mair-ah kon **ban**-yoh, kon **dot**-chah
porter	**il facchino**	eel fab-**kee**-noh
key	**la chiave**	lah kee-**ah**-veh
I have a reservation.	**Ho fatto una prenotazione.**	oh **fat**-toh oona preh-noh-tab-tsee-**oh**-neh

EATING OUT

Have you got a table for ...?	**Avete una tavola per ... ?**	ah-**veh**-teh oona **tab**-vob-lah pair ...?
I'd like to reserve a table.	**Vorrei riservare una tavola.**	vor-**ray** ree-sair-**vab**-reh oona **tab**-vob-lah
breakfast	**colazione**	kob-lab-tsee-**ob**-neh
lunch	**pranzo**	**pran**-tsoh
dinner	**cena**	**cheb**-nah
Enjoy your meal.	**Buon appetito.**	bwon ab-peh-**tee**-toh
The bill, please.	**Il conto, per favore.**	eel **kon**-toh pair fab-**vor**-eh
I am a vegetarian.	**Sono vegetariano/a.**	**sob**-noh veh-jeh-tar-ee-**ah**-noh/nah
waitress	**cameriera**	kab-mair-ee-**air**-ah
waiter	**cameriere**	kab-mair-ee-**air**-eh
fixed price menu	**il menù a prezzo fisso**	eel meh-**noo** ah **pret**-soh **fee**-soh
dish of the day	**piatto del giorno**	pee-**ah**-toh dell **jor**-no
appetizer	**antipasto**	an-tee-**pass**-toh
first course	**il primo**	eel **pree**-moh
main course	**il secondo**	eel seh-**kon**-doh
vegetables	**il contorno**	eel kon-**tor**-noh
dessert	**il dolce**	eel **doll**-cheh
cover charge	**il coperto**	eel kob-**pair**-toh
wine list	**la lista dei vini**	lah **lee**-stah day **vee**-nee
rare	**al sangue**	al **sang**-gweh
medium	**al puntino**	al poon-**tee**-noh
well done	**ben cotto**	ben **kot**-toh
glass	**il bicchiere**	eel bee-kee-**air**-eh
bottle	**la bottiglia**	lah bot-**teel**-yah
knife	**il coltello**	eel kol-**tell**-oh
fork	**la forchetta**	lah for-**ket**-tah
spoon	**il cucchiaio**	eel koo-kee-**eye**-oh

MENU DECODER

l'abbacchio	lab-**back**-kee-oh	lamb
l'aceto	lab-**cheb**-toh	vinegar
l'acqua	**lab**-kwah	water
l'acqua minerale gasata/naturale	**lab**-kwah mee-nair-**ab**-leh gab-**zab**-tah/nah-too-**rab**-leh	mineral water carbonated/still
l'aglio	**labl**-yoh	garlic
al forno	al **for**-noh	baked
alla griglia	ah-lah **greel**-yah	grilled
l'anatra	**lab**-nah-trah	duck
l'aragosta	lab-rah-**goss**-tah	lobster
l'arancia	lab-**ran**-chah	orange
arrosto	ar-**ross**-toh	roast
la birra	lah **beer**-rah	beer
la bistecca	lah bee-**stek**-kah	steak
il brodo	eel **brob**-doh	broth, soup
il burro	eel **boor**-oh	butter
il caffè	eel kab-**feb**	coffee
il carciofo	eel kar-**choff**-oh	artichoke
la carne	la **kar**-neh	meat
carne di maiale	**kar**-neh dee mab-**yab**-leh	pork
la cipolla	lah chee-**poll**-ah	onion
i fagioli	ee fab-**job**-lee	beans
il formaggio	eel for-**mad**-joh	cheese
le fragole	leh **frab**-goh-leh	strawberries
frutta fresca	**froo**-tah **fress**-kah	fresh fruit
frutti di mare	**froo**-tee dee **mab**-reh	seafood
i funghi	ee **foon**-gee	mushrooms
i gamberi	ee **gam**-bair-ee	shrimp
il gelato	eel jel-**lab**-toh	ice cream
l'insalata	leen-sab-**lab**-tah	salad
il latte	eel **labt**-teh	milk
i legumi	ee leb-**goo**-mee	vegetables

lesso	**less**-oh	boiled
il manzo	eel **man**-tsoh	beef
la mela	lah **meb**-lah	apple
la melanzana	lab meh-lan-**tsab**-nab	eggplant
la minestra	lab mee-**ness**-trab	soup
l'olio	**loll**-yoh	oil
l'oliva	lob-**lee**-vah	olive
il pane	eel **pah**-neh	bread
il panino	eel pab-**nee**-noh	roll
le patate	leb pab-**tab**-teh	potatoes
patatine fritte	pab-tab-**teen**-eh **free**-teh	french fries
il pepe	eel **peb**-peh	pepper
la pesca	lab **pess**-kah	peach
il pesce	eel **pesh**-eh	fish
il pollo	eel **poll**-oh	chicken
il pomodoro	eel pob-moh-**dor**-oh	tomato
il prosciutto cotto/crudo	eel pro-**sboo**-toh **kot**-tob/**kroo**-dob	ham cooked/cured
il riso	eel **ree**-zoh	rice
il sale	eel **sab**-leh	salt
la salsiccia	lab sal-**see**-chab	sausage
secco	**sek**-koh	dry
succo d'arancia/ di limone	**soo**-koh dab-**ran**-chah/dee lee-**mob**-neh	orange/lemon juice
il tè	eel **teb**	tea
la tisana	lab tee-**zab**-nah	herb tea
il tonno	**ton**-noh	tuna
la torta	lab **tor**-tah	cake
l'uovo	loo-**ob**-voh	egg
l'uva	**loo**-vah	grapes
vino bianco	**vee**-noh bee-**ang**-kob	white wine
vino rosso	**vee**-nob **ross**-oh	red wine
il vitello	eel vee-**tell**-oh	veal
le vongole	leb **von**-gob-leh	baby clams
lo zucchero	lob **zoo**-kair-oh	sugar
gli zucchini	lyee dzo-**kee**-nee	zucchini
la zuppa	lab **tsoo**-pah	soup

NUMBERS

1	**uno**	**oo**-nob
2	**due**	**doo**-eh
3	**tre**	treb
4	**quattro**	**kwat**-rob
5	**cinque**	**ching**-kweh
6	**sei**	**say**-ee
7	**sette**	**set**-teh
8	**otto**	**ot**-tob
9	**nove**	**nob**-veh
10	**dieci**	dee-**eb**-chee
11	**undici**	**oon**-dee-chee
12	**dodici**	**dob**-dee-chee
13	**tredici**	**tray**-dee-chee
14	**quattordici**	kwat-**tor**-dee-chee
15	**quindici**	**kwin**-dee-chee
16	**sedici**	**say**-dee-chee
17	**diciassette**	dee-chab-**set**-teh
18	**diciotto**	dee-**chot**-tob
19	**diciannove**	dee-chab-**nob**-veh
20	**venti**	**ven**-tee
30	**trenta**	**tren**-tab
40	**quaranta**	kwah-**ran**-tab
50	**cinquanta**	ching-**kwan**-tab
60	**sessanta**	sess-**an**-tab
70	**settanta**	set-**tan**-tab
80	**ottanta**	ot-**tan**-tab
90	**novanta**	nob-**van**-tab
100	**cento**	**cben**-tob
1,000	**mille**	**mee**-leb
2,000	**duemila**	**doo**-eh **mee**-lab
5,000	**cinquemila**	**ching**-kweh meb-**lab**
1,000,000	**un milione**	oon meel-**yob**-neb

TIME

one minute	**un minuto**	oon mee-**noo**-tob
one hour	**un'ora**	oon **or**-ab
half an hour	**mezz'ora**	medz-**or**-ab
a day	**un giorno**	oon **jor**-nob
a week	**una settimana**	oona set-tee-**mab**-nab
Monday	**lunedì**	loo-neb-**dee**
Tuesday	**martedì**	mar-teb-**dee**
Wednesday	**mercoledì**	mair-kob-leb-**dee**
Thursday	**giovedì**	job-veb-**dee**
Friday	**venerdì**	ven-air-**dee**
Saturday	**sabato**	**sab**-bab-tob
Sunday	**domenica**	dob-**meb**-nee-kab